Secrets from a Caterer's Kitchen

Secrets from a Caterer's Kitchen

Nicole Aloni

HPBooks

HPBooks
Published by The Berkley Publishing Group
A division of Penguin Putnam Inc.
375 Hudson Street
New York, NY 10014

First edition: February 2001

Visit our website at
www.penguinputnam.com

Library of Congress Cataloging-in-Publication Data

Aloni, Nicole.
    Secrets from a caterer's kitchen / Nicole Aloni.
       p. cm.
    ISBN 1-55788-352-1
    1. Entertaining.   2. Cookery.   I. Title.

TX731 .A62 2001
642'.4—dc21   00-061316

Printed in the United States of America

17 16 15 14 13 12 11 10 9 8 7

For Ami

One person knew I could write a book, my husband, Aminadav. His dreams for me were always grander than those I had for myself. Each page of this book bears the stamp of his creative vision.

He was a brilliant composer, he was a brilliant friend.

AMINADAV ALONI, 1928–1999

Contents

Acknowledgments

People ask me: "Why do you write about food, and eating, and drink? Why don't you write about the struggle for power and security, and about love, the way others do?" The easiest answer is to say that, like most other humans, I am hungry.

—M. F. K. Fisher
The Gastronomical Me, 1943

I WOULD LIKE to express my gratitude to those who have inspired, guided, and encouraged me.

As a teenager, watching Julia Child on television provided me with tangible proof that my dream of cooking professionally was possible. I have been fortunate as an adult to meet her, to cook for her, and to benefit from her advice. But what I appreciate most is her warmth, generosity and humor.

The gratitude to my support team for this book is profound. Jane Dystel, my agent, took a chance on an untried author and has graciously guided me through many difficult times. My editor, Jeanette Egan (my phone dials her number without being touched), was the first person, outside my group of family and friends, to believe in this book. It has been wonderful to share the arduous process of fine tuning a complex project like this with such a meticulous and knowledgeable collaborator.

The book's illustrator, Gary Hovland, has been a dream to work with; combining artistic mastery with an easygoing, "Whatever you want. Let's just make this work" attitude. His illustrations provide just the note of wry humor for which I had hoped.

Evan Lewis was hired to test recipes at the very earliest stages of this project, which she has done with care and patience. She was always an even-tempered, constructive influence—and it does get hot in the kitchen.

I cannot overstate my debt to my husband, Ami. He brought his endless creativity to everything he touched, which included the development of this project. He was truly a Renaissance man who *lived* "outside the box."

On numerous occasions I would have been stymied without the generous help of my kind and talented friends. Lee Anne Richards—astrologer, writer, and critic extraordinaire—tirelessly read, reread, critiqued, and made me laugh. Deberah Porter encouraged my dreams and taught me about mind-mapping. Leslie Marcus inspired me with her creative approach to invitations, and her faith in me. And finally, Deborah Olson who has supported every venture of mine throughout our long and action-packed friendship.

I am indebted to my chef-friends (both words of that hyphenate being equally important): Anne Dreyer, Ted Gray, Susan Kaufman (oh, how many years have we made food together?), and Jozseph Schultz, all of whom have generously allowed me to include some of their special recipes.

I would also like to thank my stepchildren, David and Dan Aloni and Dori Meshi, who shared their support, humor, and creativity.

It is one of the greatest feelings known to humans, the feeling of being the host, of hosting people, of being the person to whom they come for food and drink and company.

—Anne Lamott
"Bird by Bird"

WHILE WAITING IN the adrenaline-laced atmosphere of my dentist's office, I read a report about the anxiety levels associated with various everyday activities. The survey concluded that hosting a dinner party for eight causes more tension than undergoing an emergency root canal. I was floored. Most of my friends and neighbors would rather face an oral surgeon than have guests at their table? Yet, I know the urge to provide hospitality is almost as basic to the human animal as the need to eat. We are enchanted by the idea of hospitality, of opening our homes to friends and family, of filling them up with wonderful food and conversation. But, for many of us, entertaining has become fraught with Olympian expectations. This is partly the influence of television.

At the end of a long workday, we settle on the couch with the remote where we watch Emeril or Martha preparing beautiful, ambitious recipes. While we're being entertained, there's also a degree of intimidation that creeps in. They make it look so easy, moving from the egg whites stiffening in the giant mixer to the crispy beignets bobbing to the top of the shiny deep fryer. The feeling begins to crystallize that to entertain properly our meals and tables should look like theirs. These gourmet stars have entered through the TV screens into our kitchens and set overwhelming standards.

I have written *Secrets from a Caterer's Kitchen* to provide a solution to "hospitality anxiety" by teaching mastery of the techniques and shortcuts a caterer uses, including scores of successful menus and recipes. These menus and recipes don't just taste good, they are easy to make, manageable, spectacular looking, or all of the above. It's my goal to teach you to entertain with ease, relish, and confidence.

Introduction

Hospitality is one form of worship.

—Jewish proverb

WHEN I STARTED my own business I worked from home, like 99 percent of all beginning caterers. Until then, I had been the director of catering at the Los Angeles Music Center. The Music Center is a vast complex built around three of the most prestigious theaters in Los Angeles with several restaurants and banquet facilities for over one thousand. The theaters house many international productions including the Academy Awards, the L.A. Opera, and, at that time, the Joffrey Ballet. In this position, I directed battalions of employees. Now I was naively opening a business where I would function as the salesperson, planner, cook, truck driver, and general manager.

In the timeless "fools rush in" mode of the novice, I sold roast duckling as the main course for my first job. Fatty, splattering, smoke-producing ducks, forty of them, cooked in rounds of six, in my then boyfriend's double oven. Two long days and nights later, I transported those crispy beauties to the party site: a Victorian mansion with a gilded kitchen and one small oven. When we recognized the cooking disaster facing us, my peerless assistant, Maureen, called a party rental company and ordered the emergency delivery of two ovens. They were sold out. We settled for a transit cabinet, sort of a giant, rolling, bread warmer, and a case of Sterno. Between the transit cabinet loaded with forty-eight blazing cans of Sterno, a grill we found outside, and that very authentic, albeit miniature, oven, everyone was eventually served a piping-hot Christmas feast.

My first party was a definite eye-opener. Many lessons were vividly established in the course of that evening, which I later realized was my rite of passage from executive dilettante to independent professional. The first lesson pertained to organization. I swore (loudly) never again to plan a party without a complete understanding of the facilities. My second epiphany related to menu planning. Whole ducks are difficult and time consuming to prepare and reheat. They're awkward to eat in an elegant fashion, too. In the future I would take more than the party's theme into consideration when planning a menu. I learned "less is more" when cooking for a crowd, and that practical equals successful. A boneless duck breast could have been seared, quickly reheated, and eaten with grace. This would have been much more successful than the whole duck.

On the other hand, the charm of the home itself inspired me to do a splendid job with the third key to successful entertaining, the décor and the ambience. On that memorable Christmas, I filled the rooms with bouquets of heirloom roses and branches of clementines. I hung spiced pomanders from spruce garlands over every door. I placed antique damask overlays with dark velvet runners on the dining tables. Carolers, in opulent period costumes, performed in the library accompanied by a harpsichord. To complete the illusion, I outfitted the staff as Victorian ladies and gentlemen. Fortunately for my new career in catering, the success of the evening's theatrical and visual elements mitigated any "duck-wrestling" ire my menu had incurred.

As a result of the Victorian duck dinner episode, and many years of working with creative colleagues and clients, I developed a nearly foolproof approach to creating parties that are easy to stage, luscious to look at, and fun for the guest and host.

The Key Elements

In the years since, I have planned hundreds of events and learned my success or failure always relied on three key elements: organization, food, and ambience. You will find that understanding these elements is the secret to creating a worry-free party that looks and tastes professionally catered.

Organization

The first key is organization: the seamless coordination that allows the host to be a guest. Think lists, lists, lists. If you've been teased about your alphabetized sock drawer, here's where you will shine. A wonderful host is an organizer, a list maker, a planner, and a strategist. The details of successful entertaining can be endless. Lists and check-lists will clutter your desk, your car, and your mind. But, in the end, having accurately

The "Sizzle Factor"

I derived this expression from a speech given by the CEO of a well-known steakhouse restaurant chain. He asked his managers to concentrate on more than the quality of the food: Was the parking lot clean? Were fresh flowers on each table? Were the waiters cheerful and knowledgeable? He believed there was more to a great dining experience than good food. He said, "Hey folks, we're not just selling the steaks, we're selling the sizzle." As a caterer, I was attracted by the truth of his observation.

One of the most notable qualities a caterer adds to an event is the sizzle. This term refers to the atmosphere, the ambience—everything other than the actual food that makes your party special. Attention to how things look, sound, and smell is often overlooked by the novice. Easy-to-prepare or even purchased food can wow a group simply because of the way in which it's presented. The energy invested in creating what I call the *sizzle factor* is time well spent.

identified problems and solved them in advance is what allows you the energy and focus to create magic. The process of analyzing the festivities beforehand, and sifting through the details for problems and necessities, will also reveal welcome opportunities. For those of you not naturally given to analysis and list making, I am including useful multipurpose forms in the book. These guidelines, forms, checklists, illustrations, and menus will show you how to think like a caterer and entertain like a pro.

Food

The second key is the food: the selection and creation of an interesting and appropriate menu. There are many things to be considered in selecting a menu. Who are your guests? What is your budget? How good a cook are you? We will explore ideas about how to proceed if you are a gourmet chef, a barbecue maven, or a neophyte-microwave queen. Throughout the book I include advanced menus and recipes for the committed cook as well as simpler menus and techniques for the culinarily challenged.

My friend Vivian who is roundly regarded as a very accomplished hostess, has come up with one practical, entertaining idea that is enticing for both a fine chef and a first-timer. Years ago Vivian decided that "fussy" entertaining (in her mind that included cooking for more than thirty minutes) was for those who are not liberated. Instead, she spends her time making her rooms look beautiful and selecting glorious, emotional music. Then she serves a beautiful presentation of purchased foods complemented by her "homemade specialties." She has fun, the guests feel indulged, and at the end of the evening she's still glad she had the party.

Ambience

The third key is the ambience: sensuous fabric, shimmering steel, the smells of citrus and cinnamon, the sounds of the ocean or a harp, or the Dave Brubeck Quartet. A good host understands the importance of these components of presentation. Developing a style for your party makes choosing a menu easier and may even camouflage your lack of cooking skills or limited budget.

The Symbols

Because this is a party reference book, I have designed a series of symbols to categorize recipes and ideas by their characteristics. For example, anytime you see pie cooling in a window icon next to a recipe it means it can be completed before guests arrive! The chef's hat with the number one icon indicates a recipe that's easy to make. Menu items that are included in the recipe section of the book have the page number for easy reference.

SYMBOL LEGEND

 Easy to prepare, novice friendly

 Can be completed in advance

 Low-fat, healthy

 Complicated to prepare

 Last-minute preparation required

 Great on a buffet

Served hot

 Served cold

 Purchased

 Portable (picnic foods)

 Very pricey

 Reasonable, cost effective

 Advance preparation required

 Intermediate skills required

 Vegetarian

 Your additions to takeout food

In contrast to those warnings issued before Evil Knievel leaped the Grand Canyon, I am encouraging you to please try this at home. Use the forms, checklists, and questionnaires until analyzing a party becomes second nature to you. Together we are going to develop a comfortable, elegant, and foolproof entertaining style for you.

For more information, drop in at the party going on at my website—www.secretsfromacaterer.com.

Getting Started

If you wish to make an apple pie—truly from scratch, you must first invent the universe.

—Carl Sagan, *Cosmos*

Elements of a Party Plan

As a professional caterer, I learned to approach planning a party by asking my clients questions—lots of questions. Because you will be both the caterer and the client, you will benefit by considering similar questions to clarify your goals. Don't be embarrassed if you're caught talking to yourself. I do this so consistently while planning and preparing a party that my friends have come to assume that mumbling is a required element of entertaining. The success of your party will be determined by your consideration of the following key questions.

What is the purpose of this party?

The initial purpose of your party will probably involve an occasion like a birthday, New Year's Eve, a wedding rehearsal dinner, or maybe watching the Academy Awards with a group of friends. Another aspect of the purpose may be emotional. Are you trying to impress a new boss, a new girlfriend? Would you like to create romance or impress with your good taste? These goals are achieved with very different parties. An honest, well-thought-out answer to these questions will begin to clarify your approach to planning.

What is my budget?

Immediately following the decision to have a party comes the question. What's it going to cost? Can I afford to give the party I envision? Because this is such a defining issue, it is best to organize your thoughts about expenses before you go on to other decisions.

Every party is in essence a luxury. In some cases there is an absolute budget that must be adhered to. More often, you have a vision you want to create, little understanding of what things will cost, and a general anxiety about getting carried away. Throughout the book, recipes are included that provide delicious, elegant solutions to entertaining within a limited budget. They are identified with the symbol of a dollar sign with a line through it.

The types of parties that lend themselves to a conservative budget include: an open house, a dessert reception, a breakfast, an afternoon tea, an afternoon reception, and a potluck. Specific ways to trim any party budget include:

- **Simplify the menu (if there are fewer choices there will be less waste).**

- **Replace an expensive cut of meat with a less expensive one (instead of filet mignon, serve exotic Beef Saté, page 151).**

- **Replace an open bar with a single thematic cocktail service.**

- **Use paper plates and plastics instead of renting china and flatware.**

- **Cut the guest list.**

I have learned to employ a step-by-step approach to realistic budgeting. Using the budget form on page 9, I am reminded of all of the things that may be required for a specific party. The next step is to project reasonable costs for each necessary element by checking and comparing prices and guesstimating where necessary.

Even for a caterer, it is impossible to absolutely predetermine what the food will cost. However, if you identify the expensive ingredients (usually fish or meat or an exotic item like foie gras), and calculate their cost carefully, you will have anticipated the majority of your grocery bill.

Creating a Budget

	ESTIMATE/BID	FINAL
Invitations		
Food		
Purchased		
Made		
Alcohol/Beverages		
Rented Items *(tables, chairs, dishes)*		
Flowers/Plants		
Décor		
Entertainment		
Hired Help		
Valet		
Other		
ESTIMATED TOTAL + 5% OF THE TOTAL (FOR LIFE'S SURPRISES)		

When would I like to have the party?

This refers to both the time of day for which guests are invited, and the season of the year in which your event falls. This decision will be an important factor in menu selection, location, and perhaps, rentals.

How many guests would I like to invite?

This number may be suggested by the size of your family, the size of your home or yard, how many plates you own, or the amount of money you have decided to spend. I have a friend who always bases her invitation list on how many champagne glasses she owns. Not surprisingly, her parties have gotten smaller over the years. One thing to keep in mind when planning a party, the larger the group invited, the simpler the menu should be. That does not mean the food cannot be wonderful, exciting, and creative. But, if you are to enjoy hosting a party for thirty or forty, your energies should be focused on dishes served cold or simply reheated, and/or dishes the guests can cook or assemble for themselves like tacos, seafood bars, fondue, or *shabu shabu* (a grilled Japanese dish of paper-thin slices of beef and vegetables cooked in hot broth).

Who will make up my guest list?

All of your party plans are affected by the character of your guests. If your expected guests are the neighborhood children celebrating an eighth birthday or twenty fraternity brothers watching the Super Bowl, or a baby shower for your daughter, all of your party plans will be affected. I think it is important to have a clear picture of your guest list at the very earliest stages of party planning. To me, each of these special groups suggest different menus, décor, and music. While it may sound sexist, men and women do tend to enjoy different styles of food. And, if there are going to be a large number of small children, there must be some items planned strictly for their very finicky tastes if you want the parents to have a good time. However, men, women, and children have one thing in common, they go to a party hoping for a decadent dessert. No matter how they eat at home, at a party everyone is secretly hoping you'll give them a reason to sin. For more information on menu planning, see "How to Plan the Menu" (page 47).

What location makes the most sense for this party? Does my home accommodate the number of guests that I have in mind? If I can't have the party at home, what kind of location would be appropriate?

Near the small Southern California town where I live, it is possible to rent several locations for private parties. They include the Laguna Beach and Newport Harbor art museums, the city hall, three to four city and state parks, a state beach with picnic grounds, the train depot, the botanical garden (after dark), several art galleries, the Women's Club, the Elks' Club, the Veterans' Club, the Richard M. Nixon Library, many state historic landmark properties, private homes, and even the San Juan Capistrano Mission. These should give you ideas about where to look in your own area if you want to entertain somewhere other than your home or in a hotel banquet facility.

Will I need help, either paid or volunteer (family/friends)? If so, how many people?

Give this question serious consideration. Without exception I have been supremely grateful when I have arranged for helpers. From the comfort of your desk it is sometimes hard to remember just how hectic a large party can be. It's kind of like childbirth: our memory of the pain seems to be edited by the passing of time. Make it a rule to hire or recruit one more person than you think you'll need. This is the wisest place to splurge. Also, don't be afraid to call and ask a friend or two to commit to helping out. From my experience, people like to help with a party.

Solutions for Outdoor Entertaining

Outdoor entertaining provides an excellent solution to a number of problems, so it is important to know how to manage the challenges that can arise when Mother Nature will be the guest of honor. One December I booked two outdoor dinners to be held the following July. Any Southern California native would have agreed with me, there wasn't a chance of rain, or even cold, in mid-July. The day before the first event, the weather report predicted a 50 percent chance of rain for the following night. So, at a cost of over four thousand dollars, we erected a tent to enclose the diners. The evening turned out to be in the eighties with a glittering, cloudless sky. A week later, the day preceding the next event, the weather report predicted "clear and warming." As the first course was served, a freak twenty-minute downpour drenched everyone and everything (including the open pit barbecue where dinner was cooking). I expected the guests to panic. Instead, they spontaneously formed teams with their waiters, picked up their tables ladened with food and cocktails, and ran for cover. It became a raucous, riotous happening of a party under the porticoes. Though wet to the bone, the guests (and the staff and I) had a great time.

That party really proved that humor, and the ability to extemporize, are invaluable tools for entertaining well, indoors or out. And I learned a lesson about making absolute predictions for weather. If it is a very formal or very large event that would be difficult to move at the last minute, budget for an emergency tent, even in Southern California in the middle of summer.

Following is a checklist, which ensures that the elements affecting your party have been anticipated.

Uncomfortably Warm?

- **Rent or borrow umbrellas, fans, canopies (especially over buffets).**

- **Schedule the party before or after midday.**

- **Serve special cool drinks, including sparkling water and nonalcoholic beverages, at a table where guests can help themselves.**

- Buy extra ice and water.

- Provide squirt guns and paper fans.

- Use a water-misting system.

Too Cold?

- Rent space heaters.

- Focus the menu on dishes served warm. Spicy foods are also a good idea.

- Serve special hot toddy–type cocktails, such as hot buttered rum or a coffee table including whiskey, Kahlúa, Tia Maria, whipped cream, and chopped chocolate.

- Start an evening event as early as possible.

- Add lots of candles to the décor and fiery music for dancing.

- Hot colors like orange, red, and gold help trick the senses into feeling at ease in the cold.

Is the Party Site Frequently Windy?

- Make sure that all flowers, linens, and other décor items are secured and not likely to suffer from wind damage. Avoid umbrellas, tall or willowy floral arrangements, and balloons.

- Arrange for tables that don't require tablecloths or use cloths that are creatively tacked down or weighted at the hem.

- Try to locate as much of the party as possible in the lee of a building, fences, or trees.

- Avoid candles or open fires of any kind.

Does It Sometimes Rain on the Date You Have Selected?

This is a serious problem. If you cannot afford a tent if rain looks likely, it is best to plan on an indoor location for your party from the planning stage.

Are There Likely to Be Insect Pests?

- Arrange insect repellent candles and incense around guest seating and food areas.

- To combat the "picnic plague," one to two hours in advance place ant stakes around the party perimeter.

- Use mint and garlic plants on the buffet to discourage flying pests.

- Purchase unscented insect repellent for guests' use.

- Provide covers/screens for food served on a buffet.

Is the Party Located on a Lawn?

A lawn (especially a recently watered one) can be an unpleasant and even dangerous surface, especially for women in high heels. Check that all sprinklers have been turned off. (I have twice had sprinklers on automatic timers erupt in the middle of a garden wedding.)

Are There Any Noise or Time Restrictions?

- Ask if there are any noise/time restrictions imposed by the location itself. Restrictions are fairly common because noise/music carries so well outdoors.

- Conversely, check to see if there are unacceptable "sound effects" that might be coming from the neighboring streets or businesses at the time of your event. For example, overpowering rush-hour traffic or an adjacent restaurant patio with a noisy happy hour.

Is There Adequate Existing Lighting?

If your party will take place at night, visit the location after dark to check out the existing lighting. If it is inadequate for safety, mood, or convenience you can:

- Add luminarias (candles in paper bags weighted down with sand) to light up pathways and stairs.

- Use candles, in hurricane-style holders, to light buffets and guest tables.

- Provide camping-type kerosene lanterns. They give off a surprising amount of very attractive light. I have used seven or eight of them to provide all of the light required for a cocktail party for fifty in an unlit park.

- Check with rental companies for various kinds of useful lighting options. However, all will require an electrical outlet, which is sometimes a problem.

- Keep safety in mind when using open flames, especially in windy conditions.

What Are the Restroom Accommodations?

It is not uncommon for a park or beach area to be without restrooms. Portable toilets can be rented, but they are expensive and, except for the top-of-the-line units, not very attractive.

Organize Your Time

Timelines are worthy of considerable enthusiasm. Successful, stress-free entertaining, like other fast-paced sports, is reliant on planning, practice, and strategy. It is a very consistent equation—the more time spent planning, the more successful the outcome. My goal when organizing a party is once the guests arrive, I never have to make another decision. Of course it rarely works out that way, but I come pretty close.

Timelines

The following are samples of pre-event and day-of timelines I used to organize a cooperative family Thanksgiving for fourteen, a cocktail reception for fifty, and an elegant business dinner for eight.

Cooperative Thanksgiving (14 Guests)

Thanksgiving was my husband's favorite holiday. So we were more than happy to serve as hosts on that day with all of the traditional responsibilities involved: the creation of a beautifully decorated harvest table, a great turkey (and sometimes a duck), chestnut stuffing, my special cranberry-port relish, and pan gravy.

Because our guest list was a combination of family members and close friends, it was not only appropriate, but more fun to invite the guests to contribute to the meal. It is best if the host prepares items requiring long-cooking times, complicated last-minute preparation, or messy (nonportable) elements. The most successful dishes to farm out are baked desserts, breads, salads, soups, wine/alcohol, homemade condiments like relishes or cranberry sauce, and reheatable casseroles.

Our guests' participation allowed us the opportunity to give thanks for each other, and the year that has passed, without too much effort on anyone's part. I planned my timing to serve the meal between three thirty and four o'clock in the afternoon.

Our Thanksgiving Menu for 14

Each guest was responsible for preparing/purchasing enough to serve fourteen. Two couples conspired to provide the light hors d'oeuvres. My friend Wil brought an unusual winter salad dressed with walnut vinaigrette. My two stepsons shared the responsibility of selecting and providing the wines, a Pinot Noir and Sauvignon Blanc, which complemented the food very well. My sister and her daughter baked three pies, including our mother's Pumpkin Chiffon Pie (page 306). Our friends the Levins brought a very creative Pear and Potato Gratin with Horseradish (page 255).

I prepared the stuffing, Brussels sprouts, and the cranberry relishes. Even though two couples were bringing hors d'oeuvres, I set out bowls of my Savory Spiced Nuts (page 162) and had purchased some great olives to ensure nibbles for the first guests to arrive. I also provided the coffee and nonalcoholic beverages.

NOTE: *I have found that bread is really superfluous at Thanksgiving; it always remains untouched. But if you feel you must, purchase about a dozen rolls or two loaves of bread for a group this size.*

Thanksgiving Menu

HORS D'OEUVRES

Assorted imported olives with Savory Spiced Nuts (page 162)

Crudités with two dips

Sesame Eggplant Salsa (page 152) with Pita Crisps (page 167)

Shrimp and crab claws with rouille mayonnaise

Applejack cocktail

SUPPER

Winter salad of pear, orange, and pomegranate seeds on ribbons of spinach with walnut-pomegranate vinaigrette

Pear and Potato Gratin with Horseradish (page 255)

Brussels sprouts with crimini mushrooms in thyme butter

Glazed Thanksgiving Turkey (page 211) with Grandma Morgan's Thanksgiving Stuffing (page 265)

Cranberry Kumquat Relish (page 284)

Pinot Noir and Sauvignon Blanc

Pumpkin Chiffon Pie (page 306)

Warm apple pie with Vermont cheddar

Coffee

An apple pie without some cheese is like a kiss without a squeeze.

—Old proverb

Timeline

2 Weeks Before Thanksgiving

Check your dishes, linen, chairs, and serving pieces to see what you might need to borrow, rent, or purchase. (See pages 37–44 for quantities required; see page 86 for how to find a rental company.)

Call to confirm timing and the menu contributions of guests. Once it is decided what they are bringing, ask if they will need oven or refrigerator space when they arrive.

Order the turkey (you will need about 1 to 1¼ pounds per person, for fourteen I ordered an eighteen-pound bird).

Order the flowers (if you aren't planning to do them yourself).

Monday Before Thanksgiving

Clean out your refrigerator to make as much room as possible.

Pick up the turkey (if frozen, thaw in refrigerator).

2 Days Before

Shop for all ingredients from your prep list.

Prepare the dressing and refrigerate in a bowl.

Prepare the cranberry relish and refrigerate.

Pick up the turkey (if fresh).

Day Before

Check to be sure that the turkey is thoroughly thawed. Remove any enclosed giblets, rinse the cavity well, and pat dry. Refrigerate, covered loosely with plastic wrap.

Set up the dining table and decorate.

Pick up loose flowers or centerpiece.

Clean the house (or better yet, if you can afford it, arrange to have it cleaned).

Thanksgiving Day

10:00 A.M.

(5½ hours before serving) Preheat the oven to 325F (165C).

10:30 A.M.

Loosely fill the turkey with the dressing and lace or pin closed.

11:00 A.M.

Put the turkey in the oven, allowing about 15 minutes per pound.

The Really Important Half Hour

Plan your time so that you can shower, run a comb through your hair, dress with composure, have a glass of Champagne, and contemplate what you have wrought. Before anyone arrives, enjoy this time.

1:45 P.M.

- Open the wine.

- Put your hors d'oeuvres out.

2:00 P.M.

- Guests arrive.

- Put out the hors d'oeuvres brought by guests.

3:00 P.M.

- Remove the turkey from the oven and put the Brussels sprouts and potato gratin in to heat.

- Remove the turkey to a cutting board or serving platter and tent with foil. (Let turkey rest at least fifteen minutes before carving.)

- Ask for volunteers to help you arrange the food on serving dishes and take them to the table.

- Make the gravy with pan drippings and your favorite additions.

3:30 P.M.

- Sit down to a family-style Thanksgiving dinner.

Centerpieces

- Keep them low, no higher than your nose when you sit at the table.

- Avoid heavily scented plants or flowers.

- Combine several small vases to create an effective centerpiece. Small containers are easier to keep on hand and flowers are easier to arrange in them.

- Use anything and everything to decorate your table.

- Put the centerpiece in the most attractive location; it doesn't have to be in the center of the table. And the centerpiece can be more than one "piece."

Following are some ideas for centerpieces that go beyond flowers in a vase.

- An arrangement of hollow glass blocks filled with your marble collection.

- A tray lined with lemon leaves supporting a pyramid of tangerines and rosebuds.

- A red lacquer bowl filled with pomegranates and walnuts sprayed gold.

- Your collection of antique rolling pins in a willow basket.

- For a beach themed party: Tip over a child's sand pail in the center of the table, strew crystal sugar, seashells, starfish, the sand shovel, plastic fish, and seaweed out along the table. I have some papier-mâché lobsters I love to add to this look.

- An arrangement of candlesticks of varying heights with something as simple as rose petals nestled at their base and a silky French ribbon twined through makes a table look romantic and elegant.

Cocktail Reception (50 Guests)

This menu is a struggle-free combination of purchased dishes and items you prepare, mostly in advance. The dishes in this menu have page numbers for your reference.

Menu

PASSED ON TRAYS

Coconut Shrimp with Orange-Ginger Marmalade Dip (page 138)

Paper-Wrapped Chicken

Vietnamese-Inspired Spring Rolls (page 146)

BUFFET

Chicken Liver Pâté with Cherries and Pecans (page 137) with toasts

Duck and almonds in lettuce cups with plum sauce

Cocktail Party Walnuts (page 161)

Beef Saté (page 151)

Timeline

5 to 6 Weeks Before Party (8 to 10 weeks for December events)

Plan the guest list.

Order invitations or design and create them yourself on your computer.

Hire help (look under "Staffing Agencies" in the yellow pages, or ask a waiter or two from your favorite restaurant if they would like to moonlight).

Book a pianist.

Address the invitations.

Plan the menu (hors d'oeuvres only).

Contact the restaurant supplying the food to confirm their pricing and delivery.

4 Weeks Before Party

Mail the invitations.

Hire a valet and bartender (see pages 88–89 and 93).

Place the rental order (see page 86).

Place the liquor order (see page 118).

Do the visualization exercise (see Box on page 11).

5 Days Before Party

Based on RSVPs, confirm your order with the restaurant and finalize your shopping list.

Visit the florist and order flowers to put in your vases in the bathroom, entryway, on the coffee table, and other places. You may also want a formal arrangement completed by them.

Get out and check all serving dishes and linens.

Purchase candles, cocktail napkins, and party favors (unless this is a holiday themed party in which case purchase these items much earlier to ensure good selection).

3 Days Before Party

Shop for recipes and prepare the torta, the dip for the shrimp, the walnuts, and the pâté.

2 Days Before Party

Prepare the coconut shrimp, spring rolls, and Peanut Sauce (see page 268) for the saté.

Preceding Day

Rentals are delivered.

Set up the buffet.

Confirm order and delivery time with restaurant.

Clean house (or arrange for cleaning to be done on this day).

Check soap and towels in guest bathrooms.

Day of Party

Noon

Flowers are delivered.

3:30 P.M.

Hired staff members arrive and get your directions about room setup and food preparations.

4:00 P.M.

Liquor and ice are delivered.

The bartender checks in.

The restaurant delivers its dishes and informs the kitchen helper(s) about heating and other serving instructions.

4:30 P.M.

The Really Important Half Hour (see Box, page 18).

Kitchen helpers prepare the Beef Saté and spring rolls.

Arrange cold food on buffet.

5:00 P.M.

Valet arrives.

Adjust the lights and turn on party music unless live music is planned.

Pianist arrives, if using.

You're dressed and ready to go.

Arrange warm food on the buffet.

5:30 P.M.

Guests arrive.

8:00 P.M.

The party is over; kitchen helpers begin cleanup. Any of the subcontractors/employees not prepaid are usually paid now. Tips are generally given only to someone who provided extraordinary service.

Day After Party

The rentals are picked up.

Extra liquor is returned for credit.

Place Cards

Place cards add a soothing sense of order to a seated meal. They represent tradition in an age of curbside dining. The following are some creative options to standard cards.

- A four-inch fishbowl with one goldfish and the guest's name written on the glass decorates the table and can ultimately be a party favor.

- An individual votive candle in a glass candle holder wrapped with a raffia ribbon. Write the guest's name on the tail of the ribbon.

- A bright pippin apple with a name tag tied to the stem.

- A Christmas ornament or a Chinese fan inscribed with the guest's name.

- A snapshot of the guest in a small frame at their place.

Sit-Down Dinner (8 Guests)

Menu

Carpaccio (page 149) on Pita Crisps (page 167) with
Mustard-Horseradish Sauce (page 269)

Chicken skewers with Harissa (page 272)

Crudités with curry and yogurt-dill dips

Queen Elizabeth's California Salad (page 190)

Garlic Shrimp Sauté (page 217)

Deberah's Quick Orange Rice (page 259)

Grilled asparagus

Blackberry tarte

Coffee

Timeline

3 Weeks Before Party

Call to invite your guests and inquire about dietary limitations.

Decide on a menu based on guests' responses.

1 Week Before Party

Order the dessert if you are not going to make one. If you decide to prepare the dessert yourself, choose a recipe that can be prepared in advance.

Order a centerpiece for your table if you are not going to create it yourself. (Arrange to have it delivered the morning of the party.)

Order extra loose flowers to arrange in your vases for the bathroom, coffee table, entryway, and other areas.

Send a written reminder to guests in the form of postcard or note.

Do the visualization exercise (see Box, page 11).

3 to 4 Days Before Party

Prepare the two dips and refrigerate.

Make the sauce for the shrimp and refrigerate.

Make the salad dressing and refrigerate.

Make the Pita Crisps and wrap.

Make sauce for the Carpaccio and refrigerate.

Shop for wine and other beverages.

Order the shrimp (fresh, 15 per pound or larger).

Make the Harissa and refrigerate.

2 Days Before Party

Do all the final grocery shopping including fillet for Carpaccio.

1 Day Before Party

Clean the house (or arrange for cleaning); check bathrooms for soap and towels.

Pick up the shrimp.

Set the table.

Clean and prep the asparagus.

To Chill Bottles

Beverages chill more quickly on ice than in the refrigerator. If the bottles are well immersed in ice, it will take about forty-five minutes for beer or wine to become cold enough to serve. Chilling them in the refrigerator can take up to three to four hours or longer.

Party Day

Morning

Cut the vegetables for crudités and refrigerate.

Prepare the salad.

Clean the shrimp and refrigerate.

Pick up the dessert.

Put the fillet for the Carpaccio in the freezer to firm.

Chill white wine and water.

4:00 P.M.

Slice the fillet for Carpaccio.

Assemble shrimp in the pan, ready to bake.

5:00 P.M.

Assemble crudité tray, wrap, and refrigerate.

Fill bread basket and butter tubs.

5:30 P.M.

The Really Important Half Hour (see Box page 18).

6:00 P.M.

From this point on, at the latest, your partner or a friend whom you have asked to arrive early, begins to assume responsibility for some of these items.

Assemble the Carpaccio platter, cover with lettuce leaves, and refrigerate.

Preheat the broiler.

Put out ingredients for the wild rice.

6:45 P.M.

Set out the crudités, dips, and Carpaccio.

Adjust the lights and turn on party music.

7:00 P.M.

Put the chicken skewers in the preheated broiler.

Guests begin to arrive; your partner pours each guest a glass of wine or other beverage.

7:15 P.M.

Put the rice on to cook.

Serve the chicken skewers.

Preheat the grill.

7:30 P.M.

Arrange the salad on plates.

Pour water.

Put bread on the table.

7:45 P.M.

Put the shrimp in the oven.

Put asparagus on the grill.

Start the coffeemaker.

8:00 P.M.

Transfer cooked asparagus to the oven to keep warm.

Ask guests to be seated.

Serve the salads and offer wine or other beverage.

At this point in the proceedings, you should relax and move through the rest of your party at a casual pace, allowing yourself and your guests to enjoy each other's company. Because you planned ahead, everything flows from this point. When everyone is through with their salads (usually this takes about ten minutes) the plates should be cleared. It will then just take you a moment to step into the kitchen, remove the scampi and asparagus from the oven, add the rice, and serve eight attractive plates.

You or your partner should offer guests more of their beverages and replenish the bread and butter.

At the conclusion of the main course, it is nice to take a moment and clear the table of dirty silverware and plates, bread and butter, and unused glasses so that dessert is served on a fresh table. It's unappetizing when dessert and coffee are plunked down in the debris left over from the previous revelry.

Space Planning

MAKING INFORMED CHOICES about where to place the bar, who to seat next to your father-in-law, and where to position a make-your-own dessert table establishes the difference between a graceful event and a free-for-all. In general, you want to spread all food and beverage displays evenly around the space you are using. Not only does this eliminate congestion, it also encourages guests to mingle and interact.

- Match your group size to the party space. Spreading a small group over too large an area can be as uncomfortable as overcrowding.

- When you are using more than one dining table in a room, allow two to four feet between chair backs, when spacing the tables and chairs.

- Stand-up cocktail tables (about forty-two inches tall) are available from many rental companies. They are a great solution when there is limited space for tables, or when you want to keep guests from settling permanently in one place.

- How many seating options do you have without rentals? Besides dining-room chairs, this list could include sofas, living-room chairs, piano benches, garden furniture, and folding chairs borrowed from a friend.

- If you are planning to have dancing, make sure that you have left an open area. If dancing is very important to you, you might consider renting a dance floor.

- To determine how many square feet will be required for a table with chairs around it, add three feet to the diameter of the table. If your space is cramped, it is worth the effort to draw a scale outline of the room and experiment with different ways of arranging the tables. I have arranged a thousand rooms, and sometimes I still need to do a quick floor plan.

- For a casual buffet party, have seats for about three-fourths of the guests.

Buffet Location

- Anytime that your space will allow you to move the buffet away from a wall and allow guests to approach it from all sides, do so.

- A two-sided buffet, allowing two lines of guests to serve themselves at the same time, reduces lines and irritating waits.

- It is desirable to have a buffet close to the kitchen (for ease of replenishment) but not so close to the kitchen door as to cause a bottleneck.

- Try to have food available in at least two locations.

- Leave plenty of open space around the beginning of the buffet (where the plates are), because it is likely that guests will congregate there.

- Avoid placing a buffet or bar near the front door, bathroom door, or any other busy place.

Bar Location

There are some fundamentals to remember when deciding where to place the bar. Without exception, guests expect to get a beverage (alcoholic or not) as soon as they arrive. It is such a custom that guests are uncomfortable if they arrive and cannot quickly have a glass in their hand.

- The bar should be visible, if possible, on entry.

- Do not place the bar too near the front door or you will create a traffic jam.

- It is helpful if there is a sink nearby.

- The bar should be well lighted.

- Make sure that there is a trash receptacle nearby.

YOUR INVITATION, WHETHER written or verbal, sets the stage for your party. The pleasant anticipation conveyed by a creative invitation puts your guests in a party mood before they leave home. Use your invitation to notify guests of your intention to include them in a good time, and to give them many other cues concerning the party. When you provide the time of day, combined with an accurate description of the party, your guests know what to expect in the way of food and drink, how to dress, how long to stay, and whether they need to let you know if they are planning to attend. It is particularly important to state clearly whether the party will take place out of doors. I recall most painfully the evening reception I attended on a bluff overlooking the sea. The invitation had given no information about the location except the address. As the sun set in a vivid blaze, and the wind whipped off the whitecaps below, I was very sorry that I hadn't known to bring earmuffs and leg warmers to accessorize my strapless cocktail dress.

You also need to be aware of the assumptions created by the wording of your invitation. I attended a wedding this summer, scheduled for noon, which naturally lasted until 4:00 P.M. Nothing other than coffee and wedding cake was served. Mind you, the invitation did not specify that lunch would be provided, but the time implied that it would be. It detracted from the romance of the occasion to see the assembled family and friends constantly craning their necks, looking around to see what the heck had happened to the expected (and nonexistent) lunch. By the time the bride tossed the bouquet, the woman who caught it was more inclined to put salad dressing on it than cherish it.

The Structure of Invitations

1. **IDENTIFY THE HOST(S)—** A written invitation will begin with the name of the host(s).

example: **Maxine and Fred Walters or more formally**
Mr. and Mrs. Fred Walters

2. **EXTEND THE INVITATION**

example: **request the pleasure of your company**

3. **TYPE OF PARTY—** Cocktail, cocktail reception, open house, dinner, dinner and hors d'oeuvres, luncheon, late supper, dessert.

example: **at dinner**

4. **IN HONOR OF OR TO CELEBRATE—** Birthday, wedding, anniversary, shower, retirement, housewarming, divorce, holiday, christening, engagement

example: **to celebrate the engagement of their daughter,**
Adrian, to Mr. Paul Bocluse

5. **DATE—** Both the day of the month and the day of the week

example: **Sunday, June 14, 2001, or, more formally,**
Sunday, the fourteenth of June

6. **TIME—** Starting time only unless it is an event, like an open house or a boat party, with a specific ending time.

example: **6:30 P.M. or, more formally, six thirty o'clock**

7. **PLACE—** The address (and directions if it is unusual or hard to find)

example: **22233 Mulholland Drive (at the corner of Berry Canyon)**

8. **SPECIAL ATTIRE—** The most common suggestions are black tie, black tie optional, cocktail attire, costume suggestions, and casual or sporting attire

example: **cocktail attire**

9. **RSVP—** Respond please, followed by your phone number is absolutely necessary if you are planning on formal seating. There are other situations that also require accu-

rate guest counts: The boat you've rented will capsize with more than thirty passengers! It is standard and wise to include a cutoff date for responding.

example: **RSVP by June 1st, please, to 999-999-0099 or, more formally, reply card enclosed.**

All put together, this formal invitation looks like:

There are additional items, which may be included on an invitation: Please bring a picture that relates to the guest of honor, don't bring gifts, bring a bathing suit, or other special instructions. Written invitations should be sent out at least four weeks before the event, unless it is a wedding, in which case six weeks is more traditional.

An error on a printed invitation can create real havoc. These oversights usually occur in the numbers: the address, the RSVP phone number, or the date. The confusion caused by inviting people for Tuesday, the 14th of July, when the 14th is a Sunday, can easily be avoided by asking someone else to double check the copy. Without careful proofreading, I have seen many invitations go out with incorrect information.

> *Mr. and Mrs. Fred Walters*
> *Request the pleasure of your company*
> *at dinner*
> *to celebrate the engagement of their daughter,*
> *Adrian, to Mr. Paul Bocluse*
> *Sunday, the fourteenth of June*
> *Six thirty o'clock*
> *22233 Mulholland Drive*
> *Beverly Hills*
>
> *cocktail attire*
>
> *valet parking*
> *reply card enclosed*

A client of mine was responsible for creating a fund-raising event to preserve an historic firehouse. She and her committee decided to hold an exhibition accompanied by an artistically presented cocktail reception.

> You are covertly invited to
>
> A Surprise Birthday Party for Ami
>
> Saturday, September 14th, 1998
>
> on the Yacht *Rapture*,
>
> Johnson Marina, Dock 34
>
> Newport Beach
>
> (map and parking instructions included)
>
> 6:00 P.M. boarding, 6:30 P.M. departure (sharp)
>
> 10:00 P.M. re-dock
>
> Attire: Black Tie and Sneakers
>
> RSVP (my office number) by September 1st

On the night before the party, I dropped by with some Chinese takeout and beer for the bedraggled volunteer curators as they proudly completed setting up the exhibits. We were just tossing out the last of the white "to-go" cartons as the first of the elegant guests began to arrive. The committee had scheduled the party for June 7, but the invitations said June 6. This mistake was compounded by the omission of an RSVP number. Ouch.

If you are telephoning the invitations for a social occasion, two to three weeks is adequate. For a business event, four weeks is more appropriate. When telephoning invitations, take a minute to write out a "script" of all the information you want to impart to each invitee.

The invitations for my husband's birthday party aboard a rented yacht provide an example of how to communicate a lot of unusual circumstances. The party is on a boat that will set to sea at an exact time (nonnegotiable) and remain at sea until a set time (nonnegotiable). It is a surprise. The location is complicated, because it is not a building or home. The suggested attire is unique.

Surprise parties, while very gratifying to the surprisor and the surprisee if successful, impose some special challenges on the invitations.

1. State clearly that it is a surprise.
2. The RSVP phone number must be a number that the guest of honor will never answer.
3. The return address on the envelope needs to be for a location that the guest of honor is unlikely to visit at mail time.

My friend Rochelle's invitation to her combination job promotion to travel director of an art museum and birthday party provides a great example of a creative, casual invitation, which also includes specific instructions for guests' participation. They were produced on 8.5 × 11-inch paper with the help of a computer, scissors, and a copy machine.

Please come help me celebrate

one of the last remaining birthdays in my 30s

and

my new job in the same old place

Sunday, April 6th

International Potluck

12:30 to 5:30 P.M.

at

1111 Farout Avenue

Encino (map on reverse)

(999) 999-0000

In honor of the museum's yet to be developed but already world-

renown travel program, please bring a dish from another country to

share and your favorite travel photo. Be sure the photo's location

isn't obvious. There's a game with FABULOUS PRIZES!

(see enclosure)

RSVP by April 1st

to Rochelle (310) 123-4567

THIS SECTION DESCRIBES everything you may need to successfully "stage" your party, how to use it, and whether or not it is an item worth purchasing.

Tables

Whether you are trying to determine how many tables to rent or how many people you can fit at your dining-room table, the rule of thumb when calculating a table's seating capacity is two feet of linear space per person (place setting). This includes the ends of the table, which in some cases are broad enough to seat two or even three people.

Following is a list of some standard table sizes available from rental companies and how many guests they each accommodate (the name commonly used by rental companies to identify each type of table is in parenthesis).

- 24-inch round (cocktail) table seats two to three casually (not often used for full meal service)

- 36-inch round (cocktail) table seats four casually

- 60-inch round table comfortably seats eight, or ten with a squeeze

- 72-inch round table is great for ten, or twelve with a squeeze

- 6-foot × 30-inch rectangular (banquet) table seats eight

- 8-foot × 30-inch rectangular (banquet) table seats ten, or twelve with a squeeze

NOTE: *Rental companies also frequently stock special children's height tables and chairs.*

Creating a Beautiful Buffet

There are five underlying principals of a great-looking buffet:

1. Use lavish quantities of the decorating materials you have selected.

2. Be bold with your color choices, and bold can mean all black, all gold, or the excitement created by contrasting purple and yellow.

3. Arrange the food at various heights and angles.

4. On a buffet, bigger is better. Big baskets, boxes, platters, or trays filled with bountiful quantities of food are inviting.

5. There should be some focal point for the buffet. It doesn't have to be in the center, and it doesn't have to be flowers. A bushel basket of corn-stalks combined with cattails at the end of the table might be just the right touch for a fall buffet.

A flat, orderly arrangement on a buffet is not appealing. On the other hand, the visual movement created by a variety of levels and angles is engaging and exciting. To create the levels for an attractive buffet, place sturdy, flat objects like boxes, bricks, and crates on the table. These objects will support the trays and platters of food. A tablecloth or a decorative fabric is then draped across these homely pedestals. Flowers, fruits, and beautiful vegetables can be arranged around these levels for a professional-looking buffet table. If guests will approach the buffet from all sides, take that into consideration when placing centerpieces and other décor. Make sure things look beautiful from every angle.

Only elevate trays or platters of cold foods. Hot items need to rest firmly on the table for safety. Everything else should be either at varying heights or at least titled on an angle. Baskets or bowls of breads, fruits, and candies need a wedge under one side; use a brick or a small bowl, so the contents spill out onto the table in a sumptuous jumble.

To avoid renting tables and to conserve space, I have used the kitchen island, patio tables, children's tables, a covered spa, the fireplace mantel, and a rolltop desk as buffets. An easy, amusing display based on something you own can be created from a wheelbarrow. Line it with plastic wrap (for obvious reasons) then cover the plastic completely with cabbage leaves. Miniature or cut vegetables are arranged on the cabbage as a dramatic crudité display. Hollowed acorn squash can hold the dips. It takes about fifteen minutes longer than to place the same vegetables and dip on a tray, but what a difference.

Linens

The lavish use of linens or fabrics layered and draped on guest and buffet tables is one of the basic elements in a "catered look." This simple technique makes any party look more special and beautiful. The materials can come from myriad sources—1940s tablecloths, a sari, a Mexican serape, velvet yardage, a quilt, or flags. Depending on your theme, any of these items make a festive contribution to your tables.

The purchase of several tablecloths (as a rule of thumb twice as many as the number of tables you normally use for a party) is a very good idea. Select colors or patterns that complement or match each other and do not require dry cleaning. (I find I hesitate to use cloths I know will have to be dry cleaned every time they're used.) Fabric napkins that coordinate are necessary for formal parties. For casual, outdoor, or children's parties good-quality paper napkins are perfectly appropriate.

Rental companies have a selection of solid color linens, including napkins, and a varying selection of prints and damasks that you can get to use as a base for your more interesting personal additions. They usually also offer pregathered "skirting" to cover the sides of a buffet table. While this is a timesaver, the look it creates is really typical of a hotel and rather industrial looking.

If a table is not particularly attractive, which includes virtually all rented tables, it is best to use a cloth large enough to drape all the way to the floor. Since most tables are twenty-eight to thirty inches high, add fifty-six to sixty inches to the diameter of a round tabletop for floor-length coverage. The addition of a shorter overlay cloth adds a sense of luxury and personalizes even rental linens.

To cover a six-foot rectangular (banquet) table is more challenging. No cloth is readily available that covers it all the way to the floor evenly. A caterer will generally order a banquet cloth (156 × 90 inches) and box the corners.

To cover an eight-foot rectangular (banquet) table you need a 156 × 90-inch cloth. Because these are not always available, you may need to allow for two cloths and overlap them.

Creative Chafing Dishes

If you are serving warm food on your buffet, there are some creative options to a standard chafing dish or warming tray. The basic elements of a chafing dish are a frame, which holds a pan of food over a source of gentle heat, and the heat itself, like a votive candle or Sterno. A chafing dish is designed to keep food warm for up to three hours. I have invented my own chafing dishes by stacking bricks or glass blocks to support the food pan and slipping a Sterno (on a plate to protect your table) under the pan. For a casual party or barbecue, the bricks add a warm, earthy tone to your buffet. Glass blocks or pieces of polished slate lend themselves to a more formal table. Whatever the material, it should only take a few minutes to assemble and provide an attractive, practical solution to keeping food warm and appealing. Plus, chafing dishes are expensive to rent. You can reuse the bricks or glass blocks to build these more interesting chafers over and over again.

Food Heating/Holding Elements

You cannot serve a dish that needs to be eaten warm on a buffet without some accommodations for keeping it warm. A chafing dish, fondue pot, electric hot tray, or warming (votive) candles under a sheet of marble are some common options for keeping food warm. A large coffeemaker and portable convection oven are the most practical purchases for extra cooking and heating.

Chafing Dish: Typically a chafing dish is a metal container for food, resting in a larger pan filled with hot water, with a heat source, such as a candle or Sterno, under the pans.

Every catered buffet you've seen no doubt featured one (or ghastly sight, a military row of eight or ten) chafing dish patiently offering hot food. If used correctly, chafing dishes are an excellent way to keep moist foods, like lasagna or cassoulet, warm. If used to hold cuts of rare meat, or delicate fish, or tender vegetables, they simply overcook the food within minutes. As long as you understand their appropriate use, a chafing dish adds a lot of flexibility to your entertaining menus. I have an attractive four-quart chafing dish for my home that I use at nearly every party.

Coffeemaker (twenty-four cup or larger): You will almost always serve coffee, and for even ten people you will likely need fourteen to fifteen cups in the course of a party. So, purchasing a buffet-type coffeemaker/server (such as West Bend) is a practical investment that should last for years of entertaining. I have also used mine to serve hot cider and hot, mulled wine. Be sure to clean it well with a baking soda and water solution before and after using it for any beverage besides coffee.

Toaster Oven or Convection Oven: Although convection ovens are a little more expensive than toaster ovens (usually about $120), they are much larger and more powerful. For many purposes, convection ovens provide you with the cooking flexibility of adding another full-sized oven to your kitchen when needed.

Warming Tray: For any style of buffet, including the family Thanksgiving dinner, a hot tray is another useful tool for maintaining the temperature of "dry heat" (crispy) dishes like crab cakes, tarts and quiches, pizza and calzone, and borek and spanakopita.

Serving Utensils

There are a wide variety of serving utensils available: cute salad servers carved to look like pine cones or zebras, cake servers decorated with cutouts of Winnie-the-Pooh, cheese knives with bowling pins or French waiters as the handle. Clearly you can indulge your personal style, whatever it is. However, in terms of practicality, flexibility, and usefulness, there are some basic types of serving pieces that an average host will find necessary to purchase.

Cheese Knives, Wedges, and Pâté Spreaders: Cheese, in all of its wonderful incarnations—from rock-hard Cheddar, gooey Camembert, springy Gruyère, to spreadable cream cheese is a classic element of entertaining. Cheese is never going to go out of style and a beautiful cheese board is one of the easiest hors d'oeuvre solutions. An attractive selection of small cheese knives, slicers, and spreaders is a great, basic purchase.

Serving Spoons and Forks: Serving spoons are the most flexible utensil after tongs. In a pinch, you could even serve lasagna with an attractive spoon (and I have). The serving fork is especially useful for serving slices of meat. The most practical serving spoon or fork has an eight- to ten-inch handle. Longer and they overpower some platters, shorter and they tend to slip in to saucy dishes like chili or stew and disappear. Fishing the serving spoon out of the bouillabaisse, in front of the guests, is an extremely embarrassing but common occurrence.

Spatulas: Unless it is a casual barbecue or picnic, your kitchen spatula, while effective, will look out of place on a buffet or dining-room table. Purchase at least one handsome,

The Cheese Course

Cheese is probably the best of all foods, as wine is the best of all beverages.
—Patience Grey

Whether as part of an hors d'oeuvres table, or offered as a separate course at the end of a meal, the simple presentation of a variety of cheeses is a timeless favorite. The artful selection of a good cheese board should include four to seven cheeses. They should present a composition of contrasts in texture, appearance, and flavor: creamy, firm, semisoft, or hard; covered in ash, herbs or leaves; salty, pungent, mild, or sweet.

Fifteenth-century French philosopher, Rabelais, described the marriage of wine, bread, and cheese as "the Holy Trinity." I couldn't agree more. However, I add fruit to this ideal. I always include pears, apples, apricots, grapes, and/or dried fruits in any cheese presentation. Both red and white wines can be excellent with cheese. Experiment to find your favorite combinations. Slices of baguette or plain crackers are best with everything except intensely flavored blue cheese. These strong cheeses are mellowed when served with a robust dark or nut bread, like walnut pumpernickel.

Allow cheeses to come to room temperature before serving. It's best to leave the cheeses uncut and provide guests with a separate knife or spreader for each type of cheese. Once they are cut they begin to lose aroma and moisture.

On a buffet, cheese is most successfully served on a wooden cutting board or marble slab so

party spatula or cake server. You will need it to serve wedges of quiche, squares of strata or lasagna, slices of pie, and brownies.

Tongs: These are my favorite utensil, period. Use large, long-handled ones for the grill and sautéing. Every professional chef I know uses sturdy tongs for just about every kitchen task except cutting. Use short-handled attractive ones for serving salads, sliced meats and cheeses, cut fruit, rolls, pastry, and pasta. Small tongs are for serving sugar cubes, tiny tarts, bonbons, butter balls, or ice.

guests can slice and spread with ease. When cheese is offered as a course during a seated dinner, I suggest using a small tray or flat basket lined with greens because it is easier to pass at the table.

The following are examples of two cheese selections with accompaniments.

CHEESE SELECTION 1

Saint Nectaire (creamy, coated in ash, complex flavor)

Gruyère (firm, nutty, mild)

Maytag Blue (spicy, salty, crumbly blue cheese)

Buchette de Banon (fresh, soft, mild goat cheese, wrapped in leaves)

Dry California Jack (hard, tangy, salty)

Accompany this board with baguette slices, crackers, nutty pumpernickel, and red and white wines. Decorate with sliced apples, grapes, and dried apricots.

CHEESE SELECTION 2

Huntsman (beautiful layers of Stilton and creamy Cheddar, sharp, salty)

Emmentaler (firm, nutty, mild)

Chevre, fresh (mild, creamy, tangy)

Brie de Meaux (the queen of the Brie family, creamy, pungent, sweet, rich)

Accompany this presentation with the same breads as above, red and white wines, pears, apples, and toasted walnuts.

Work and Buffet Tables

A sturdy card table or a six- to eight-foot folding table can solve a world of space problems, and they're easy to keep on hand. Just make sure they are strong enough to hold hundreds of pounds. I frequently use my six-foot folding table as extra kitchen space while I am preparing for a large party. The day of the party I wipe it off, move it to the living room, and transform it into a buffet. The look can always be concealed with artfully draped linens. I recommend this as one of your first entertaining purchases.

Dishes and Flatware

At a dinner party, where you serve a three-course meal, you will need the following per guest:

FLATWARE

> Knives (1 or 2, depending on menu)
>
> Salad/dessert forks (0 to 2, depending on menu)
>
> Dinner forks (1)
>
> Teaspoons (1)
>
> Soup/dessert spoon (0 to 2, depending on menu)

CHINA

> Salad/dessert plates (1 or 2, depending on menu)
>
> Soup bowl (1, depending on menu)
>
> Underliner for soup bowl (1, depending on menu, can be a salad plate)
>
> Bread and butter plate (1)
>
> Dinner plate (1)
>
> Cup/saucer (1 of each)
>
> Creamer, sugar bowl, salt shaker, pepper grinder, butter dish (1 of each for every table)

GLASSWARE

> White wineglass (1, if served)
>
> Red wineglass (1, if served)
>
> Champagne flute (1, if served)
>
> Water glass (1)

For every ten guests, I allow for one extra of everything, to allow for breakage and other complications.

When the entire meal is served buffet style, I generally plan on one dinner plate plus one salad plate per person for the main course. This gives guests the opportunity to have second helpings, or to take a small amount of something they only want to sample. You

Buffet Etiquette

Make sure there is a practical serving implement with every dish and a bowl for guests to discreetly discard toothpicks, shrimp tails, or other refuse that accumulates at the buffet table.

will need a third plate for dessert. If you have a seat for everyone, it is thoughtful to have silverware and a water glass preset on the tables. Beverage glasses and coffee mugs should be located on the buffets or bar. I usually use a mug when coffee is being served from a buffet. It is much easier to handle than a cup and saucer when you are walking around. When the seating arrangements are more casual, silverware wrapped in a napkin should be placed at the *end* of the buffet.

Again, for every ten guests, I allow for one extra of everything. In addition, I find that there is always a use for some extra fabric napkins, such as lining bread baskets, wrapping wine bottles, or covering a mid-party spill on the buffet.

MRS. B WAS a committed hostess and a much sought after interior decorator. Together we had executed many innovative and successful parties in her luxurious home. I still feel the same disbelief today as I did on that afternoon when I took this call. "Nicole, I'm having forty people to the house for dinner. They are all of my most important business associates. Everything served must be white."

"White?"

"Or clear. Clear would be okay."

"White or clear?"

"Oh, and I would like to have several entrée choices at the buffet. Of course, there has to be an elegant beef dish."

"White beef?"

An accomplished caterer is expected to serve a menu that acknowledges the reason for the party, the season, the budget, the location, and the guest of honor's favorite food. The successful fusion of these variables, and often there are many more, is one of the main qualities that distinguishes a catered party from that of a novice. That's why I enjoy designing a menu.

"Yes, I've just rethought the house and everything is white, carpets, furniture—everything. An absolutely blank canvas, and I want it to stay that way. I don't want to spend the evening worrying about red wine dribbles or crumbling strawberry tarts. I'm always stressed out when I give a party anyway, so please, be creative and find a delicious, beautiful way to present a color-free party. And I would just as soon that the guests don't realize that's how the menu was chosen."

Even though a career spent in the catering trenches had pretty well numbed me to surprise, this request shocked me. I had never been asked to plan a menu from such a completely visual perspective. Within the next three months I had two other clients, ones that Mrs. B and I had in common, request white menus. All white definitely enjoyed a vogue.

Menu for the All-White Supper Buffet

Note: in order to compensate for the bland tones of the food, everything was served on colorful dishware and garnished with lots of fresh herbs and edible flowers.

Baked Brie en croûte, layered with almonds, kirsch, and brown sugar

Endive and mushroom vinaigrette

Cauliflower Gruyère gratin

Potato soufflé

Chevre and Prosciutto Ravioli (page 142) filled with chicken mousse and served with thyme butter

Chicken roulade with white truffles and hazelnuts

Veal scallopini (white beef!)

White Chocolate Cheesecake en Croûte (page 292)

For the beverage service, instead of the usual complete bar, which would include bourbon, red wine, and Kahlúa, just to mention a few potential disasters, we limited the choices to white wine, Champagne, and festive clear cocktails: vodka lemon drops, a martini bar, Ramos fizzes, and gimlets. To tie all of this together I placed a table near the bar draped in silver lamé. Three large silver tubs of crushed ice were filled with bottles of

Champagne, vodkas, gins, and white wines, establishing the theme. The bar itself was decorated with a pretty pyramid of martini glasses and Ramos goblets.

Once I accepted that Mrs. B was serious, I had a lot of fun making this idea work. Requests from other clients for a vegetarian Indian wedding, a nostalgic World War II mess hall dinner, and a menu that reflected the music of Gershwin were also fun to research and plan. As a caterer, I could respond to these diverse circumstances, because I had developed a large repertoire of recipes and a trained kitchen staff on which to rely. Because you aren't likely to have either, how do you handle creative, appropriate menu planning?

My solution is a series of party strategies. Even though I had help and experience, like most successful caterers I often had five or six parties in progress at the same time. In response, I had to develop the techniques for planning menus that this chapter imparts. They are as relevant to the home party planner as they are to a busy, professional caterer. The most significant of these tactics is learning to analyze the fundamental characteristics of your party.

The Essentials of Menu Planning

Each party is complex and unique, yet there are common issues that must always be considered.

Know Your Limitations

Taking a realistic look at how much time you can (or want to) invest, how many serving dishes you have, or your ability to flambé crepes tableside will guide you in making choices you can live with.

Establish Your Budget

This is usually a major factor in deciding on a menu (see page 8).

Give Consideration to the Tastes and Preferences of Your Guests

Are your guests health conscious? kosher? staid? cosmopolitan? vegetarian?

Balance the Challenges: Divide and Conquer

No professional caterer ever tries to prepare absolutely everything they serve. It's not practical, and there are specialists at things like dim sum or pastry that can do a better

job than you would. Think of the grocery store, bakery, specialty market, and restaurants as part of your team and delegate certain elements. Observe the following proportions:

- 0 to 20 percent challenging or new recipes

- 60 to 70 percent easy-to-prepare or all-done-ahead-of-time recipes

- 20 to 40 percent items that are purchased and you just need to open, serve, slice, heat, or garnish

NOTE: *Never plan to include a recipe in a party menu that you haven't prepared at least once before.*

Balance Flavor, Color, and Texture to Create Interest, Variety, and Harmony

Do serve:

- An appetizer that reflects the entrée that is to follow. Example: Vietnamese-inspired Spring Rolls (page 146) followed by Ginger Roast Duck Breast (page 209).

- A dinner plate of contrasting colors and textures. Example: Barbecued Pork Ribs (page 231), Spinach in Black Bean Sauce (page 251), and Herb-Roasted Corn on the Cob (page 253).

- A light dessert following a rich meal, a rich dessert following a light repast. Examples: Smoked Salmon and Asparagus Strata (page 234) paired with Evan's Summer Cooler (page 309) or Chicken Piccata (page 201) followed by Susan's Apple Bread and Butter Pudding (page 296) with Whiskey Caramel Sauce (page 288).

Avoid:

- Overuse of one cooking method such as deep-frying. For example, a main course of fish and chips followed by beignets.

- A strong flavor such as blue cheese in more than one dish.

- Mixing distinct ethnic flavors, such as a first course of sashimi followed by enchiladas.

- Foods on a plate that are all one color such as chicken, mashed potatoes, and cauliflower; add some visual interest.

Select the Style of Service That Fits Your Party

Any group larger than ten, maybe twelve, should not be served plate service by an individual. Give yourself a break and provide a buffet as the most common style you employ when entertaining. However, whether you decide on a buffet, a picnic, or a formal sit-down meal, you must select recipes that are suited to that style. (For more information on styles of service, see page 106–113.)

Observe and Celebrate the Seasons

Both the dishes you select and the style of the meal are most exciting when they reflect what is best in the market and the season of the year.

Create Drama

Another caterer's tool is the inclusion of intentionally dramatic elements. Try to elicit at least one "wow" in every menu.

Plan Recipes and Quantities That Are Appropriate to the Time Frame of the Event

Portions are usually smaller at a lunch than at dinner. Similarly, if a cocktail reception is scheduled from 4:30 to 6:00 P.M., you may be able to serve only nibbles; what I think of as a hint of food. On the other hand, if you have invited guests for a party lasting from 6:00 to 9:00 P.M., the thoughtful and practical host should serve enough cocktail fare, and hors d'oeuvres to provide a filling meal. See page 32–33 for more information about the right way to communicate with an invitation.

Menu Problem Solving: Tying It All Together

The creation of a menu, which balances fantasy with reality, is an art and a science. It is also a skill that can be learned. The simplest way to explain this process is to provide you with some examples of problem-solving menus. That is the term I use to describe the process of translating the reason for each party, plus the answers to all of the essential questions on pages 49–51, into a great menu.

Entertaining Crown Royalty

One of the most daunting menu requests I ever had came shortly after I started working at the Los Angeles Music Center. I received a call from the mayor's office. He said, "We are planning a state luncheon honoring Queen Elizabeth, the second. The occasion calls for a formal menu requiring the use of one utensil. Cost is no object. The theme is California cuisine."

At first I thought I had misunderstood part of the conversation, *"One utensil?"*

He replied, "We have been informed, by the head of protocol, that members of the British royal family do not use a knife and fork at the same time! Oh, and the menu must be confined to strictly local ingredients."

I put the one-utensil quandary on hold and asked about the queen's favorite foods. Her favorite was salmon, the worst possible answer. What kind of American salmon could possibly compete with Scottish salmon? Our German chef had the answer. According to Hugo, the finest salmon in the world is the chinook salmon of Oregon.

Menu for Queen Elizabeth II and five hundred Local Dignitaries

Queen Elizabeth's Salad (page 190)
Firestone Chardonnay

Salmon quenelles with lobster sauce
Asparagus bundles
Wild rice with pine nuts and morels

Lemon sorbet in lemon shells
Black walnut crisps

Windsor Vineyards Champagne

Sample Parties

Sample Party #1

> **Occasion:** Introducing your daughter's fiancé and his family to your family
> **Date/time:** Summer, 6 to 9 P.M.
> **Type of event:** Cocktail reception
> **Number of guests:** 25
> **Budget:** moderate to high
> **Where:** Your garden
> **Guest profile:** 50 percent strangers

I discovered weeks later there was one more tiny, little complication. Legally, only members of the Columbia River Treaty tribes can catch the chinook salmon.

After a great deal of thought, I submitted the following menu for approval.

The queen's meal was made still more difficult because she could not be addressed unless she spoke first. So, "May I take your plate?" or "Would you like some more water?" were all out of the question. We had to stay alert and try to sense her mood. The event was a wonderful success, made possible by the cooperation of the Columbia River Treaty tribe, the British Embassy, the staff of the *Yacht Brittania*, and the United States Navy.

Following are menus created for more everyday occasions that can be accomplished by an average host and, where noted, the novice host as well. Following my divide and conquer philosophy, I indicate which dishes to prepare and which you should purchase. Recipes that are in this book have the page numbers included for convenience.

- Summer fruits are highlighted.

- The food should be elegant and easy to eat, befitting this somewhat formal occasion.

- The food should be light and mostly cold, acknowledging the weather.

- There should be enough food to provide a light supper, which is necessary given the time frame of the party.

- A full bar can be included, because it is more cost effective than just wine with a group of twenty-five or more; besides it feels indulgent.

- Only one dish requiring last minute attention should be included, and it can be handled by the hired help so you are free to mingle with your new family.

- Your daughter loves saté dishes and her fiancé's favorite is salmon.

Engagement Menu A

Sun-Dried Tomato and Pesto Torta (page 156) with Herb-Garlic Crostini (page 168)

Sesame Eggplant Salsa (page 152) with Pita Crisps (page 167)

Savory Spiced Nuts (page 162)

Chicken and Beef Saté (page 151), passed

Prosciutto with melons and plums

Good green or black olives

Cheese selection plus crackers

Grapes and berries to accompany cheeses

Poached salmon (purchased or made) with Orange-Dill Sauce (page 273)

Heart-shaped strawberry tart (purchased or made)

Skewers of fig and cherries with chocolate fondue (made)

Basic Bar (see page 120)

Champagne (for toasting)

Menu B

If your budget is more generous, these would make wonderful additions to the preceding menu, but they would require additional help.

Grilled baby lamb chops with Rosemary Pesto (page 277), passed

Warm Gorgonzola apple tartlets (purchased)

Spicy Honeyed Shrimp (page 148)

Sample Party #2

Occasion: Your spouse's birthday

Date/Time: Fall, 7:30 P.M.

Type of Party: Dinner

Number of Guests: 10 guests

Budget: Moderate

Where: Your house

Guest Profile: All close friends, you know they are adventurous eaters. They have been over so many times they know all your special recipes by heart, so you decide to take a whole new direction.

ADDRESSING THE ESSENTIALS

• Your guests enjoy creative, ethnic foods.

• Your husband loves chicken.

• You would prefer a simple menu that you can prepare over a couple of evenings after work.

• The flavors should be spectacular, but the cost moderate.

• The cake should be big enough for fifty candles.

• The menu should be suitable to be served at a casual buffet, leaving you free, once any last minute dishes are cooked, to enjoy the party.

• Everything on the menu should be available in September.

Menu

Coconut Shrimp with Orange-Ginger Marmalade Dip (page 138)

Samosas (purchased)

Braised artichokes with orange mayonnaise

Paisley-Patterned Summer Soup (page 176)

Tandoori-Flavored Chicken (page 206 or purchased)

Aromatic Basmati Pilaf (page 261)

Mint-Cilantro Raita (page 285 or purchased)

Roasted Balsamic and Honey Onions (page 281)

Fruit chutney (purchased)

Naan (purchased)

Mile-High Coconut Cake (purchased)

Indian beer and hot tea

Sample Party #3

Occasion: Super Bowl Sunday

Date/Time: Late January, noon

Type of Party: Brunch buffet

Number of Guests: 20

Where: Your home

Budget: Low

Guest Profile: Family, neighbors

ADDRESSING THE ESSENTIALS

- All of the food should be prepared the day before, so there is no rush to be ready by noon.

- The menu should be based on sturdy food that can safely sit out during the several hours of the game.

- The total cost for the menu can't exceed five to six dollars per person, excluding alcohol.

- The style of the menu should suggest a tailgate party—casual, hearty, comfort food.

- There must be plenty of food so everyone can graze throughout the 3 to 4 hours the game lasts.

Super Bowl Menu

Bloody Mary Soup (purchased) with Herb-Garlic Crostini (page 168)

Mediterranean Bean Spread (page 163) with sliced vegetables and baguettes

Peanuts and pistachios in the shell

Beer and pitchers of Sangrita (page 169)

Chain Gang Chili (page 230)

Corn tortillas

Winter Fiesta Salad (page 191)

Ankica's Crisp Ideas (page 300)

Coffee

Sample Party #4

Occasion: Baby shower for Deberah
Date/Time: Spring, 11:30 A.M.
Type of Party: Brunch buffet
Number of Guests: 20
Where: Your home
Budget: Low
Guest Profile: Women of various ages

ADDRESSING THE ESSENTIALS

- While this should be an elegant menu, the cost can be controlled by serving a casserole (the strata) and other creative entrées.

- Combining the Champagne and orange juice reduces the liquor costs (the guest of honor can have the orange juice).

- Guests like to indulge at a party, yet women are always watching their weight, so some dishes that address both needs should be included.

- The party begins at 11:30 A.M., requiring a relatively light menu.

- Deberah loves fruit, white chocolate, and smoked salmon.

- Everything possible should be made ahead of time, so that you are free to be the MC for the games and activities.

Baby Shower Menu

Pastries, bagels, and croissants (purchased)

Jams and butter

Cinnamon Toast Spread (page 288)

Grilled turkey sausage

Smoked Salmon and Asparagus Strata (page 234)

Banana-walnut griddle cakes (made)

Fresh fruit compote with vanilla yogurt sauce (made)

White Chocolate Cheesecake en Croûte (page 292) with berries

Fresh orange juice and Champagne

Coffee

I must warn you, angst is guaranteed when you ignore the preceding entertaining menu guidelines. I will always think of my personal Waterloo as the "great omelet/shower marathon." "I am a chef," I mused. "What could be easier to serve than omelets for a bridal shower brunch I am hosting? Only 15 guests—no problem." It was fun for everyone except me, the hostess-chef who chopped, flipped, and folded omelets, instead of sipping, chatting, and playing safety-pin games. I had forgotten my own rules of simplicity and do-ahead. Play it safe, follow the rules, learn from my mistakes, and your entertaining will be a breeze.

Create Drama: The "Wow" Factor

Cooking is like love. It should be entered into with abandon or not at all.
—Harriet Van Horne

Give me the luxuries of life and I will willingly do without the necessities.
—Frank Lloyd Wright

Drama, Luxury, Surprise, and Beauty

Following are some of my favorite ways to make a splash.

- Fresh fruit glazed with egg white and confectioners' sugar to garnish a cake.

- Butterfly (by removing the backbone) a chicken or other fowl and grill flat.

- Black beans, red lentils, orzo, tiny river rocks or rock salt to line a tray of passed hors d'oeuvres.

- Salmon trout *en papillote* (baked in a parchment envelope) to be opened at the table.

- A Napoleon appetizer made by layering crisp phyllo pastry or deep fried wonton layers with savory fillings.

- A stuffed chicken breast baked in a pastry purse, tied with a ribbon of lemon-grass.

- A fish cooked whole, head-on—deep fried, roasted, or steamed.

- A wild rice waffle as the base for a savory appetizer.

- Edible flowers and flower petals included in salads and desserts or sandwiched between glass plates.

- Heart-shaped ravioli on a brilliant red sauce for a Valentine appetizer.

- Baby squash served with their blossoms attached, battered and fried.

- Salmon cut into strips and interlaced to create a basket weave square, for steaming (one of a myriad of stunning presentations from the great John Sedlar's career).

- Fresh morel omelet.

- Venison, bison, or ostrich steaks.

- A sampling of regional oysters with simple sauces and Champagne.

- A ten-inch porcini mushroom as an entrée.

- Crisply fried Maryland softshell crabs in a nest of tempura parsley.

- Jumbo Thai prawns grilled in the shell served on a giant banana leaf.

- Fine caviar combined with a vodka tasting.

- Tiny chocolate boxes or sacks filled with peach mousse, berries and edible flowers (an easy and stunning idea from Judith Olney's *The Joy of Chocolate*).

- Homemade coffee bean ice cream sandwiched with fudgy cookies.

- Blackberry and blueberry sorbets served in hot-pink tulip glasses.

- Sweet tamales of walnut and cinnamon in *crema fresca*.

- Wild berry shortcake with *fraise des bois* (tiny wild strawberries), loganberries, and golden raspberries.

- Peaches (with the stem on) poached in red wine with cardamom-vanilla sauce.

- Chocolate Pâte with Fresh Plum Sauce (page 305).

Celebrate the Season

Summer ends, and Autumn comes, and he who would have it otherwise
would have high tide always and a full moon every night.

—Hal Borland, *Sundial of the Seasons*

Your guests feel "catered to" when you serve dishes involving an ingredient you grew yourself. Foods with a short season or those that have come freshly into season are also a "wow." There is primordial satisfaction in eating something that is perfectly ripe, just here, just now. If it's May, plan to revel in the fresh, lively spring produce: artichokes, cherries, sorrel, asparagus, ramps, strawberries, sugar snap peas, wild mushrooms, and softshell crabs. The season's special flowers, tulips, freesia, daffodils, peonies, and lilies of the valley, need nothing but simple vases to make your table resonate with spring.

If planning for November, serve a menu based on foods flourishing at this time of year. For me, fall evokes a yearning for hearty food and things that come from the

Spring Tea Party Buffet

My all-time favorite buffet table was created for a summer tea party. Fresh, bright green sod was cut to cover the entire eight-foot tabletop. We used sphagnum moss to cover the edges of the "lawn." Individual tulips and lilies were inserted into the sod, as if they had bloomed there. Trays of pastries, cookies, scones, and fruit were placed on the grass. As romantic as you can get, it was not very expensive or difficult, just a little messy to set up.

forest and the earth: pumpkin flan, warm duck salad, venison stew. There are many muted winter desserts I find every bit as sensual as the brightly colored summer treats—a Sterling apple tart with gingersnap cream or aromatic Bosc pears with Stilton cheese and Port. And, my absolute favorite fall indulgence: chestnuts, simply roasted and eaten warm from the fire, or used as a luxurious ingredient in stuffings and sauces.

A Dramatic New Year's Eve: Piquenique in Provence

My husband and I wanted to host a New Year's Eve party, but we weren't interested in another black-tie occasion. Instead we opted for a more lighthearted party: a French picnic. Our invitations clearly stated that this was to be a picnic and recommended casual clothes and a beret as the appropriate costume.

To set the tone for the evening, we leaned my bicycle next to the front door with a basket of lavender on the handlebars. As guests entered, we gave them a small basket holding their silverware, napkin, wineglasses and a little tub of Tapenade (page 267). Throughout the evening a selection of popular French songs (lots of Edith Piaf) interspersed with recordings of Ravel and Debussy filled the house. The mantel was covered with jars of honey, jars of olives, and piles of brilliant, yellow lemons.

All of the living room furniture was moved out of the way and picnic blankets spread on the floor. On each blanket was a small vase of sunflowers. I covered the dining room table with a red-and-white checked cloth and scattered fall leaves casually across it. All the food was served in some kind of basket or rustic bowl. I found some realistic plastic ants at the toy store, which I glued snaking up the sides of the baskets. The ants became the highlight of the décor. People pulled them off the baskets and slipped them into each other's food and dropped them into cocktails. We found them everywhere the next day, including in the dog's bowl.

The menu was based on ingredients I associate with Provence and dishes that are practical for a picnic. And, of course, we served only French wines.

New Year's Piquenique

Tomato, chevre, and basil salad

Grilled asparagus with hollandaise

Pâte de foie gras

Tart pissaladière (Onion, olive, and anchovy)

Garlic sausage with selected mustards

Provencal cheese board: Picodon, Saint Marcellin and Roquefort with pears

Baguette and pain de campagne

Pignola Lemon Tarte (page 301)

Tarte tatin with Calvados whipped cream

Coffee

THERE ARE *SECRETS* that most caterers rely upon which I urge you to incorporate into your entertaining.

Develop a Specialty

Pardon me, how do I get to Carnegie Hall?
Practice, practice, practice . . .

Martin was a successful caterer. The first time I was a guest at a party he catered the entrée was a wonderful, baked lemon chicken. Six months later, I attended another party prepared by Martin, lemon chicken was served from the barbecue. That Christmas a friend's law firm employed Martin for their holiday open house. Surprise, lemon chicken skewers, garnished with festive red and green pepper rounds.

    I was introduced to Martin at this event as a fellow caterer. When I mentioned how much I liked the lemon chicken, he beamed. He confided that he had opened his catering business based on the fact that he loved to throw parties and that everyone loved his lemon chicken. To the best of my knowledge, his business continues to flourish. Hot or cold, whole or pieces, skinless or skewered, lemon chicken remains his trademark.

While I wouldn't encourage you to specialize to this extreme, I think it is important to note that even his repeat customers were satisfied. Lemon chicken is a popular entrée, and he turned out perfect lemon chicken every time. An excellent dish, like good news, does bear repeating.

If you don't intend to make cooking and catering your life's work, but you love to entertain, become a specialist. Don't be misled into thinking that you must be a master of every cuisine to be a splendid host. Select dishes that you personally love and work on them. Make them for yourself and your family. Experiment with the recipes; do them until they are your "own," meaning that you understand the concept or technique so well you needn't rely on a recipe. You don't need to look up how to make chicken soup, because you've done it a hundred times. This is the first step in creating a safety zone for yourself when entertaining, and a way to "wow" your guests. Be the first on the block to know everything about gnocchi, dim sum, grilling, couscous, or sushi.

The following are general techniques which, when mastered, will give a cook the confidence and ability to create myriad variations with more flair than the lemon chicken guy (as I always think of him). It takes time to become proficient at any of them, but investing a few hours can give you your own repertoire. And, on your way to Carnegie Hall, you and your family will get to eat both your successes and failures.

1. Phyllo Pastry

This delicate Middle Eastern pastry dough is available in the frozen food section of virtually all grocery stores. Once you master the techniques for handling these feathery

Phyllo Pastry Tips

When you buy a box of phyllo pastry you get about 24 paper-thin leaves of dough. Regardless of how many sheets your recipe calls for, each leaf must be coated with oil or butter before stacking the next one on top. To save time and mess, use a spray bottle to apply the oil or oil/butter to the layers as you assemble. Gourmet cooking stores sell spray bottles especially made for oil. Because the sheets are fragile, expect to waste a few as you separate them into single layers. Leftover sheets of pastry can be tightly wrapped and refrigerated for a few days.

leaves of pastry, phyllo can be used as the basis for hors d'oeuvres, entrées, and desserts. Included in this book are recipes using phyllo pastry dough for: Mushroom Strudel in Phyllo Pastry (page 236), Lamb and Mint-Pesto Borek (page 150), and White Chocolate Cheesecake en Croûte (page 292).

2. Fresh Pastas

With the purchase of a simple pasta roller (hand-cranked or electric), you can create sheet pasta in an endless variety of flavors and a rainbow of luscious colors such as crimson beet, spring green basil, and a lovely lemon yellow. The filled varieties, such as ravioli and tortellini, give you the most flavor variations. These filled pastas, which I usually make oversized, are also the most dramatic. They can also be frozen, uncooked, up to several weeks in advance. Four-inch-square "pillow" raviolis, served in a pool of bright sauce, make a stunning, simple appetizer. Included in the recipe section of the book are recipes for Basic Pasta Dough, (page 313), including how to infuse the dough with fresh herbs (page 313), two versions of pillow ravioli (pages 142 to 143), and Pappardelle with Feta and Olives (page 235). There are as many variations as you wish to explore. For parties I do not generally bother to make fresh pasta if what I want is a noodle. Fresh noodles, of a very good quality, are available almost everywhere; and they're time-consuming to make in quantity.

3. Crepes

Crepes are intimidating until the third one, but producing a perfect crepe is simple from then on. They can be made in large batches and frozen to be thawed and filled or sauced as needed. There are an endless variety of preparations based on the crepe. (Hey, there's an entire chain of restaurants that serves nothing else for breakfast, lunch, and dinner.) See the recipes for Basic Crepe Batter (page 312) and Peach-Caramel Crepes (page 299)

4. The Grill and Barbecue

Many cuisines around the world glorify food cooked over an open fire. Whether you prefer the flavors of Greece, or those of Tunisia, you will find a broad range of recipes for the grill. This is another arena in which practiced skill gives you a wonderful range of foods to prepare in an expert fashion. This is a great basic technique for entertaining because grilling provides open-ended possibilities: hot dogs for your six-year-old's birthday and rack of lamb for a Valentine dinner. Recipes that employ this technique are: Skewered Lamb Ruffles with Almond Mint Pesto (page 219), Spicy Honeyed Shrimp (page 148), Grilled Vegetables with Balsamic Vinaigrette (page 262), Quick

Grilled Pizza (page 159), Grilled Scallops with Bacon (page 213), and Herbed-Roasted Corn on the Cob (page 253).

5. Stir-fry

If you are comfortable being in the kitchen at dinnertime, stir-fry cooking affords end-less flavor variations and lots of fun for guests, whether they just watch you perform or lend a helping hand. There are a few necessities for great stir-fry: a good, hot pan; a small amount of oil or other liquid; and time invested, in advance, to slice all your fresh ingredients so they are ready to add rapid-fire. Chinese, Mongolian, Moroccan, Cali-fornian, and Japanese cuisines all provide a sizzling variety of recipes for stir-fry.

6. Desserts

I have prepared many parties with a budget so limited we could only afford to serve one luxurious dish. Generally the one splurge should be saved for dessert. Time spent per-fecting chocolate fantasy deserts, the perfect pie, or luxurious homemade ice creams will create many grateful guests! See the desserts section (page 290 to 311) for ideas to get you started.

Of course, there are other excellent multipurpose techniques you could pursue: sushi and sashimi, ethnic cuisines, smoking (stovetop and freestanding), or bread and pizza making.

Purchased Menu Additions

*I lift my eyes unto the hills from whence
will come my help: from the bakery on
Main Street, the chocolate lady on Mel-
rose, the cheese shop on Rodeo Drive.*

—Caterer's prayer

Whether you intend to entertain once a month or once a year, plan to divide and conquer. Whenever it's feasible, a menu that's all homemade is really special. But, for the
occasions when that's not practical (for a whole grocery list of reasons), plan a menu
including dishes or ingredients you can purchase. Search out bakeries, specialty grocers,
and mail-order sources whose products you enjoy. In addition, small caterers will often
prepare individual dishes for you to pick up. Purchase and sample products that appeal
to you. When you find a winner, begin to incorporate it into your entertaining repertoire along with your own specialties.

When you consider that an average three-course dinner, preceded by light hors
d'oeuvres, (the most common dinner format) will require preparation of eleven to fifteen recipes, purchasing even one item is a good idea. *Most* caterers coordinate their
efforts this way. Focus on what you do best (or enjoy the most), and develop resources
for quality items to fill in the gaps. And remember, just like a magician, part of the
caterer's strategy is not to disclose their secrets.

I realize this breaks with romantic illusions about the parameters of gracious
entertaining, suggested by your mother and Martha Stewart. I think it's time for a
change in attitudes. The quality and variety of prepared foods and gourmet or artisanal
ingredients have improved dramatically in the last ten years. Part of the discomfort a
caring host has felt with serving "store-bought" items has been the expectation that
these dishes couldn't be as good as homemade. It just isn't true anymore. If you are

selective, there are quality products available (locally and from mail-order sources) that will be a genuine complement to your lovingly prepared recipes. (See "The Gourmet Network," page 317).

Expand the Possibilities: Think Outside the Box

When your cooking skills are unsteady, time is limited, or your kitchen is less than ideal, I suggest you explore some of the following alternatives to traditional entertaining: Interactive cooking, a sophisticated potluck, and dressed-up takeout are all excellent ways to express hospitality that can be accomplished by anyone, anywhere, anytime. Even on a boat with no galley, with less than an hour before guests arrive, or in a park without electricity, it's possible to use one or more of these ideas to create a smashingly successful party.

In the course of the six months that my kitchen was being remodeled (read: nonexistent) there were still birthdays and holidays that demanded attention. Fluffed up takeout and creative potlucks saved the day. And, the resulting festivities were as joyful as any that I have given. Take comfort in the knowledge I gained through this experience; people arrive in your home wanting to enjoy themselves. If you genuinely want to show your friends a good time—everything works.

Interactive Cooking

In this approach to low stress entertaining, the main elements of the menu are prepared in collaboration with your guests. The preparation of the meal becomes an adventure with the focus placed on the pleasure of the shared process. When you make your invitation, let guests know they will be participating in the preparation of the meal (this is an excellent icebreaker for unacquainted guests). You provide all (or some) of the ingredients, cookware, and recipes for dishes that add up to a complete meal. When your guests arrive you provide a festive beverage, hors d'oeuvres, and the cooking assignment. I have hosted parties like this many times with great success. Even noncooks get into the fun; recipe questions become conversation starters. This communal cooking, which concludes by sitting down to a shared meal, was the very exciting format of my French cooking school.

The menu you select should be fairly simple, and the recipes should take less than an hour and a half to complete. Limit the number of guests invited to the number with whom you feel you can comfortably share your kitchen space. Also, plan the menu so only one dish requires the use of each piece of kitchen equipment, that is, oven, cooktop, cutting boards, grill, or microwave.

In another approach to cooperative entertaining, you can include recipes in the party invitation and allow guests to choose which dish they would like to make from your suggestions. For the party, they bring the ingredients for their dish to prepare at your house.

Menus for Cooperative Suppers

HORS D'OEUVRES
(prepared by host)

Cocktail Party Walnuts (page 161)

Hors d'Oeuvre Twists (page 166) wrapped in smoked salmon

Skewered Lamb Ruffles with Almond Mint Pesto (page 219)

COOPERATIVE SUPPER
(total preparation time: 1 hour)

Wilted spinach salad with mint and Montrachet cheese and sherry vinaigrette

Grilled Scallops with Bacon (page 213)

Quick Risotto Reggiano with Asparagus (page 238)

Sugar snap peas with shallots and lemon zest crisps

White chocolate raspberry fool

Coffee

HORS D'OEUVRES
(prepared by host)

Blue Cheese Pâté (page 164)

Spicy Honeyed Shrimp (page 148)

Herb-Garlic Crostini (page 168) with Skordalia (page 165)

COOPERATIVE SUPPER
(total preparation time: 1 hour)

Grilled eggplant with Artichoke Pesto (page 276)

Salsiccia all'Uva (page 233)

Evan's Summer Cooler (page 309)

The Sophisticated Potluck: Creativity and Graciousness

A wonderful example of the fine art of the potluck was the creation of my friend Leslie for her fortieth birthday. She wanted to host a great, big, rollicking birthday party. She set the stage with her droll, intriguing invitation.

The National Academy of Culinary Puns & Silliness presents

"The Pomme de Terre" Awards Ceremony

(and not incidentally the 3rd annual 39th birthday of its

founder and president Leslie M.)

To enter the potluck awards, bring an edible dish whose title

falls into any of the following categories:

- **Namesakes**
  Examples: Cole Porterhouse Steak Sandwich on Andrew Lloyd Webbers Bread, James Garni, Carrie Gefiltefisher
- **Musical Munchies**
  Examples: It's Havarti and I've Rye If You Want, Too (The Leslie Gore Appetizer), The Grapeful Dead
- **Literature**
  Examples: The Bread Also Rises, Bonfire of the Canapés
- **Geography**
  Examples: Seoul Food, The Leaning Tower of Pizza
- **That's Entertainment (movies, TV, plays)**
  Examples: Tender Is the Bite, Who Flamed Roger Rabbit?
- **Puns, Proverbs and Cliches**
  Examples: Nice Pies Finish Fast, A Steak in Time Serves Nine

In this delightful invitation she turned the hackneyed, although convenient and cost-effective, potluck idea into an opportunity for creativity and whimsy. At the party itself, the dishes, with their titles, were displayed, by category, around the house. Guests voted for their favorites, while eating them, and "prizes" were awarded. With originality and humor like this, a potluck can be a classy affair.

To facilitate the perfect potluck, plan to have extra serving dishes, serving utensils, platters, and baskets on hand for items brought by your guests. Frequently someone will bring bread in a bag or cheese in the grocery packaging. Because many people do not visualize how food will be served, you should be prepared for this.

"Dressed Up" Takeout: Restaurant Favorites with Homemade Touches

A wonderfully relaxed party can be arranged in a short time by planning a menu based on reheatable dishes from a favorite restaurant. Dishes that are supposed to be served cold are also obvious choices. The host personalizes these items with fresh additions of her own. This approach allows everyone the luxury of spontaneous entertaining.

The following menu is based on one of my favorite dishes, *sopa de tortilla*, from a local Mexican restaurant. I prepare simple quesadillas and a salad, chop some garnishes, and get out all my colorful plates and linens. I have a rustic enamelware Dutch oven that I use to serve the soup and multicolored bowls for everything else. Once I am home from the restaurant, this meal can be on the table in twenty minutes. Ole!

Mexican Menu

Brie-Mango Chutney Quesadillas
(page 158)

Sangrita (page 169)

Guacamole (page 282)
Salsa cruda
Tortilla chips

Sopa de tortilla
Bowls of chopped cilantro, shredded
Monterey Jack cheese, pepitas, minced
jalapeño chiles, lime wedges, and
crispy tortilla strips

Coconut ice cream topped with
Kahlúa chocolate sauce
Coffee

Karen, a close friend of mine, is the product of a traditional Jewish family. Her husband is from Pakistan and is a Moslem. As this party chronicle began, Karen was moving into a new home, working full time, and was nine months pregnant with her second child, a boy. She planned to observe Jewish tradition and celebrate her son's *bris* eight days after his birth. She obviously couldn't plan the exact date, but she had decided she wanted to celebrate the occasion with a luncheon for fifty friends and family. Under the circumstances, I suggested she order food from a favorite restaurant. Karen and Syud made this convenient solution more interesting by using their diversity as a theme. They combined dishes from their favorite Israeli restaurant, desserts from an Indian restaurant, and Syud's preparation of two of his family's recipes. Karen hired waiters on standby from a staffing agency she found in the Yellow Pages, ordered flowers, and waited. After the baby's birth, all they needed to do was call the guests and notify the help, florist, liquor store, and restaurants. The party was painless for Karen, if perhaps not for the guest of honor, and we all enjoyed the personal flair of the menu. Two years later Karen's friends are still talking about her innovative celebration.

Karen and Syud's Menu

Baba Ghannoush (page 155 or
purchased)
Hummus and pita

Middle Eastern cucumber salad

Roast chicken with tahini sauce
Falafel with all of the trimmings
Pilau
Shami kabobs

Gulab jamen and rusmalei (Indian
desserts)
Tropical fruit skewers with mint
Mango Lassi (page 172), tea, and wine

Here are some examples of how to order, prepare, and garnish menus based on popular cuisines. No matter whose number you dial, give some consideration ahead of time to the serving dishes you will need. Generally to-go food packaging is strictly functional so you will need to transfer the food. Serving a purchased pizza on your rustic maple cutting board surrounded by fresh basil transforms a good delivered pizza into a colorful company dinner.

Some other examples of how to make a purchased dish feel homemade include:

- **Arranging an antipasto on a slab of marble.**
- **Filling Grandma Rose's soup tureen with Thai curried coconut shrimp soup.**
- **Packing a foie gras pâté into a terra-cotta pot lined with fresh green leaves.**
- **Stacking calzone and pizza on your turn of the century pie rack.**
- **Serving tamales from your Chinese bamboo steamer.**

How to Order

Italian

Order: Your favorite sauce for pasta (cook the pasta at home), any casserole-type dish such as lasagna or manicotti, calzone, soups, an antipasto platter, tiramisu, and cannoli.

Garnish: Bunches of fresh green herbs like basil, oregano, or chives, rosemary branches, and bay laurel.

Make: Whole Roast Garlic with Herbs (page 283) or fresh mozzarella with pesto salad.

Buy: Italian wines, Italian beer, Campari, Proseco.

Mexican

Order: Saucy, moist specialties like enchiladas or chicken in mole sauce, grilled dishes like soft chicken tacos and carne asada. Tamales of every kind are endlessly forgiving, as is any soup. The refried beans, salsas, and seasoned rice that generally accompany entrées are very manageable side dishes. Avoid fried items like hard-shell tacos, taquitos, chile rellenos, and chimichangas; fried foods just never reheat well.

Italian Menu

Antipasto platter

Whole Roast Garlic with Herbs (page 283) with Herb-Garlic Crostini (page 168)

Pasta é fagiole soup

Pan rustica

Osso buco

Campari and soda

Wine

Serafina's Tiramisu (page 291 or purchased)

Garnish: Fresh cilantro sprigs, whole jalapeño chiles, red pepper rings, dried chile pods, avocado or citrus leaves, and hibiscus blossoms.

Make: Hearts of romaine with toasted pumpkin seeds, fruit bowl with Triple Sec splash, Traditional Margaritas (page 171), Guacamole (page 282)

Buy: Mexican beer, tortilla chips, tortillas, salsa, and tropical sorbets

Chinese

There is a reason why Chinese restaurants have such a strong association in our minds with takeout food. Many of their traditional dishes travel well. If there is a restaurant with a good dim sum selection near you, an assortment of six to seven can make an elegant supper, with a soup for starters. They will no doubt provide sauces, but freshen everything up with the addition of the Spicy Vinegar Dipping Sauce (page 279).

Order: Mu shu dishes, dim sum, dumplings, Peking duck with all of the accompaniments, any soup, any nonfried noodle dish, steamed rice (avoid any dish described as "crispy").

A Chinese Theme

A Chinese theme is one of the easiest to create, even for a beginner. Drape the buffet and guest tables with red, black, and shiny gold fabrics. As a centerpiece, tip a large wok on its side, spilling out tangerines, pomegranates, and red chopsticks tied with gold ribbons. Light the party with strings of Chinese paper lanterns and place flickering red candles around the room on shiny brass dishes from the import store.

To create a lively movement of guests throughout the party, set the food up in several locations. On the main table, place a wok on bricks over a candle or Sterno offering kung pao chicken, served in white to-go containers. Arrange plates of chicken pyramid dumplings with a spicy dipping sauce and Sesame Eggplant Salsa (page 152) with wonton crisps on little trays and set them throughout the room. In an open area, set a table where guests can learn to assemble their own mu shu pork.

To include the bar in the theme, offer Chinese beers and pitchers of iced oolong tea.

Garnish: Cilantro, parsley, snow peas, shredded bok choy cabbage, flower blossoms, ginger branches, anything gold, orchids.

Make: Personalized Fortune Cookies (below), Sesame Eggplant Salsa (page 152) with wonton crisps, Chicken Pyramid Dumplings (page 145), and melon, orange, and lychee skewers with mint.

Buy: Chinese beer, Chinese rice wine, oolong tea, green tea–ginger ice cream, lychee nuts, and chopsticks.

Chinese Menu

Paper-wrapped chicken

Any soup

Lotus root salad

Kung pao shrimp

Noodles with roast pork and bok choy

Asparagus and mushrooms in black bean sauce

Steamed rice

Chinese beer and Chinese rice wine

Date and Orange Wontons (page 295)

Melon, orange, and lychee skewers with mint

Personalized Fortune Cookies (page 77)

NOTE: *For a casual, grazing-style party I frequently use white takeout containers with the handle and arrange them and baskets of chopsticks near the food. They are the world's easiest dish if you don't have a seat at a table. You can fill your little tub, wander, and munch.*

Personalized Fortune Cookies

For a theatrical, creative dessert use tweezers or a wooden pick to remove the fortunes from fortune cookies bought at your local Chinese restaurant. Write your own personal messages, slip them into the cookies with a knife, and dip the ends in chocolate. Serve these with green tea ice cream and candied ginger slices. The puzzled look on your guests' faces when they open a "standard issue" fortune cookie, just like ones they've eaten all their lives, and pull out a message personalized for them, quickly turns into delighted laughter.

Lists, Lists, and More Lists

REMEMBER, I WARNED you about lists. To really have a relaxed party, first you'll have lists everywhere. For dressed up takeout it is a short list. For a foray into elegance, there are several lists involved. Once you have decided on a menu, write out all of the elements for each dish, including all the sauces, garnishes, and accompaniments involved. From this master list you will then compile the following "sub-lists." If you have planned your menu based on "The Essentials of Menu Planning" (page 49), your preparations should involve mostly do-ahead tasks.

Master Shopping List

This list must include every item you need to purchase to prepare your menu. This includes both food and nonfood supplies, such as parchment paper, ramekins, paper towels, trash bags, skewers, or Sterno.

Order List

A master list of every food item that must be ordered in advance, such as a birthday cake, shucked oysters, a boned leg of lamb, and any item you are buying from a restaurant or gourmet shop.

Preparation List

A master list addressing all the kitchen operations, such as shred cabbage, grate carrots, or make coleslaw dressing. This list should be organized by days. Group the tasks that can be done a week ahead, two days ahead, or the day before. Every caterer organizes kitchen time with preparation lists. It helps you to plan your time and also ensures that you don't forget a minor but key element like the sauce for the lamb or the dressing for the salad.

Knowledge of what is possible is the beginning of happiness.

—Santayana

Knowledge is of two kinds: we know a subject ourselves, or we know where we can find information upon it.

—Samuel Johnson

WHEN THE SCOPE of the event you've planned exceeds your abilities, or facilities, it's time to consider seeking help. Or you may simply want to hire professionals to make your life easier. In either case, you will be most successful when you understand what to expect, who to hire for what, and how to find the best. Often these contractors will not only provide the services for which you have contacted them, especially a caterer, but may help you resolve other needs as well. Experienced professionals are a great source of references for other suppliers. Following is a detailed explanation of how to get the most out of collaborations with commonly used services for entertaining—caterers, rental companies, valet services, florists, and wedding coordinators.

Engaging the services of some of these consultants will not necessarily increase your expenses. Often their networking and experience allow them to save you more than their fees.

Caterers

The art of dining well is no slight art, the pleasure not a slight pleasure.
—Montaigne

This subject is very close to my heart. I spent many hectic years as a caterer, yet I honestly felt (most of the time) that I was in the fortunate position of making dreams come true, à la Walt Disney or Glinda the Good. There is an elusive human magic in the air at a wonderful party that I have always found exhilarating. When you need the services of a caterer look for someone who has this passion.

When Do You Need a Caterer?

I have devoted this book to showing you how to duplicate a caterer's techniques without the caterer. However, it is the wise person who understands her or his limitations. A once-in-a-lifetime wedding or sit-down supper for one hundred is not an occasion to do on your own.

What Are the Responsibilities/Services of a Caterer?

What does a caterer bring to the party that will simplify your life and enhance your event? This will vary dramatically depending on whether you have arranged for your neighbor to drop off her fabulous manicotti and cannoli (or orange chicken and pot stickers) or you have engaged a full-service catering company.

In the drop-off scenario, your neighbor's assistance may merely include written instructions for reheating. A full-service caterer typically provides a great deal more than just food. You should expect creative menu proposals and the willingness to incorporate your suggestions about the menu as well. The caterer's services will also include professional uniformed staff directed by a party manager whose job is to supervise the staff and take care of any problems, similar to a maître d' in a restaurant. The calculation and the ordering of rentals and liquor is also generally handled by the caterer. The catering staff will move furniture and rentals, set the tables, prepare, and serve the food and drinks, and clean everything up. The standard is that your home or facility should be returned to its pre-party condition by the catering staff, everything clean, put away, and leftovers packaged and left for you. The more experienced companies can also help you find a special location, contract for a valet, costume the waiters, and provide centerpieces and entertainment.

Another option is to contract the food and the location in one package at a hotel, club, or restaurant. While this can be a more cost-effective option, in my experience, there is usually a sacrifice of charm and intimacy.

How to Find a Reliable Service

Catering is such a personalized service that I always liken it to choosing a hairdresser. They can make or break your day and once they've started the job, there's no turning back. The safest way is to get the name of the caterer at a party that you are enjoying; second best, use referrals. In any case, if you have questions or hesitations ask to:

- **See another party they have set up (before the guests arrive so you don't intrude).**

- **Have them provide references, for a party similar to the one you are planning, who you can call.**

- **Schedule a tasting of the proposed menu. There may be a nominal charge for a tasting, but it is money well spent if you have concerns.**

Typical Costs/Paperwork

Catering a meal in your home or other special location is more expensive than taking the same number of people to a good restaurant. This has consistently shocked my clients as they read their contract, always bottom line first, and calculated. "Why, we could go to Spago for less than this." Absolutely. A catered party is actually the creation of a restaurant for one day—your day. However, for a price, you are able to create a unique and intimate experience that cannot be duplicated in a restaurant or hotel. To duplicate the food and service of a fine restaurant in your home will cost roughly 20 to 30 percent more than the same meal at the restaurant. However, your liquor bill can provide some balance, because a restaurant typically marks their wine and liquor up by 200 to 300 percent over what it will cost you at the liquor store.

A full-service caterer or facility will give you a contract that lists the exact menu. In some cases even the exact quantity of an expensive or unusual item will be specified, such as 325 prawns or one pound of Sevruga caviar. There will be separate line items describing the number and type of staff, special décor, rentals, liquor, and any extras like valets, costumes, entertainers, and so on. It is common for a caterer to add a service charge (or gratuity) from 15 to 22 percent of the total food bill. Some caterers will ask you to pay a preparation fee for the proposal, which will apply as a credit toward your party if you decide to hire them. You are

Caterer Checklist

_____ **Contract complete**

(To include: detailed menu with pricing, staff with pricing, timing, guest count, taxes and gratuity. Optional caterer responsibilities, which can be itemized on the contract: flowers/décor, rentals, valet service, entertainment, liquor)

_____ **Menu selection**

_____ **Tasting (if necessary)**

_____ **Insurance**

_____ **Staff attire**

_____ **Arrival time**

_____ **Guest count confirmed**

_____ **Have liquor and rentals been ordered?**

_____ **Have flowers or other décor been addressed?**

usually expected to put down a deposit to secure the date and pay the balance the day of the party.

If you need to adjust something to stay within your budget, your caterer will be able to give you suggestions, which will usually focus on simplifying the menu or décor. However, do not try to economize by cutting down on the number of staff; this is a fatal mistake. Having an adequate staff is what allows you to enjoy your own party.

Unless it is a simple drop-off menu, you should always have a contract. There are so many variables involved in party planning: menu changes, guest count additions, unexpected rentals, and more. It all needs to be summarized in a contract, and updated as you go along. Insist on proof of insurance along with the contract.

Spread the table and contention will cease.

—English proverb

Do I Need This Service?

There are several scenarios in which a rental company saves the day. If you need to compensate for excessive heat, cold, or rain at an outdoor location, a rental company will be a must. They can provide a tent with heaters for a cold, wet winter evening or canopies and fans for a party held on a sizzling summer day. The need for special equipment that you'll never want to purchase, like a dance floor, a giant barbecue, or a hundred-cup coffee urn, also necessitates using a rental companies' services.

Another motivation for hiring a rental company is to have the luxury of serving a large group on matching dishes, glasses, and linens. For a casual party, who cares if you've mixed your blue china with your neighbor's yellow ones. But for a formal party, the right accoutrements matter. And I don't know many people who own twenty matching dinner plates, let alone that many Champagne flutes, soup bowls, salad plates, and butter knives! Fortunately, in the last ten years rental companies have become much more sophisticated. Frequently they offer an upscale line of china and glassware that is quite beautiful and doesn't look rented at all. Always order more of everything than "just enough." The rule of thumb is about 5 percent extra to allow for accidents and unexpected guests.

What Are the Responsibilities/Services of a Rental Company?

Basically they must deliver clean, working supplies and equipment at a specified date and time. When the rentals are delivered, check in everything yourself; don't just take their word for it. Errors in counting are common in their busy warehouses. Also, check to make sure that all equipment is in working order. You really are out of luck if you don't discover that the barbecue is broken until you're putting the steaks on to cook. It's much better to figure it out when the equipment is delivered and can be repaired or replaced, which is their absolute obligation.

For a large dinner party I once checked in a crate that was labeled as containing two hundred dinner knives; when opened, it actually contained two hundred butter knives. We discovered the mistake while setting the tables, and the rental company probably shaved a few driving laws to correct the delivery before dinnertime. I was desperately glad when I saw their van pull up, because there is no acceptable explanation for serving prime rib with a dinner fork and butter knife.

How to Find a Reliable Company

I use several criteria to assess the quality of a rental company:

- What does the equipment on display in their showroom look like? Do I like the quality and style of their dishes, linens, and flatware? While most companies will have the standard white china and simple flatware, the fabrics they select for linens, styles of upscale tableware, and equipment vary widely.

- Is the staff knowledgeable about their equipment and helpful in assisting me to determine what I will need?

- Do they carry a comprehensive selection of items?

- Are their charges in line with other companies in the area?

- If you are using a caterer, is this their preferred rental company? Because it is usually the caterer who calculates the actual quantities of equipment, checks all supplies in, and sees that everything is repacked for return, it is important that they work well together.

Rental Company Checklist

_____ **Contract**

_____ **Review contract and double check that you have not omitted anything**

_____ **Check delivery time/place**

_____ **Arrange for pickup time**

_____ **Double check quantities of everything upon delivery**

_____ **Double check quantities of everything for return**

Typical Costs/Paperwork

Rentals can quickly become as expensive as the food. When you place your order, which, by the way, can be canceled or adjusted up to two days before delivery, you'll receive an itemized bill listing everything you've ordered and the prices. When considering the total cost of rentals, it is important to know that you will be charged the replacement cost for any broken or unreturned items.

Following are prices on commonly rented items from reputable companies in Los Angeles, Chicago, and Miami.

ITEM	LOS ANGELES	CHICAGO	MIAMI
60-inch round table *(seats up to 10)*	$8.90	$7.50	$12.00
Folding chair *(white wood)*	$2.05	$2.90	$5.00
Chiavari chair *(fancy, ballroom)*	$8.35	$7.75	$8.15
1 dinner plate *(white, bone china)*	$0.51	$0.45	$0.60
1 fork, knife, or spoon			
(silverplate)	$0.52	$0.55	$0.55
(stainless)	$0.31	$0.30	$0.32
Napkin	$0.72	$0.60	$0.40
Bar glass			
(all purpose, 6–8 ounce)	$0.57	$0.42	$0.50
banquet cloth			
(120 × 72-inch)	$10.40	$8.10	$14.00
8-quart chafing dish			
(stainless)	$34.25	$20.00	$18.00
(Siverplate)	$56.00	$42.50	$45.00
10-foot square canopy	$165+del	$125+del	$140+del

TIP: *The liquor store where you're purchasing your bar supplies will often loan glasses at no cost; this is a fairly common courtesy.*

Do I Need This Service?

You should consider hiring a valet service if you have invited more people with cars than can be parked in a one- to two-block radius of your party. Under these circumstances, providing parking assistance is a thoughtful, gracious gesture—if it fits into your budget.

There are also some unique locations, a hilltop meadow, for instance, where it would be very kind to provide just a shuttle service. For these special locations, with long ascending driveways and plenty of parking at the bottom, a shuttle, which could be as cost-effective as enlisting your cousin and her minivan, expresses to your guests that you care about them and their blood pressure.

On the other hand, if the area surrounding your party is unsafe, or there is *no* available parking, you are obligated to make some kind of arrangements for helping your guests dispose of their cars. Otherwise, you must have the party somewhere else.

There's one last reason to hire a valet. It is a universally recognized signal to the arriving guests that this is going to be an elegant affair.

What Are the Responsibilities of a Valet Service?

Basically, they need to park cars and return them in the same condition as received. In addition, they should provide signs which announce their presence to arriving guests. The attendants should be in uniforms, so your guests can distinguish them from some-

Valet Service Checklist

_____ **Contract (including certificate of insurance)**

_____ **Number of attendants**

_____ **Uniforms**

_____ **Adequate signage**

_____ **Tipping (prepaid or not)**

_____ **Permit (if necessary)**

one who just wants to take a joyride in a car with all four hubcaps. This brings us to a very important topic when considering valets: their insurance. They are taking responsibility, at your request, for possibly hundreds of thousands of dollars worth of automobiles, and they must be completely, adequately, and currently insured! Otherwise, you're next on the insurance food chain. All of this should be covered in the contract, which you must definitely request from any valet company you hire.

A competent valet service should schedule a site inspection of your location. At this time, discuss exactly where they will position their check-in station and ask them to estimate how long they think it will take them to retrieve each car when guests are departing. Check with them to see if a permit is required from the city at your location.

How to Find a Reliable Service

As always, personal references are the best. Also, any restaurant with valet parking is using one of these companies. Call a favorite restaurant for a referral. If I didn't have firsthand experience with one company, I would definitely interview at least two before committing.

Typical Cost/Paperwork

A valet charges based on four factors: how many attendants will be required, how many hours they will be on site, how challenging will it be to park the cars, and do you wish them to refuse tips from guests. There is generally an up-charge if you want the valets to refuse any offer of a tip from a guest. They will expect to be paid more up front for agreeing to refuse this potential revenue. An average fee for parking thirty cars (a party for fifty), with no tips accepted, is currently about $225 on the West Coast.

Florists

Flowers always make people better, happier and more helpful; they are sunshine, food and medicine.
—Luther Burbank

Do I Need This Service?

To the simple question, "Do I really need flowers if I'm giving a party?" My answer is always, "Yes." The placement of colorful, living things in your home is an ancient symbol of hospitality and welcome. Whether you purchase cut flowers to arrange yourself, or engage a florist to deliver finished bouquets is immaterial. It's just not a party without at least a bud vase in the bathroom. One of my favorite clients creates stunning casual arrangements from collections of flowers, greens, and branches gathered from her yard.

How to Find a Reliable Company

A florist's style, the look and the quality of the flowers she uses, varies so dramatically that I always visit the shop if I have not seen her work before. If I am unsure that my descriptive powers are adequate—"I would like something tall, in yellows, for about forty dollars"—I order a sample arrangement, before my event.

What Are the Responsibilities/Services of a Florist?

In addition to the obvious—providing you with fresh flowers and plants, loose or arranged—a full-service florist often provides decorating help. The florists I work with have undertaken jobs as small as rosebud napkin rings to projects as complex as decorating a large tent with vibrant fabrics, rugs, furniture, and pillows to create an exotic Moroccan atmosphere. Natural or floral wedding arches and *chupahs* are generally created by the florist as well as the other wedding flowers.

What They Cost

A wonderful florist, Walter Hubert of Silver Birches in Pasadena, was the first to show me the grades, or quality levels, of flowers available to a florist. A rose is not a rose, exactly. Top-quality flowers, handled well, can be expected to look fresh and inviting for at least a week. Lesser-quality flowers, generally older, may be dead the next day. This quality and freshness is reflected in higher prices. A top florist will also have access to a wider selection of rare or unusual blooms, like peonies, garden roses, delicate dahlias, and lilies of the valley.

There are two factors to consider when evaluating a florist's charges. There is the intangible value of a style that appeals to your sense of beauty, and the cost of the type and quality of flowers they use.

A simple bud vase can range from four dollars to twenty-five dollars. A centerpiece of roses or lilies, suitable for a dining table, can range from thirty-five dollars to two hundred dollars. A bridal bouquet represents one of the greatest ranges in pricing. I have seen an elegant bride carry a floor-trailing arrangement that cost a thousand dollars and a beautiful, romantic bouquet that cost fifty dollars.

Wedding Coordinators

*Weddings seem to be magnets for mishap and for whatever craziness lurks
in family closets. In more ways than one, weddings bring out the ding-
dong in everybody involved.*

—Robert Fulghum

Do I Need This Service?

A wedding is a truly unique social gathering. In discussions with experienced coordinators, they have expressed that it is common for weddings to be the first large scale
entertaining undertaken by the bride, and her mother. So, there is a lot of unknown
territory for the families involved in planning a big wedding. It is also the nexus of
intense emotions and perhaps lifelong fantasies. In my opinion, management of this
emotional hurricane is the best and most authentic reason to hire a professional to take
charge. If you can afford it, their objective, knowledgeable approach will allay a lot of
the attendant anxieties. Not all, mind you.

This is the only entertaining service I can think of where the value is more
emotional than practical. If you're planning a wedding of any size, you are already
committed to spending a lot of money, even if you don't realize it yet. The additional
fees for a coordinator are a wise investment in your enjoyment of the occasion.

The degree of their involvement in your planning will depend on many ele-

Wedding Coordinator Checklist

_____ **Contract completed (to include who is responsible for invitations, flowers, valet/
limousine, bride/groom gifts, rehearsal, rehearsal dinner, ceremony, reception,
music, gifts)**

_____ **Fee established**

_____ **Timeline established**

ments. However, it is generally accepted that selecting a coordinator six months before the wedding is a minimum.

What Are the Responsibilities/Services of a Wedding Coordinator?

A really good wedding coordinator provides many services. She brings you the best suppliers in your area, is familiar with the rules and guidelines of the facility you have chosen, suggests ways in which to make the bride's fantasies come true, and quietly manages the traditional festivities so that the families can enjoy the occasion like guests.

After one or more meetings with the members of the wedding party, the coordinator will help them to establish a budget and time line. However, the coordinator's most valuable service is opening her Rolodex. An experienced coordinator will give you recommendations for all of the other suppliers you are going to need: florists, limousines, bands, invitations, dresses, linens, and so on. Depending on how involved you want the coordinator to be (time equals money), she will provide written organization and supervision of: the wedding rehearsal, the rehearsal dinner, the ceremony, and the reception/party. She might continue to tie up loose ends with the thank-you notes and final billing process from the suppliers.

How to Find an Experienced Coordinator

The facility that you have selected, if you have, will almost always have a short list of preferred coordinators. This at the very least assures you that they understand how to work in this location. As always, personal references or experience are the best. There are also bridal fairs held in most major cities throughout the year where suppliers of every variety present themselves. This is a good way to begin if you do not have a location or any personal recommendations.

As you make your selection, do consider the potential influence of this person who will be so intimately involved in your wedding. In the worst case, the coordinator can take over the wedding. I catered a wedding where the coordinator assumed the persona of General Patton, commanding officer of the day, directing the bride and groom at every moment, and creating a wedding which fulfilled her expectations—and no one else's.

What Do They Cost?

A wedding coordinator bases her fee on several elements: the size of the wedding party and guest list, the number of events to be coordinated, and the complexity of the plans.

You should anticipate spending from five hundred dollars to ten thousand dollars or more, depending on these choices.

Other Services

Other special service businesses that exist to assist the occasional party giver include:

- Costume companies who supply special outfits for the staff or costumes for the guests.

- Entertainment agencies will provide you with anything from an orchestra, to a clown, a belly dancer, trained dogs, a juggler, or a DJ.

- Location finders make it their business to know all of the places, from private homes to parks, that can be rented for a party.

- Bartender services will provide professional bartenders, the bars themselves, glassware, and usually the alcohol (if your caterer is not handling this).

- Balloon companies provide balloons and the tanks to blow them up.

- Invitation specialists will not only print invitations, but can design a custom concept invitation package. Also, many of these companies now own equipment that produces a handsome handwritten script for addressing envelopes.

- Children's party planners specialize in providing all of the elements geared to the under-ten group—clowns, games, pony rides, pool sports, magicians, trampolines, face-painting, water slides, and more.

The Fundamentals

How Much to Serve

The questions I am asked most often by those in the throes of party planning relate to calculating food quantities for a group.

- **How much chicken should I bake for fifty people?**

- **How many heads of cabbage do I need to make coleslaw for one hundred?**

- **How many pounds of fresh pasta should I buy to serve twenty-five people spaghetti carbonara?**

I hope the following chart will relieve you of those middle of the night anxieties. To be honest, caterers call each other to hash out these figures, too.

Quantities throughout are approximate, estimated on the high side, which is a must for party planning.

Shrimp, caviar, lobster, crab, oysters, mussels, and smoked salmon will be the cause for great enthusiasm on a buffet, and are expensive exceptions to the quantity guidelines. Your guests will eat every piece you serve so the quantities should be based on what you want to spend.

Caveat: I just gave a party for eighty good friends. I served hors d'oeuvres from a buffet, including some of my well-known recipes. All of my seasoned guests headed straight for their old favorites and consumed twice the normal quantity of these dishes. I couldn't believe it. Bottom line: Don't expect to be 100 percent accurate, serve a variety of dishes, always prepare a little extra, and don't worry if you run out of one thing on a buffet.

Hors d'Oeuvres

The wider the variety of tastes you offer, the more your guests will consume. The same instinct that caused Marco Polo to explore the Far East and return with exotic spices and tea, makes us feel the adventurer's obligation to sample every hors d'oeuvre offered.

Hors d'Oeuvre Fundamentals

- For hors d'oeuvres preceding a meal (I recommend this event last no more than one hour), there should be at least four different tastes (6 to 8 per person). For twelve guests at this type of party, make between 75 and 100 pieces.

- When hors d'oeuvres are the only food offered at a three-hour reception there should be at least six tastes (12 to 15 per person). For twelve guests at this kind of reception make between 144 and 180 pieces.

- To calculate for hors d'oeuvres not in pieces (like cheeses, pâtés, and dips) assume 1 ounce is equal to 1 piece.

- Create a balance between hot and cold dishes.

- Plan a balance between individual bites versus platter presentations (such as whole cheeses, pâtés, and sides of smoked fish).

- If you're having twenty to twenty-five guests or more for hors d'oeuvres, you *must* include some of the "bulk" type items in your menu. Otherwise you will find yourself making hundreds of little things.

- If you're hosting forty to fifty people or more, you must also include some purchased dishes.

- After my calculations, I always add a nibble like nuts or olives to my shopping list as insurance.

NOTE: *Recipes for dishes with page numbers can be found in the recipe section. The remaining dishes in each menu are suggested purchases.*

Hors d'Oeuvres Menu for Reception Preceding Dinner for Twelve Guests

New potatoes with Baba Ghannoush (page 155; 1 recipe) and caviar (20 pieces)

Sun-Dried Tomato and Pesto Torta (page 156; ½ recipe) with Herb-Garlic Crostini (page 168)

Melon wrapped with prosciutto (20 pieces)

Poached shrimp with lemon chutney (25)

Skordalia with Crudités (page 165; 1 recipe)

Total of 105 pieces

Menu When Hors d'Oeuvres Are the Meal for Twelve Guests

Stuffed grape leaves with Lemon-Parmesan Aïoli (page 135)

Grilled Scallops with Bacon (page 213; 2 recipes)

French cheese board (43; 1 pound)

Carpaccio (page 149; ½ recipe) with Mustard-Horseradish Sauce (page 269) and toast

Sesame Eggplant Salsa (page 152; ½ recipe) with Pita Crisps (page 167)

Cheese biscuits with prosciutto spread (25 pieces)

Orange chicken wontons (25 pieces) with ginger sauce

Total of 150 pieces

Everything After Hors d'Oeuvres

It is a well-documented phenomenon that the average human being cannot resist the urge to take a little of everything from a buffet. They even take things they're not totally sure they'll like. Everybody winds up with more food on their plate than they can possibly eat. The first rule of buffet menu planning is: Make individual portions smaller than standard serving sizes. Cut the fish fillets, the steaks, the lasagna, and the chicken to half their normal serving size when offering them in combination.

Hors d'Oeuvres Menu for
Reception Preceding Dinner for Twenty-five Guests

Warm Figs Stuffed with Gorgonzola and Pecans (page 135; 50 pieces)

Smoked Salmon and Avocado Rosettes (page 135; 50 pieces)

Chicken Liver Pâté with Cherries and Pecans (page 137; ½ recipe)

European cheese display with fresh fruit (page 43; 2 pounds)

Cocktail Party Walnuts (page 161; 2 recipes)

Total of 164 pieces, plus nuts

Menu When Hors d'Oeuvres Are the
Meal for Twenty-five Guests

Warm Brie and Pear Tartlets (Page 135); 50 pieces)

Coconut Shrimp with Orange-Ginger Marmalade Dip (page 138; 2 recipes)

Carved fillet of beef, with tiny rolls and horseradish mousse (4 pounds)

Tortellini Skewers with Lemon-Parmesan Aïoli (page 135; 50 pieces)

Gravlax (page 153; 1 recipe) with Dill-Mustard Sauce (page 269) and pumpernickel

Mushroom-walnut pâté (2½ pounds) with Herb-Garlic Crostini (page 168)

Crudité display with two dips (3 pounds)

Three varieties of stuffed olives (3 pounds)

Total of 375 pieces, plus olives

Hors d'Oeuvres Menu for
Reception Preceding Dinner for Fifty Guests

Spicy Honeyed Shrimp (Page 148; 5 recipes)

Chicken Pyramid Dumplings (page 145; 2½ recipes)

Peppered ham (4 pounds) with biscuits and ginger mustard

Blue Cheese Pâté (page 164; 2 recipes) with rye crisps and green apples

Roasted nuts (3 pounds)

Total of 337 pieces, plus nuts

Menu When Hors d'oeuvres Are the
Meal for Fifty Guests

Lamb and Mint Pesto Borek (page 150; 7 recipes)

Smoked fish platter (6 pounds: sturgeon, albacore, whitefish, salmon, oysters, clams)

California cheese board with Champagne grapes (page 43; 6 pounds)

Beef Saté (page 151; 5 recipes)

Mediterranean Bean Spread (page 163; 3 recipes) with pita and grilled eggplant (3 pounds)

Polenta squares with grilled wild mushrooms (100 pieces)

Hors d'Oeuvre Twists (page 166) with prosciutto (100 pieces)

Total of 688 pieces

How to Use the Chart

- The individual serving portion for a plated meal is in column two.

- Quantities in the third column are for twelve guests served from a buffet, the fourth column indicates quantities for twenty-five and so on.

- Quantities suggested assume there will be a choice on the buffet of at least two entrées, two or three vegetables, two or three salads, plus bread and two or three desserts.

- Weights or quantities are for the raw or untrimmed weight of the item you need to purchase.

- The buffet quantities provide a half-size portion of each dish for every guest.

- The letters "NR" indicate that this item is not recommended for the number of guests in that column.

Food Quantity Chart

Menu item	Individual portion/ a plated meal	12 guests served from a buffet	25 guests served from a buffet	50 guests served from a buffet	75 guests served from a buffet	100 guests served from a buffet
SOUP (HOT OR COLD)						
Served as a first course	8–10 oz	2½ qts	5 qts	2½ gals	3½ gals	4½ gals
As the entrée course	1½–2 cups	1 gal	2 gals	4 gals	5½ gals	7–8 gals
GREEN SALADS						
romaine or iceberg lettuce	¼ head	2 heads	4 heads	8 heads	11 heads	14 heads
red leaf or butter lettuce	⅓ head	3 heads	6 heads	12 heads	16–17 heads	21 heads
mesclun mix	1 cup	8 cups	16 cups	30 cups	40 cups	55 cups
shredded cabbage (coleslaw)	½ cup	3–4 cups	6–8 cups (about 1 head)	12–16 cups (1–2 head)	16–20 cups (about 2½ heads)	24 cups (about 3 heads)
tomato, cucumber, radish, mushroom, etc., as garnish	3–4 slices	1½ cups	3 cups	6 cups	7½ cups	10 cups
croutons (medium size)—increase measures if using jumbo size	3–4	1 cup	2 cups	4 cups	5 cups	6½ cups

Menu item	Individual portion/ a plated meal	12 guests served from a buffet	25 guests served from a buffet	50 guests served from a buffet	75 guests served from a buffet	100 guests served from a buffet
dressing, on the side	1–2 tbsps	1½ cups	3 cups	1½ qts	2½ qts	3 qts (96 oz)

FRUIT SALAD						
combined, roughly chopped (berries, melon, mango, citrus, papaya, grape, pineapple, kiwi, etc.,)	⅔–1 cup	6–6½ cups	3 qts	6 qts	9 qts	12 qts

STARCH SALADS						
you need the quantities indicated plus herbs, chopped vegetables, garnishes, and dressing						
potato	½ (medium)	2½	5	10	15	20
pasta, rice, couscous, or bulgur	2 oz	1 lb	2 lbs	4 lbs	5½ lbs	7 lbs

BREAKFAST MEATS						
sliced bacon	2–4 slices	1 lb	2 lbs	4 lbs	5 lbs	7 lbs
sausage (link or patty)	¼ lbs	2–2½ lbs	4–5 lbs	8–10 lbs	12½ lbs	16–17 lbs
Canadian bacon	2–3 oz	1½ lbs	3 lbs	6 lbs	8 lbs	10½ lbs

POULTRY ENTREES						
boneless chicken, duck, or turkey	½ lb	3½–4 lbs	7–8 lbs	14–16 lbs	19–22 lbs	24–28 lbs
bone-in chicken pieces	¾–1 lb	7–8 lbs (2 birds)	14–16 lbs (4 birds)	28–32 lbs (8 birds)	41 lbs (11 birds)	49–56 lbs (14 birds)
bone-in duck pieces	1½–2 lbs	12 lbs	24 lbs	48 lbs	66 lbs	84 lbs
whole turkey	1 lb	9 lbs	18 lbs	36 lbs	50 lbs	63 lbs

BEEF, LAMB, PORK ENTREES (ALL WEIGHTS ARE FULLY TRIMMED)						
boneless roast cuts (tri-tip, top loin)	½ lb	3½–4 lbs	7–8 lbs	14–16 lbs	21 lbs	26–27 lbs
T-bone, porterhouse steaks	16–24 oz	5 lbs	NR	NR	NR	NR
bone-in roast (leg, prime rib)	14–16 oz	7–8 lbs	15 lbs	30 lbs	41 lbs	50 lbs

Menu item	Individual portion/ a plated meal	12 guests served from a buffet	25 guests served from a buffet	50 guests served from a buffet	75 guests served from a buffet	100 guests served from a buffet
CHOPS						
pork	one (14 oz)	NR	NR	NR	NR	NR
veal	one (12 oz)	NR	NR	NR	NR	NR
lamb	4 chops	3–4 racks (20–28 chops)	6–7 racks (42–49 chops)	13–14 racks (84–98 chops)	18–19 racks (119–130 chops)	21–28 racks (147–196 chops)
baby back ribs, pork	1 lb	7–8 lbs	14–16 lbs	28–32 lbs	38–44 lbs	50–60 lbs
spareribs, pork	1 lb	7–8 lbs	14–16 lbs	28–32 lbs	38–44 lbs	50–60 lbs
beef short ribs	1 to 1¼ lbs	10 lbs	20 lbs	40 lbs	55 lbs	70 lbs
GROUND AND CHOPPED MEAT						
ground meat	½ lb	3½–4 lbs	7–8 lbs	14–16 lbs	21 lbs	26½ lbs
chopped meats (for stroganoff, ragout, chili, stew, etc.)	5–6 oz	3 lbs	6 lbs	12 lbs	16½ lbs	21 lbs
SEAFOOD						
soft-shell crab	2	12	45	50	75	100
fillet or steak	6–8 oz	4 lbs	8 lbs	16 lbs	22 lbs	28 lbs
trout (cleaned, 1 lb each)	1 fish	10 fish	20 fish	40 fish	55 fish	70 fish
shrimp, large (16–20 per lb)	5–7	3–4 lbs	7 lbs	14 lbs	19 lbs	24 lbs
Maine lobster (1½–2 lbs each)	1	12	25	NR	NR	NR
lobster tail (8–10 oz, shell on)	1	12	25	50	75	100 (ouch!)
lobster medallion	5–6 oz	3½ lbs	6¼ lbs	12½ lbs	18 lbs	25 lbs (ouch!)
king crab legs	10–12 oz	6 legs	NR	NR	NR	NR
scallop meat	4–6 oz	2½ lbs	5 lbs	10 lbs	13¾ lbs	17½ lbs
BIVALVES IN THE SHELL (OYSTERS, CLAMS, MUSSELS—MEDIUM TO LARGE)						
as an entrée	6–10	50–80	100–160	200–325	NR	NR
as an appetizer	4–6	40–60	80–120	160–240	NR	NR

Menu item	Individual portion/ a plated meal	12 guests served from a buffet	25 guests served from a buffet	50 guests served from a buffet	75 guests served from a buffet	100 guests served from a buffet
VEGETABLES (AS A SIDE DISH)						
asparagus, sugar snap pea, carrot, cauliflower, beets, broccoli, green beans, etc.	3–4 oz	2 lbs	4 lbs	8 lbs	11 lbs	14 lbs
potato, yam, turnip	1 medium or 5–6 oz	3 lbs	6 lbs	12 lbs	16½ lbs	21 lbs
eggplant	⅓ medium	3 medium	6 medium	12 medium	16 medium	21 medium
corn on the cob (to serve on a buffet, break each cob in half)	1 ear	10 ears	18–20 ears	35 ears	45 ears	55 ears
corn kernels, peas, lima beans	3–4 oz	1¾ lbs	3½ lbs	7 lbs	9½ lbs	12¼ lbs
zucchini, summer squash, chayote	4–5 oz	2 lbs	4 lbs	8 lbs	11 lbs	14 lbs
spinach, chard (1 bunch = 1 lb = 1 cup, cooked)	⅓ bunch	3 bunch (3½ lbs)	6 bunch (7 lbs)	12 bunch (14 lbs)	16 bunch (19 lbs)	23 bunch (24½ lbs)
GRAINS AND LEGUMES						
white rice	3–4 tbsps	2½ cups (17½ oz)	5 cups (2 lbs)	2½ qts (4 lbs)	3½ qts (5¼ lbs)	1 gal (6 lbs)
wild rice and brown rice	2–3 tbsps	2 cups (¾ to 1 lb)	1 qt (1½ lbs)	2 qts (3 lbs)	2 qts+ 1 cup (4¼ lbs)	3½ qts (5¼ lbs)
dried beans, bulgur, barley, lentils	¼ cup	2½ cups (15 oz)	1 qt (1½ lbs)	2 qts (3 lbs)	2 qts + 1 cup (4¼ lbs)	3½ qts (5¼ lbs)
couscous	⅓ cup	2¾ cups (1 lb)	5½ cups (2 lbs)	2½ qts (4 lbs)	3½ qts (5½ lbs)	5 qts (7 lbs)
polenta	⅓ cup	2¾ cups (1 lb)	5½ cups (2 lbs)	2½ qts (4 lbs)	3½ qts (5½ lbs)	5 qts (7 lbs)
PASTA, AS AN ENTREE						
linguine, fettuccine, angel hair (dry)	2–3 oz	1½ lbs	3 lbs	6 lbs	8¼ lbs	10½ lbs
linguine, fettuccine, angel hair (fresh)	4 oz	2 lbs	4 lbs	8 lbs	11 lbs	14 lbs
tortellini, ravioli, and other filled pastas, fresh or frozen	4–5 oz	2¼ lbs	5 lbs	10 lbs	12¼ lbs	15¾ lbs

Menu item	Individual portion/ a plated meal	12 guests served from a buffet	25 guests served from a buffet	50 guests served from a buffet	75 guests served from a buffet	100 guests served from a buffet
PASTA SAUCE						
cream sauce	½ cup	4½ cups	2½ qts	5 qts	8 qts	10 qts
tomato- or vegetable-based sauce	½–⅔ cup	6 cups	3 qts	1½ gals	12 qts	12 qts
COMPOSED OR CASSEROLE ENTRÉES						
quiche	one 4" wedge	one 10" tarte or cake pan	two 10" tarte or cake pans	four 10" tarte or cake pans	three 13" × 9"× 2" baking pans	four to five 13" × 9" × 2" baking pans
filled crepes	2–3 crepes	16–24 crepes	3–4 dozen crepes	6–8 dozen crepes	9½ dozen crepes	12–13 dozen crepes
lasagna, strata	1–1½ cups	one 9" × 9" pan (8–12 cups)	two 9" × 9" pans (16–24 cups)	three 13" × 9" × 2" pans (32–48 cups)	four 13" × 9" × 2" pans (55 cups)	five 13" × 9" × 2" pans (70 cups)
BREADS						
dinner rolls	1½	18–24	3½ dozen	7 dozen	10 dozen	120 dozen
muffins, pastry, croissant	1½	18–24	3½ dozen	7 dozen	10 dozen	120 dozen
DESSERT						
ice cream, sorbet, gelato	6 oz	2 qts	1 gal	2 gals	2¾ gals	3½ gals
layer cake, angel food cake	1 slice	one 8" cake	two 8"cakes	four 8" cakes	five to six 8" cakes	seven 8" cakes
sheet cake	one 2" × 2" piece	less than a ¼ sheet cake	¼ sheet cake	½ sheet cake	½ + ¼ sheet cakes	1 full sheet cake
cheesecake	one 2" wedge	one 9" pie plate or springform pan	two 9" pie plates or springform pans	four 9" pie plates or springform pans	five to six 9" pie plates or springform pans	seven 9" pie plates or springform pans
pie, tarte	One 3" wedge	one 9–10" pie plate	two to three 9" pie plates	four 9" pie plates	six 9" pie plates	seven 9" pie plates
bars, brownies (cut approx 1" × 2")	1–2	16–18	2½–3 dozen	5½–6 dozen	8 dozen	10 dozen
cookies	2–3	1½–2 dozen	3–4 dozen	6–8 dozen	9–10 dozen	12½ dozen

Menu item	Individual portion/ a plated meal	12 guests served from a buffet	25 guests served from a buffet	50 guests served from a buffet	75 guests served from a buffet	100 guests served from a buffet
trifle, tiramisu, bread pudding bowls	1 cup	one 9" × 5" bowl (2 qts)	two 9" × 5" bowls (1 gal)	four 9" × 5" bowls (2 gals)	five 9" × 5" bowls (2¾ gals)	seven 9" × 5" (3½ gals)
cobbler, slump	1 cup	one 9" × 9" × 2" baking pan	two 9" × 9" × 2" baking pans	three 13" × 9" × 2" baking pans	four 13" × 9" × 2" baking pans	five 13" × 9" × 2" baking pans
mousse	¾ cup	one 8" × 5" bowl	two 8" × 5" bowls	four 8" × 5" bowls	five 8" × 5" bowls	seven 8" × 5" bowls
bowls		(6–7 cups)	(3–3½ qts)	(6–7 qts)	(2+ gals)	(2¾ gals)
MISC						
coffee (ground)	2 tbsps (¼ oz)	¾ lb	1½ lbs	3 lbs	4½ lbs	6 lbs
cream/milk for coffee	1–2 tbsp	1 cup	2 cups	1 qt	1 qt + 1½ cups	1 qt + 3 cups

Styles of Service: Seated, Buffet, or Both

There are more choices for serving a menu than just "stand up" (buffet) or sit down. How you combine these styles will impact the flow of your party, guest interactions, and what kind of a menu you can best serve. A caterer approaches each event as though it were an empty stage. They are the director and your guests the actors. The party created is the play. Mastery of the different styles of service is one of a caterer's most important tools in staging the play. Making innovative use of your space, and combining some of the serving options described on the following pages, can introduce an alluring layer of drama and spontaneity to your event.

Plated Service

In the kitchen you arrange the food on each plate and then serve them to your guests. This is frequently preceded by cocktails and buffet or passed hors d'oeuvres.

Advantages

- Your control over portion sizes allows you to serve expensive or exotic ingredients (nobody puts lobster on a buffet).

- You can establish the pace of the meal and therefore the party.

- It's easy to create dramatic presentations.

- You can most easily create an elegant or romantic mood.

Disadvantages

- This style requires a lot of planning and much of your time is spent sweating in the kitchen instead of mingling with your guests and enjoying the party. You may wind up feeling like a waiter/waitress.

Best for

- Two to eight for a special occasion.

- Maximum of twelve to fourteen, if you have help.

Plated Menu

Carpaccio (page 149)

Mushroom Strudel (page 236)

Crudité baskets with curried yogurt

Fresh pea soup with Pistachio Mint Pesto (page 277) on toast

Baked Sea Bass with Caribbean Salsa (page 214)

Mashed Mapled Sweet Potatoes with Glazed Nuts (page 258)

Cappuccino crème brûlée

Coffee

A Pretty Plate

"Food on a plate" is a good subject for a watercolor. It's also an opportunity for creativity and imagination. There are a few basics principals that must be observed when arranging food on a plate, then let your imagination take flight!

- It is more appetizing to see some space around each element on the plate. The sauce from the entrée oozing into the asparagus appears sloppy and unappealing. For this reason, it is much easier to present food on an oversized (buffet) plate.

- If you plan to entertain often, owning unique plates is an effective shortcut to creating a beautiful table. Unexpected shapes, like squares or rectangles, are effective; colored plates or clear plates stacked on an unusual material like steel or bamboo also create visual excitement. I have oversized black dinner plates, square glass salad plates, and glass soup bowls with a black and gold rim. This eclectic combination creates an interesting table even before the colorful food is introduced.

- When planning your menu consider how recipes will look when they are completed. How will they look when united on one plate? There should generally be some green and some red or orange on an entrée plate.

- Garnishing the plate with fresh herbs should be limited to an herb that is an ingredient in the dish being served. Flowers are appealing decorations on a plate, especially for salad or dessert. However, you must be sure they are edible and nonpoisonous. Use flowers like roses, nasturtiums, chive blossoms, or squash blossoms that were grown without pesticides.

- The plastic squeeze bottles available in every kitchen store allow you to paint with a sauce. They're especially useful for desserts, where drama is always crucial. Use an intensely red raspberry puree to draw swirls of color on a deep chocolate dessert. Put the bright green Yemenite Zhoug Relish (page 286) in a squeeze bottle and paint dots of color on the rim of an entrée plate featuring Skewered Lamb Ruffles with Almond Mint Pesto (page 219), on a bed of rice.

- If the main course is something messy, like cassoulet or risotto, it's best to put any accompaniment on a separate plate to be served on the side. When the entrée plate presents a single item, sprinkle a minced herb, lemon zest, or grated cheese around the rim of the plate to frame the dish.

Family Style

All of the food is brought to the dining table in serving dishes and passed around the table or served by the host. Thanksgiving dinner is usually served like this.

Advantages

- The food is easy to assemble and get on the table.

- Because you are using large serving dishes, you don't have to worry about food getting cold quickly.

- This serving style develops a sense of camaraderie for a casual gathering of friends or family.

Disadvantages

- Guests never really get a chance to admire the food's appearance.

- It can be awkward with everyone passing dishes to and fro at the table.

- This presentation is not appropriate for a formal or business occasion.

Best for

- Family holidays, potluck, events including a lot of young people.

Family-Style Menu

Quick Grilled Pizza (page 159)

Buttermilk fried chicken

Grilled Vegetables with Balsamic Vinaigrette (page 262)

Classic Mashed Potatoes (page 256)

Cilantro Slaw (page 187)

Iced tea and beer

Hot fudge sundaes with all the trimmings

The All-Purpose Grape

Grape clusters in every color are great as accents on platters or the table itself. Their drapey and malleable shape easily conforms to any surface. Use them to grace cheeses on a board, or sliced ham on a platter. I love to see lush grapes cascading over the edge of a table. Every caterer knows that if you have a case of grapes in the truck you can decorate almost anything.

Casual Buffet

All of the food is presented on one or more buffet tables and guests serve themselves. The menu for a casual buffet could feature only hors d'oeuvres, just desserts, or a full meal.

Casual Brunch Menu

(all at room temperature)

Grilled corn and fennel salad

Marinated shrimp and snow peas

Galette of onions and olives

Mediterranean cheese board (page 43)

California Chicken Salad (page 192)

Turkey Tonnato (page 210)

Small rolls

Biscotti and fresh fruit

Chocolate Pâté with Fresh Plum Sauce (page 305)

Advantages

- You can use the buffet tables themselves to decorate the party.

- All (or most) of the food can be in place before the party begins, freeing you for other tasks.

- You can offer a variety of dishes, which eliminates the challenge of pleasing every palate with only one entrée or dessert.

- Guests can help themselves to what they like, when they like.

- It is not necessary to seat everyone at once, so you can invite more guests than will fit around your table.

Disadvantages

- You cannot control how much food is taken and must prepare more than "just enough."

- In most cases you will have considerable leftovers.

- If there are hot or warm items some attention will have to be given to maintaining the temperature and possibly making adjustments.

- The buffet will need to be replenished or tidied several times during the course of the party.

Best for

- A large group or an open house with guests arriving over an extended period of time.

- A casual buffet is best if there are no hot dishes included.

Formal Buffet Option

With this option there is someone serving the guests from the buffet. If all of your guests are seated, and there are more than twenty people, the host should invite guests to the buffet a few at a time to eliminate waiting in line.

Advantages

- The addition of server(s) allows people to move through the buffet more quickly. For a large party this can be an important consideration.

- The server determines how much is served; which is useful if you are serving something expensive, or you have concerns about quantities.

- A large roast or whole turkey can be carved to order, which adds a sense of indulgence and professionalism.

- Because someone is assigned to paying close attention to the buffet, it is easier to serve hot dishes.

Disadvantages

- The added expense of, or effort to find, servers.

Best for

- A formal occasion when you would like to invite more than twelve to fifteen guests.

Formal Buffet Supper Menu

HORS D'OEUVRES
(could be on a separate table from main buffet)

Crudités with two dips

Warm Brie and Pear Tartlets (page 135)

Smoked trout mousse with toast

MAIN BUFFET
Seeded Roast Roots (page 250)

Warm White Beans with Prosciutto and Sage (page 252)

Grilled zucchini and asparagus salad

Chicken with Artichokes and Olives (page 203)

Roast loin of pork with cherries

DESSERT
(use the same table as had been used for hors d'oeuvres)

Tulip cookie baskets filled with vanilla cream, liqueur soaked plums, and peaches, and toasted pine nuts

Chocolate Pâté with Fresh Plum Sauce (page 305)

Coffee

Buffet and Tray

Food is served at buffets and small finger foods are circulated on trays.

Buffet and Tray Dinner Menu for Twenty-four

PASSED

Lamb and Mint Pesto Borek (page 150)

Coconut Shrimp with Orange-Ginger Marmalade Dip (page 138)

The Quesadilla Concept (page 158) made with chevre

BUFFET

Melon wrapped in prosciutto and thyme and drizzled with Port

Cheese board with crackers, grapes, and white peaches (page 43)

Savory Spiced Nuts (page 162)

Cocktail Party Walnuts (page 161)

Roast Tenderloin of Beef with Gorgonzola (page 227)

Tandoori-Flavored Chicken (page 206)

Aromatic Basmati Pilaf (page 261)

Mint Cilantro Raita (page 285)

Carrots with sherry and ginger

Serafina's Tiramisu (page 291)

Flourless Chocolate Cake

Individual fruit tarts

Coffee

Advantages

- Provides the ultimate in terms of "catering" to your guests. If they are too engrossed in conversation to go to the buffet table, or the line is too long, someone brings them a nibble, creating a relaxing combination of luxury and elegance with practicality.

Disadvantages

- You must have one or more hired people to help. (You may have teenagers who love this kind of helping out.)

- You definitely can't take this on by yourself unless there are fewer than eight guests.

Best for

- A special occasion when extravagance is appropriate; especially useful if you expect the party to be crowded, making it difficult for guests to circulate.

- This option is also thoughtful if there are elderly or physically challenged guests.

Mixed Service

One or more course or element of the meal is served at a buffet and one or more is served at the table. For instance, hors d'oeuvres and an appetizer are served on a buffet, and guests are seated for a plated entrée. For dessert and coffee, attention is again focused on the buffet. This provides an opportunity to stretch and chat after dinner and to create a special, personalized dessert.

Advantages

- This combined style allows you to combine the best of plate service (presentation and a sense of indulgence) and the buffet (choices and ease of service). Guests get to mingle and still feel indulged by your attention.

- This is one of the most successful party styles. The participatory theater of the buffet and the relaxation at the table for the entrée course provides an excellent style for all but the most formal events. It was my clients favorite style.

Disadvantages

- For more than eight people, you will need servers.

- You may have to explain to guests what to do, but this is part of the fun.

Best for

- A group of six to twenty.

Mixed Service Menu

APPETIZER BUFFET

Iced seafood display

Sun-Dried Tomato and Pesto Torta (page 156) with Herb-Garlic Crostini (page 168)

Chicken Pyramid Dumplings (page 145)

Whole Roast Garlic with Herbs (page 283) with Pita Crisps (page 167)

ENTRÉE PLATE

Party Prime Rib (page 224)

Pear and Potato Gratin with Horseradish (page 255)

Grilled wild mushrooms

DESSERT TABLE

White and dark chocolate bags to be filled with each guest's selection from assorted berries, amaretto, whipped cream, custard, and raspberry sauce

Coffee

Liqueurs

How to Set the Table

These are some examples of appropriate ways to set the table for casual, formal, and takeout menus. Each illustration is followed by a menu, which would be served in this manner. If you follow these guidelines, you are likely to be on safe ground. However, there are many other correct and attractive ways to arrange glassware, napkins, and flatware. The only really rigid rules are: forks to the left of the plate, knives to the right, spoons to the right of the knives, glasses above the knives. Unless of course, as in illustrations for the formal table setting with soup and the very formal place setting on the next page, flatware for an entire course has been placed above the center of the place setting. I like this style for several reasons: It keeps the silverware from sprawling too far across the table and shows clearly what to use for a particular course.

In most cases you will notice that I've not included the silverware required for dessert and coffee in the initial place setting. Unless you're trying to fill space on the table, impress your guests with how large your silver service is, or you know that you won't have an opportunity during the meal to bring out additional flatware, set the table with the necessities for everything up to dessert. It's better to clean the table after the main course, then bring out the flatware and coffee cups with the dessert. Using this approach, you avoid having a cluttered table and conceivably embarrassing a guest with too many choices. Many, many people are confused by three forks, or three spoons of varying sizes, no matter where they are placed.

Basic/Casual Table Setting for Salad, Entrée, and Dessert

Formal Table Setting with Soup As the Entrée Preceeded by Salad

What to Do with Chopsticks for a Menu Featuring Chinese Takeout

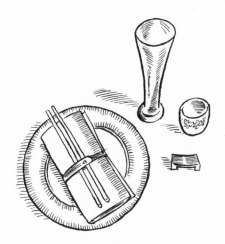

Very Formal, Including Place Card and Bread Plate

Beverage Service

*It was my uncle George who discovered that alcohol was a food well in
advance of modern medical thought.*

—P. G. Wodehouse, *The Inimitable Jeeves*

- The most cost-effective approach to serve liquor to a group of twenty or more is a full bar. Hard liquor is much less expensive in quantity than even average wine.

- I recommend the use of an all-purpose nine- to eleven-ounce stemmed glass for everything. (An assortment of specialty glasses is unnecessary and more expensive whether you buy or rent them.)

- The one exception to use of the all-purpose glass is when serving Champagne. Naturally, if you are serving Champagne, it is of a good quality with lovely, fine dancing bubbles. This treat must be served in a flute-shaped glass to protect the effervescence that makes Champagne so special. Whether you want to buy twelve or rent them will depend on how often you plan to include Champagne in your bar.

- Don't serve Champagne unless you can afford something of at least moderate quality (nine dollars and up per bottle depending on where you live).

- If you are planning to entertain several times per year, purchase a simple, sturdy stemmed glass in quantity. Pottery Barn, Pier 1 Imports, and Crate & Barrel are some stores that usually stock moderately priced glasses that would fit your needs. Keep the boxes they come in to store the glasses between parties.

- A great solution to lines at the bar, particularly a problem if most of the guests will be arriving at the same time, is to have a table or two with trays of prepoured white wine, Champagne, and mineral water near the entrance. At least half of the people will be happy with one of these choices and the stress is taken off the bartender(s).

- Avoid using plastic glassware for cocktail service unless it is a backpacking picnic or there is a safety issue (near a pool or on a boat).

- A cocktail party (average length 2½ to 3 hours) involves the heaviest liquor consumption, except for a wedding (see below).

- For an evening wedding, you should generally increase the standard liquor consumption figures quoted below by about 75 percent.

- Quantities for a full bar: For every eight guests allow one quart of alcohol plus wine and mixes. On the West Coast we calculate that the alcohol should be balanced 50 percent vodka, 30 percent scotch/bourbon, 10 percent gin, and 10 percent tequila or rum. You will need to adjust this for your community. Geographic regions definitely have different alcohol preferences. Southerners, for instance, consume much more bourbon and Scotch than western residents who prefer vodka and wine.

- There are approximately 16 drinks in a fifth of liquor.

- Quantities for wine: Allow one-half bottle per person; do not pour more than five to six ounces per glass. On average you will get five glasses from a bottle of wine.

- Quantities for sodas and mixes: Buy one bottle of each for every eight people.

- Quantities for mineral water: Buy two bottles for every eight guests.

- One pound of ice per person is usually enough for use in cocktails and to chill wine and beer. (To chill bottles, see Box, page 25.)

- Even though there is often less alcohol consumed at a luncheon or seated meal than at a cocktail reception, I always use the preceeding figures unless there is a special theme for the party, or I know my guests' unique preferences and can purchase especially for them.

- There will definitely be bar supplies left over, so be sure to purchase brands that you personally enjoy.

Stocking the Bar

All liquor, unopened wine, and mixes will keep for the next time you entertain so stock your bar with a generous hand. The other option, of under buying and running out of a guest's favorite alcoholic indulgence, is at least as unpleasant as being short one serving of crème brûleé—ouch!

Shopping List for a Cocktail Reception for Thirty Guests (a very effective size)

Basic Bar

1 bottle rum or tequila (depends on personal taste and where you live)

2 bottles gin

3 bottles vodka

1 bottle Scotch

1 bottle bourbon

> ## To Keep Cold Beverages Cold
>
> To help cold beverages, like iced tea, iced coffee, lemonade, or punch retain their flavor and stay chilled on a hot day, freeze some of the same beverage in a coffee can, ice cube tray, dessert mold, or Bundt pan. Use this custom-flavored ice to chill the beverage instead of watering it down with plain ice. Rose petals, lime slices, mint leaves, and sweet cherries encased in ice are simple garnishes to add flair to your beverage table. A glass pitcher of rosy hibiscus iced tea looks gorgeous with little raspberries floating in the ice cubes. A jug of spicy Sangrita (page 169) is exotic filled with lime juice ice cubes showing a sliver of jalapeño chile in the middle.

9 bottles white wine (Chardonnay, Chablis, or Vouvray)

6 bottles red wine (Merlot, Cabernet Sauvignon, or Pinot Noir)

12 bottles of beer (regular and light)

6 large bottles each tonic, soda, cola, and a diet soda

6 to 7 bottles mineral water

Lemons and limes

Large green olives

40 pounds of ice (15 pounds for cocktails, 25 pounds for chilling bottles)

NOTE: The popularity of red wine as a beverage is escalating. So, consider your guest list when deciding on the quantity of red and white wine needed.

Expanded/Elegant Bar

To the basic bar inventory, add: 4 to 6 bottles of brut Champagne (adjust the white wine quantity accordingly), 2 quarts fresh orange juice, 1 quart fresh grapefruit juice, 1 bottle each: of Cognac (VS or better), Bailey's Irish Cream or Kahlua, dry vermouth, Campari, dry sherry, Grand Marnier or Triple Sec, and coffee.

C'est Tout—It's the Ritz

To the elegant bar inventory add: Calvados, vintage Port, poire eau de vie, crème de menthe (green or white), Dubonnet, Irish whiskey, XO Cognac.

Wine and Water only (a very popular option these days)

12 bottles white wine

12 bottles red wine

12 quarts sparkling mineral water

10 quarts assorted sodas (diet and regular)

Bar Supplies

Basic Bar for a Cocktail Reception for Thirty Guests

 100 glasses

 150 cocktail napkins

 Wine opener, small knife, bar towel

 Ice bucket and tongs for cocktail ice (could be as simple as a bowl)

 Cooler or ice tub large enough to hold wine and ice (and beer if served)

Expanded/Elegant Bar

 35 Champagne flutes

 Cocktail shaker

 Kosher salt for margaritas

 Pretty swizzle sticks (they come in everything from little cacti to top hats)

Bar Setup

A regular five- to six-foot table can be used very effectively; however, make sure that you have protected the surface if it is a good piece of furniture. An actual bar from a rental company has the advantage of being an easier height for a bartender to work at. This height also serves to camouflage the ice tub and other sundry supplies that aren't particularly attractive, but needed behind the bar to make things work.

Mixes

Homemade versions of the following recipes are a very noticeable improvement over the commercial mixes normally served. They are quick and easy to assemble, well worth the time invested. This is a place where the novice can imbue his party with a sense of creativity and adventure.

 Bloody Mary Fantastico (page 169)

 Brazilian coffee

 Caiparinha

 Eggnog (page 170)

Exotic iced teas (Japanese green, Red Zinger with rose petals, mango with peach)

Flavored vodkas (lemon, grapefruit, orange, chile, vanilla)

Hot Buttered Rum (page 172)

Traditional Margaritas (page 171)

Sangrita (page 169)

Protecting Wine Labels

If you are serving a white wine or Champagne that is expensive or one that might be left over and served at another party, protect the labels from water damage by slipping each bottle into a small plastic bag before placing it on the ice to chill.

How to Equip a Kitchen

The Basic Kitchen (getting started)

Purchase the best-quality knives you can possibly afford, even if you can only purchase one at a time. Good knives will last a lifetime if properly cared for.

BAKING EQUIPMENT

> 9 × 5-inch loaf pan
>
> 9-inch Pyrex pie plate
>
> 9-inch round cake pans (2)
>
> Baking pans (2)
>
> Cookie cutters
>
> Cooling rack
>
> Hot pads/mitts (4)
>
> Kitchen towels, all cotton (6)
>
> Muffin pans, preferably nonstick (2)
>
> Pastry brush
>
> Rolling pin

BLENDER

CUTTING BOARDS

> (large), 1 hardwood, 1 hard plastic

ELECTRIC HAND MIXER

GRILL

> (start with whatever size is appropriate to your outdoor space; a hibachi is better than nothing. The easiest is attached to either a propane tank or natural-gas line for instant heat, no fire building required; although you do sacrifice a lot of the smoky, woodsy flavors of real charcoal.)

INSTANT-READ THERMOMETER

KNIVES

> 2 (3½-inch) paring
>
> 8-inch serrated bread
>
> 8-inch chef
>
> 5½-inch utility
>
> 10-inch carving
>
> Sharpening steel

MICROWAVE WITH CAROUSEL

MINI FOOD PROCESSOR

POTS AND PANS

Collapsible steamer basket

Deep, about 12×16-inch, roasting pan with rack

Microwave cookware (glass or plastic), 1 cup, 2 cup, 1 quart

10-inch cast-iron skillet

2 nonstick sauté pans with lids (8 and 10 inch)

$2\frac{1}{2}$- and $4\frac{1}{2}$-quart saucepans with lids

8-quart stockpot with lid

13×9-inch shallow roasting pan

4-quart casserole with lid

PRESENTATION/SERVING EQUIPMENT

12 all-purpose wineglasses

12 tumblers/water glasses

2 trays or platters (cheese board, carved meats, pastries)

3 handsome, sturdy baskets (bread, salad, crudité)

Candleholders

Cloth for the dining table, with napkins

Salad bowl large enough to serve 12

Salad servers, serving forks, and spoons

Serving bowls, small, medium, and large

TIMER THAT INCLUDES MINUTES AND HOURS

UTENSILS/TOOLS

Barbecue tools (extra-long handled spatula and tongs)

Box grater

Can opener

Citrus reamer

Corkscrew

Ice cream scoop (the paddle type is best)

Pepper mill with a heavy steel grinding mechanism

Pizza wheel

Salad spinner

Spatulas (2 metal, 1 rubber)

Set of measuring cups (glass or stainless)

Set of measuring spoons (stainless)

Set of nested mixing bowls in stainless or glass

Slotted spoon, long-handled

Spoons, long-handled stainless (2)

Stainless colander (8 to 12 inches wide)

Teakettle

Tea strainer

Tongs, stainless, 10 to 12 inches (2)

Vegetable peeler (heavy duty)

Whisk, stainless, 8 to 10 inches

Wooden spoons, long-handled (3)

Thermometers

An instant-read thermometer is an absolute necessity, especially when cooking a large piece of meat like a turkey or a roast. Cooking meat based solely on elapsed time is just not practical. You must know what the internal temperature of the meat is to accurately determine when it's done to your liking. An oven thermometer is a valuable ally, too. It can be used to check on both your oven and your grill. An oven temperature can be off by as much as a hundred degrees. If you don't have a grill with a temperature indicator, put in your own oven thermometer as a safeguard against overcooking.

The Intermediate Kitchen (add the following)

AUTOMATIC LIGHTER

BAKING EQUIPMENT

Mini muffin pans (2)

2-quart soufflé dish

9 × 5-inch loaf pans (2)

9-inch fluted tart pans with removable bottoms (2)

Coated canvas piping bags (2) and a set of decorating tips

Crème brûlée/custard cups (12)

Marble pastry board

Pastry brushes, small and large

Springform pans, 6 and 8 inch

CANDY/DEEP-FRY THERMOMETER

stainless steel with clip for side of pan

ELECTRIC FRYING PAN WITH TIGHT FITTING LID AND THERMOSTAT

ELECTRIC ICE CREAM MAKER

FOOD PROCESSOR

11-cup capacity, purchase grater and slicer blades also

IMMERSION BLENDER

KNIVES

10-inch chef

12-inch chef (if you're comfortable with this size, it's very efficient)

Heavy Chinese cleaver

POTS AND PANS

13-inch cast-iron frying pan

2-layer bamboo steamer

6-inch crepe pans (2, to be used only for this purpose)

Baking dishes appropriate for strata or lasagna (2, attractive enough to take to the table)

Cast-iron rangetop griddle/grill

Copper-bottomed omelet pan (use only for this purpose)

Double boiler with lid

Enclosed deep-fat fryer with removable basket

Large enamel Dutch oven with lid, 6 to 8 quart

Small saucepan with lid, 1 cup

Wok (heavy) with lid and cooking ring

SCALE THAT MEASURES IN OUNCES AND GRAMS UP TO 5 POUNDS

SPICE MILLS/COFFEE GRINDERS

2 (keep one for sweet, one for savory)

UTENSILS/TOOLS

Bulb baster

Cheesecloth

Chef's choice knife sharpener

Cocktail shaker

Ladles, stainless steel, small and large

Measuring cup–type fat separator

Meat mallet

Oyster shucker

Pizza stone

Small mortar and pestle (wooden or marble)

Strainer for stir-fry and deep-fry, long-handled

Zester, heavy duty

PRESENTATION/SERVING EQUIPMENT

Buffet linens (2 to 3)

Cheese and pâté knives (8)

Crab crackers (2)

Dining tablecloth with 12 matching napkins

Electric hot tray

Flat cheese trays (2)

Napkin rings/wraps (12 or more)

Platters: bamboo, terra-cotta, silver, Lucite, marble or glass. Attractive, not too fragile (hectic party hands) and remember that the bordering design will be most important since the center will generally be covered with food. A few really large pieces are invaluable (at least 20 inches).

Set (at least 12 each) of red wine, white wine, and water glasses

Silver or other handsome pitchers (2)

Tiny seafood forks (12)

Votive candle holders (at least 12, buy them every time you see them on sale, you can't have too many)

Wine/champagne cooler

The Semiprofessional Kitchen

(if cooking is your major hobby or you want to cater on a small scale)

BAKING EQUIPMENT

12-inch tart pans with removable bottoms (2)

5-inch deep springform pans (2)

Charlotte mold

Jelly-roll pan

Pizza peel

FONDUE SET

FREESTANDING SMOKER

FREESTANDING MIXER, 10-QUART

Purchase dough paddle, dough hook, balloon whisk, meat grinder, and sausage stuffer attachments.

KNIVES

Mandoline, stainless steel

Boning knife

LARGE, HEAVY-DUTY GRILL WITH ROTISSERIE ATTACHMENT AND THERMOMETER

PASTA MACHINE

POTS AND PANS

Couscoussière

12- to 14-quart stockpot

Fish poacher

PRESENTATION/SERVING EQUIPMENT

4- to 6-quart chafing dish

Small salt and pepper saucers for the table, 6 pairs with spoons

Caviar serving bowl with outer bowl for crushed ice

Champagne flutes (12)

Food covers for outdoor buffet platters (4 to 5)

Freestanding wine bucket

Handheld cheese grater for parmesan

Horn spoons for caviar (2)

Linen collection (variety of napkins and cloths for dining and buffet tables)

Pedestals for buffet décor (4 to 6)

Specialty cocktail glasses (martini, margarita, 8 each)

TORTILLA PRESS

UTENSILS

Barding needle

Chinois strainer

Ginger grater

Poultry shears

Hospitality on Hand: The Party Pantry

An arsenal of easy-to-use, multipurpose ingredients is the secret weapon for anyone who wants to feel delighted by drop-in guests. My party pantry inventory relies on high-quality, brightly flavored products from around the world, including handcrafted food products from America. Many of these ingredients are available through the purveyors listed in the Gourmet Network (pages 317–326).

FROM THE PANTRY

Albacore tuna in spring water

Anchovy fillets in olive oil

Anchovy paste

Bread crumbs

Canned beans: cannellini, black, garbanzo

Capers

Caponata

Chicken broth

Chinese chili oil

Chipotle chiles in adobo

Chutneys

Clam juice

Crackers and crisps: pita crisps, bagel chips, bread sticks, water biscuits, crostini, tortilla chips

Dijon and whole grain mustard

Dolmades (stuffed grape leaves)

Glass noodles

Hearts of palm

Herbs: basil, bay leaf, oregano, marjoram, rosemary, tarragon, thyme

Horseradish sauce

Instant polenta

Kosher salt

Lemon and orange peel

Lump crabmeat

Madeira

Mayonnaise

Nam pla (fish sauce)

Oils: extra-virgin olive oil, virgin olive oil, walnut oil, peanut oil, toasted sesame oil

Olives

Plum tomatoes

Pomegranate molasses

Port

Rice paper wrappers (Thai or Vietnamese)

Roasted red peppers

Salsas

Sherry (dry)

Spices: black peppercorns, caraway seeds, cardamom, cayenne pepper, chili powder, Chinese 5-spice powder, cinnamon, coriander (ground and seeds), crab boil, cumin seeds, curry powder, dill seeds, fennel seeds, garam masala, garlic powder, ginger, mustard (ground and seeds), paprika, poppy seeds, red chili flakes, sesame seeds, white pepper

Soy sauce (regular and low-sodium)

Sun-dried tomatoes in olive oil

Tabasco sauce

Tamarind paste

Toasted nori (yakinori)

Tomato paste in tubes

Vermouth (dry)

Vinegars: raspberry, sherry, rice wine,
and balsamic

Wasabi in tubes

Water chestnuts

Worcestershire sauce

IN THE FREEZER

Unless you have an extra-large freezer, this list may seem unrealistic. However, these are all items that hold well in the freezer and work in multiple recipes. Select those that appeal to your tastes.

Artichoke Pesto (page 276) and other
pestos

Bacon

Breads: party rye, pumpernickel,
baguette, pita

Butter (unsalted)

Cheeses: crumbled blue cheese, small
wedges of Brie, cream cheese,
Parmesan cheese (whole or grated),
crumbled feta cheese

Chicken tenders

Chiles: dried ancho, pasilla, Thai

Cocktail Party Walnuts (page 161)

Dried wild mushrooms

Fruits packed without sugar

Ground turkey and beef

Lemon juice

Mini tart shells

Nuts: almonds, walnuts, pine nuts,
macadamia nuts

Orange juice concentrate

Phyllo pastry

Pizza dough

Prosciutto or Parma ham

Puff pastry

Sausages (see Gourmet Network, pages
317–326)

Wrappers: wonton and Vietnamese cha-
gio (Filipino lumpia)

HEART, n. Figuratively, this useful organ is said to be the seat of emotions and sentiments . . . It is now known that sentiments and emotions reside in the stomach, being evolved from food by chemical action of the gastric fluid.

—**Ambrose Bierce,** *The Devil's Dictionary*

MY FIRST POSITION after cooking school was as the chef at a sixteenth-century French chateau in Burgundy: a gray stone castle rising regally from a thousand acres of manicured farmland. The staff spoke no English, the dining-room table sat forty, and I was overwhelmed and overwrought. A month into my contract, the guest list introduced a new facet of intimidation. Two sitting heads of state, one of France's most beloved chefs, and thirty assorted cognoscenti were arriving for a three-day conference. Intimidated is actually too tame a description; I became frozen with the conviction that I had learned absolutely nothing at school. Nonetheless, the owner, Madame F, insisted I plan an ambitious, traditional menu to celebrate the first night of the conference. Because of our remote location, the more exotic ingredients would be delivered by private plane. *Mon dieu!*

That morning I got up at 5:30 A.M., looked out my bedroom window at the emerald fields dotted with placid, portly sheep, and threw up. But by 3:30 P.M., lunch had been served, the sauces were finished, the

---

The Menu

Barquettes aux Champignons Sauvage

Bouchées de Cocktail aux Escargots

Caviar

Huitres au Champagne

Consommé Madrilene

Tournedos Rossini

Fenouil et Carottes Braisées

Pommes Noisettes

Bavarois au Chocolat

Fraise des Bois

dessert was chilling, and the butlers were decorating the dining table. For this gala occasion, the center of the vast table was covered with a collection of porcelain miniatures from India and golden lilies. In the kitchen, I was exhausted but gratified with my efforts. Every preparation had been completed, and I felt safe to go up to my room for a short nap, before the grand dinner service began.

My assistant, Rajiv, a graceful young man from Sri Lanka, had one responsibility in my absence. He had to prepare and serve an early supper to the twenty-five kitchen and household staff before I returned at 5:00 P.M. From then on, the staff would be completely occupied assisting me in serving the formal dining-room menu.

I returned to the kitchen at five o'clock sharp and found everyone just sitting down to supper. As I stood at the end of the kitchen, frowning at Rajiv for starting their dinner late, I realized their entrées looked chillingly familiar. Even those steaks sloshed with ketchup and mango pickle were still unmistakably my airlifted tournedos. I felt as if I were in a nightmare playing in slow motion as butlers, vegetable washers, and dairy workers began to slice the irreplaceable fillets of Charolais beef.

I have no doubt the next couple of minutes live on as a unique memory for these simple, country folks. Howling with dismay, I gathered up the tails of my apron to form a pouch and ran up one side of the vast kitchen table and down the other ripping the meat from their plates.

As I rescued the dripping beef, I never stopped interrogating Rajiv. "What did you think you were doing?"

"You said there was beef for their dinner."

I groaned. "Can't you tell the difference between *filet de Charolais* and a roast from Aix?"

Suddenly there was a *whoosh* and a *thud* from the kitchen window behind me, a general intake of breath, then absolute, gelid silence. I spun around. Rajiv had responded to my outrage with spontaneity and heart. He had leapt from the open third-floor window, presumably to his death.

In one wild gesture he settled so much; he short-circuited my rage and expressed his most sincere sorrow. We all rushed to the window to view the body, frantically squeezing together in horror. Looking up at us was a smiling Rajiv; for that moment, we were united in hysterical laughter. It was only twenty feet to the cobbled courtyard, and we had forgotten Rajiv grew up in a traveling carnival.

This laughter was a brief interlude. My mind snapped back to focus on the soggy weight in my apron. I dumped the meat onto a baking sheet for inspection. I closed my eyes and tried deep breathing to slow my racing heartbeat. There was no question of throwing the meat away and starting over. This was it, in terms of prime beef, for over three hundred miles. In the following hour, I trimmed fork prints, rinsed off bottled condiments, rebrowned, and prayed out loud.

Thankfully the truffled sauce and foie gras were fresh and fine. Still, I served this recycled delicacy with considerable anxiety. At the conclusion of dinner, Madame F sent the butler, Jean-Pierre, to request my presence in the dining room. I demurred weakly, pointing out the sauce-encrusted quality of every stitch of my clothing, from apron to sneakers.

"Nonsense," insisted Jean Pierre, "Madame was quite clear."

Damn! I cringed at the thought of being fired in front of everyone. As he urged me toward the dining room, I wondered what quirk of her aristocratic upbringing made her wait until after dessert and coffee to sack me.

I entered the glittering hall to a round of enthusiastic applause and encouraging smiles and crystal goblets being sedately tapped with sterling knives.

"Merci, beaucoup. C'etait sublime."

I bowed my head in a mixture of pride, shame, gratitude, and disbelief.

Everything ends this way in France—everything. Weddings, christenings, duels, burials, swindlings, diplomatic affairs—everything is a pretext for a good dinner.

—Jean Anouilh
Cecile

Appetizers, Hors d'Oeuvres, and Beverages

I don't like to eat snails. I prefer fast food.

—Graffiti on a Southern California freeway

An hors d'oeuvre is a welcoming nibble to wake up the appetite with an announcement of good things to come.

Because they are usually finger food, eaten without the use of utensils, there are some caveats you should consider for hors d'oeuvres, especially if they are tray passed. Keep them bite size, and keep them tidy. Avoid even delicious recipes if the servings will be an awkward size, have a drippy sauce, or a crumbling texture. It is also important to be judicious with quantities. Don't overwhelm people with too much food before a meal, guests should sit down to your beautiful table with an appetite. On the other hand, if the hors d'oeuvres are to be the meal, make sure there are some more substantial items served from a buffet with small plates and salad forks, if necessary. Finally, make them beautiful, little jolts of color and flavor.

A Warm Welcome

While hors d'oeuvres are the first food served, you can suggest the flavor of your party before guests have tasted a thing. Light the entryway with luminaries (votive candles, nestled in sand or soil in the bottom of a brown paper lunch-size bag), have music playing outdoors, or fly a flag or balloons to identify your house. Decorate the door and entryway. Sprinkle flower petals or confetti from the street to your door, like Hansel and Gretel in reverse.

Cocktail Mixes

Quickly, bring me a beaker of wine, so that I may wet my mind and say something clever.

—Aristophanes

Homemade cocktail mixes are a wonderful choice for hosts at any level of expertise. For the novice, they are a simple way to make a cocktail party creative. For the accomplished host, they add the finishing touch. I put out the mix in a pitcher or punchbowl (depending on how many guests are expected) chilled with flavored ice cubes. This avoids diluting the flavors, while keeping the beverage cold. These special cubes are also very pretty, since I generally include a snippet of an herb, flower, or chile pepper. A bottle or two of the appropriate alcohol, a bowl of plain ice, and glasses are displayed next to the mix.

Easy Combinations

The hors d'oeuvres I serve most often are simple combinations of excellent ingredients. The following suggestions are some of my favorites.

- **Tortellini Skewers with Lemon-Parmesan Aïoli** Cook purchased fresh tortellini, then skewer, 2 to 3 per skewer. Serve with a dipping sauce of lemon-Parmesan aïoli (prepared mayonnaise, lemon juice, lemon zest, a little minced garlic, and freshly grated Parmesan cheese whipped together). These can be tray passed or presented on a platter on a buffet.

- **Warm Brie and Pear Tartlets** Fill purchased mini tart shells with a slice of Brie and finely diced ripe pear. Sprinkle a little minced fresh thyme or lavender on each and drizzle lightly with honey. Place on a greased baking sheet. Bake in a 375F (190C) oven for 7 to 8 minutes, until the cheese is bubbling. Serve immediately.

- **Skewered Bocconcini with Prosciutto** Start this several hours before serving. Cut thick rosemary stems into 3-inch lengths. Use the rosemary to skewer 1 to 2 bocconcini (fresh mozzarella balls). Wrap and set aside for 1 to 2 hours in the refrigerator. Cut very good proscuitto into 3 × 1-inch strips. Arrange on a baking sheet in a single layer and drizzle with extra-virgin olive oil, a dash of balsamic vinegar, and freshly ground black pepper. Wrap and refrigerate for 1 to 2 hours before using. To serve, wrap each bocconcini with a marinated prosciutto strip.

- **Warm Figs with Gorgonzola and Pecans** Cut ripe, fresh figs in half. Dust lightly with sugar, place on a greased sheet pan and bake in a 400F (205C) oven for about 7 minutes, until the sugar begins to color. Remove from the oven. Use the back of a spoon to press a hollow in the center of each half. Fill the hollow with crumbled Gorgonzola cheese and top with a pecan half. When ready to serve, return to a 350F (175C) oven for 5 to 7 minutes, until the cheese begins to melt. Serve immediately.

- **Smoked Salmon and Avocado Rosettes** Mash a ripe avocado with a squeeze of lemon juice, salt, and pepper and 1 to 2 tablespoons cream cheese or mascarpone. Set aside in the refrigerator. Cut very good smoked salmon (not lox) into 4 × 1-inch strips. Cut firm dark bread, such as German rye, into small squares. Wrap each salmon strip around the end of your finger, then sit this roll, standing upright on the bread. Drop a spoon of avocado mousse in the middle and gently spread the edges of the salmon back to form a "rosette." Garnish with a sprig of dill or a sprinkle of cumin seeds.

- **Corn Muffins with Smoked Turkey and Jalapeño Jelly** Purchase mini corn muffins. Slice almost in half and spread one side generously with jalapeño jelly and the other with softened butter. Fill with finely sliced smoked turkey breast and some watercress leaves.

- **Artichoke Hearts with Seared Scallops** Purchase artichoke hearts packed in water and drain well. Prepare Orange-Dill Sauce (page 273). In a sauté pan over medium-high heat, sauté fresh bay scallops in butter with a little salt and pepper 1 to 2 minutes, tossing to brown evenly. To serve, put a dollop of Orange-Dill Sauce in each artichoke heart and top with 2 or 3 seared scallops and a sliver of orange peel.

- **Grilled Chicken Skewers with Tamarind-Chipotle Sauce** For dipping sauce, puree ½ cup tamarind paste or pomegranate molasses, 1 teaspoon sugar, ⅔ cup pine nuts or slivered almonds, ⅓ cup peanut oil, 2 chopped garlic cloves, salt, and white pepper in a blender. Stir in 3 to 4 teaspoons minced chipotle chile in adobo (with some juice) to blend. The sauce will keep up to one week. Makes 1 cup. Drizzle chicken tenders with peanut oil and season with garlic powder, Kosher salt, and black pepper. Grill or broil until cooked through, 2 to 3 minutes. Serve on skewers or with wooden picks with the sauce.

- **Olivada with Focaccia** In a food processor, puree 2 to 3 cups of plump pitted black olives such as kalamata. When smooth, drizzle in 2 to 3 tablespoons extra-virgin olive oil. Add a splash of Cognac and a generous amount of coarsely ground black pepper. Serve with sliced focaccia or baguette.

- **Lemon-Basil Crostini** Slice a baguette into very thin rounds. Dry out on a sheet pan in a 300F (150C) oven for about 10 minutes. Meanwhile, in a food processor, puree 2 tablespoons cream cheese, ¼ cup soft unsalted butter, ⅓ cup grated Parmesan cheese, ¼ cup fresh lemon juice, pinch lemon peel, pinch sugar, pinch granulated garlic, 1 tablespoon minced basil, and salt and white pepper to taste. Spread generously on baguette slices and bake in a 350F (175C) oven about 10 minutes, until bubbling and crispy.

- **Dolmades (Stuffed Grape Leaves)** Drain purchased dolmades. Drizzle with fresh lemon juice and extra-virgin olive oil. Season with black pepper and minced cilantro, mint, or parsley; toss to coat. Garnish with roasted red peppers and pine nuts.

Chicken Liver Pâté with Cherries and Pecans

This luscious, velvety pâté is easy to make, and keeps, refrigerated, for days. It is the perfect centerpiece for a casual cocktail party menu in which everything else is purchased—olives, cheeses, nuts, great bread, and crackers, c'est tout. Spread the pâté on sliced green apples and crackers or crostini.

MAKES 8 TO 10 SERVINGS

---

2 sprigs parsley or other fresh herb

½ cup dried cherries or cranberries

1 cup chicken broth

Freshly ground coarse black pepper

1 pound chicken livers, trimmed

1 medium onion, chopped

1 cup unsalted butter, cut into chunks

1 clove garlic, peeled

1 teaspoon salt

¾ teaspoon freshly grated nutmeg

2 to 3 tablespoons brandy, poire eau de vie, or Calvados

½ cup chopped pecans or walnuts

Line a 3- to 4-cup terrine or mold with plastic wrap. Spray with cooking spray. Arrange the parsley or other fresh herb and a few dried cherries or cranberries in the bottom of the mold. This creates the decoration for the top of the pâté when unmolded.

In a medium saucepan, bring the broth, pepper, and 2 to 3 cups of water to a boil. Add the livers and onion and reduce the heat. Simmer until cooked through, 10 to 12 minutes.

Drain the livers and onion. Let cool and transfer to a food processor. Add all remaining ingredients except the dried cherries and pecans. Process until smooth.

Fold in the remaining cherries and transfer to the lined mold, tap the mold gently on the counter to settle out any bubbles, and smooth the top. Cover and refrigerate for at least 4 hours or up to 4 days before unmolding to serve.

To serve: Loosen the plastic wrap, invert the mold over a serving plate and turn out. Remove the plastic wrap. Gently press the chopped pecans into the sides of the mold.

Coconut Shrimp with Orange-Ginger Marmalade Dip

While some time is required to prepare these incredible treats, you can do it all ahead of time except for the actual frying. The unsweetened coconut required in this recipe is most commonly found in health food stores. It is also necessary that you start with uncooked, unpeeled shrimp.

MAKES 8 TO 12 SERVINGS

BATTER

1½ cups warm beer

1½ cups all-purpose flour

3 tablespoons butter, melted

4 eggs, separated

½ teaspoon Kosher salt

¼ teaspoon ground white pepper

¼ teaspoon paprika

COATING

¾ cup freshly grated Parmesan cheese

¾ cup chopped blanched almonds

¾ cup chopped unsweetened dried coconut

¾ cup finely broken dry capellini pasta (see Tips on page 139)

2 pounds raw large shrimp (21 to 25 per pound), peeled and deveined, leaving the tails attached

3 cups canola oil, for frying

Orange-Ginger Marmalade Dip (page 270)

Prepare the dip up to 2 days ahead and refrigerate.

Prepare the batter: With a whisk, mix the beer, flour, butter, egg yolks, salt, pepper, and paprika into a smooth batter. Let rest for 1 hour at room temperature. Reserve the egg whites.

Prepare the coating: In a large bowl, toss the Parmesan cheese, almonds, coconut, and capellini until combined.

Rinse the shrimp thoroughly and pat dry with paper towels. Set aside. Beat the egg whites until stiff but not dry. Fold the egg whites into the beer batter.

Holding the shrimp by the tail, dip each one into the beer batter, and coat thoroughly. Transfer the battered shrimp to the coconut mixture and use your hand to press the mixture onto the shrimp. As they are coated, transfer them to a sheet pan lined with plastic wrap or foil. Prepare all of the shrimp, cover, and refrigerate for up to 6 hours, or freeze (see Tips on page 139).

Cook the shrimp: Heat the canola oil in a heavy, deep pan (wok or Dutch oven) to 375F (190C). If you don't have a deep-frying thermometer, drop in a spoonful of the batter to test the oil temperature. It should drop to the bottom, then bob back to the surface, and become golden in 1 to 2 minutes. If it sinks to the bottom of the pan and stays there, the oil is not hot enough. If it immediately burns, the oil is too hot.

Gently slip the shrimp, in batches, into the hot oil. Do not overload your pan with too many shrimp at one time. Depending on the size of the pan, 3 to 6 pieces at a time is probably the most that can safely be cooked in one batch. Using a strainer or slotted spoon, roll the shrimp around in the oil to cook evenly. Fry until golden, 2 to 4 minutes. Remove from the oil and drain on paper towels. Keep the cooked shrimp warm on a baking sheet in a 325F (165C) oven while the remaining shrimp are cooked. Lay a paper towel over the top of the cooked shrimp and they will hold, without drying out or overcooking, for up to 30 minutes.

Serve 3 to 4 shrimp as an appetizer or 5 to 7 as an entrée. In either case, the Orange-Ginger Marmalade Dip should be presented in a small bowl or endive leaf on each plate.

TIPS

The shrimp can be prepared completely through the coating stage and frozen for up to 2 weeks. To freeze the shrimp successfully, lay the coated shrimp out on a baking sheet lined with plastic wrap or parchment paper so that they do not touch. Cover tightly and freeze. Do not defrost before deep-frying.

To break up the pasta: Break up the pasta strands into short pieces and enclose in a cloth towel. Use a rolling pin or other heavy object to roll over the pasta and crush it into tiny bits about the size of a grain of rice.

VARIATION

Dip ripe banana chunks in the batter and coating and fry along with the shrimp. They are really great offered together, as a sort of fritto misto.

Crab Cakes with Green Sauce

The patties can be mixed and shaped up to 1 day before cooking and serving. These are superior if you use lump meat from the blue crab. Because the cakes are baked rather than fried, they require less last minute attention from the host and have a lighter taste.

MAKES 8 SERVINGS

Green Sauce (page 270)

½ pound lump crabmeat, preferably blue crab

¼ cup minced green onion

1½ teaspoons minced fresh basil or cilantro

¼ cup finely diced celery

2 to 3 tablespoons mayonnaise

1¼ teaspoons fresh lemon juice

¾ tablespoon Old Bay seasoning

⅛ teaspoon dry mustard

⅛ teaspoon Dijon mustard

½ egg, beaten

About 4 tablespoons fine bread or cracker crumbs

Kosher salt

Freshly ground coarse black pepper

Fresh herbs

Prepare the Green Sauce up to 4 days in advance and refrigerate.

Pick through the crabmeat to remove any cartilage, being careful not to break the chunks. Combine the crabmeat, green onion, basil, and celery in a large bowl.

In another bowl, combine the mayonnaise, lemon juice, Old Bay seasoning, and mustards. Gently fold the mayonnaise mixture into the crab mixture. Gently mix in the egg. Sprinkle in 2 tablespoons of the bread or cracker crumbs, salt and pepper to taste, and fold together being careful not to break up the crab chunks. The mixture should be moist, but manageable. If it is too soft to form into cakes, add a little more bread crumbs.

Form into 16 to 20 about 1-inch-diameter cakes. Press all sides of the cakes into the remaining crumbs. Place on a flat tray, wrap, and refrigerate 1 hour or up to overnight before cooking.

Preheat the broiler. Place the cakes on a greased baking sheet. Broil for a total of 3 to 5 minutes, turning once, until lightly browned. Hold in a 200F (95C) oven for up to 30 minutes.

To serve: Top each crab cake with a dollop of the sauce and an herb leaf.

VARIATION

To fry: Place a large heavy-bottomed frying pan (cast iron is best) over medium-high heat. Add 2 to 3 tablespoons canola oil to the pan to coat. When oil is hot, carefully add the cakes, in batches, and brown on both sides, 1 to 3 minutes per side. Remove to paper towels to drain. May be held in a 300F (150C) oven for up to 30 minutes.

Barbecued Oysters

The hardest part of preparing this dish is selecting very fresh oysters. I usually prepare both of the quick sauces, because the rest of the dish takes virtually no time. This simple preparation makes a very festive first course presented either on a large platter or on individual plates.

MAKES 8 SERVINGS

Roasted Red Pepper Sauce (page 278) or Vietnamese Chili Sauce (page 280)

4 dozen fresh oysters

4 lemons, cut into wedges

Prepare the sauces up to 3 days in advance and refrigerate. Preheat the grill to hot.

Wash the oyster shells well and discard any oysters that remain open when pressed.

Place the oysters on the hot grill with the cupped side of their shells down. Remove when the shells pop open, or after no more than 6 minutes (some shells seem to stick slightly and not open, even though the oyster within is perfectly cooked).

Serve immediately on a tray or plates lined with black beans or rock salt to keep the oysters from rolling around. Serve with lemon wedges and sauces.

Chevre and Prosciutto Ravioli

I call them "Pillow Ravioli" because I like to make them in 3- to 4-inch squares. When cooked, they look like tiny, fluffy pillows. There are many filling and sauce combinations that work beautifully.

MAKES 16 TO 20 RAVIOLI

Basic Pasta Dough (page 313) or wonton wrappers (see Variation on page 143)

Fresh Tomato Sauce (page 267)

CHEVRE AND PROSCIUTTO FILLING

1 tablespoon minced garlic

½ cup chopped shallots

1 tablespoon unsalted butter

½ cup chevre

¼ cup pine nuts, toasted (page 315)

1½ ounces prosciutto

⅓ cup ricotta cheese, drained

2 teaspoons minced rosemary

1 egg yolk

Freshly grated Parmesan cheese

Prepare the Basic Pasta Dough and Fresh Tomato Sauce.

Prepare the filling: Sauté the garlic and shallots in the butter in a sauté pan over medium heat until soft, about 5 minutes. Let cool. Combine all the ingredients in a food processor and pulse to mix thoroughly. Chill for at least 30 minutes before using.

To assemble the ravioli: Lay 1 (about 9 × 4-inch) sheet of dough on the work surface. Place 1 tablespoon of filling centered on each third of the strip. Cover with another pasta sheet. Press the pasta sheets together, starting at each ball of filling and working toward the edges. Press out any air pockets and get a smooth seal.

Use a pastry cutter or knife to slice the filled strip into three large ravioli. Cover and refrigerate until ready to cook. Proceed with remaining sheets of pasta and filling.

To cook: Lightly oil a sheet pan; set aside. Bring a large pot of salted water to a rolling boil and slip in half of the ravioli. Stir them gently to make sure none have stuck to the bottom of the pan.

Reduce the heat to medium-low so that the water gently simmers. The ravioli are done when they come to the top, about 2 minutes. Remove with a slotted spoon, drain well, and place on the oiled pan while you cook the second half.

To serve: Place 2 or 3 ravioli on each plate; top with a spoonful of the sauce and a sprinkle of Parmesan cheese.

VARIATION

If you're short on time 40 (3½-inch square) wonton wrappers make a great substitute for the fresh pasta. Place 1 tablespoon filling on each square, brush the edges with water, press on a second wrapper, and seal. Cook as you would the pasta.

Shrimp Ravioli with Saffron Cream Sauce

Seafood and saffron is such a great marriage of flavors. In this recipe, the very easy Saffron Cream Sauce adds an elegant finish to the ravioli.

MAKES 16 TO 20 RAVIOLI

Basic Pasta Dough (page 313) or
Wonton wrappers (see Variation, page 143)

SHRIMP FILLING

½ pound raw peeled shrimp

⅓ cup minced fresh cilantro or basil

1 tablespoon orange juice

2 teaspoons grated orange zest

3 tablespoons minced onion

3 cloves garlic, peeled

1 egg

2 tablespoons freshly grated Parmesan cheese

1 teaspoon minced jalapeño chile

½ teaspoon Kosher salt

¼ teaspoon ground white pepper

SAFFRON CREAM SAUCE

2 pinches saffron threads

1 tablespoon boiling water

2 cups whipping cream

Salt

Ground white pepper

2 tablespoons freshly grated Parmesan cheese

¼ cup chopped green onion

Prepare Basic Pasta Dough.

Prepare the filling: In a food processor, combine all the filling ingredients and pulse until finely chopped. Chill for at least 30 minutes before using.

To assemble and cook the ravioli: Follow the directions on page 140.

To prepare the Saffron Cream Sauce: In a small bowl, combine the saffron threads and boiling water. Let steep until the water cools. In a small, heavy-bottomed saucepan, combine the cream, saffron and water, a pinch of salt, and a pinch of white pepper. Simmer over high heat until reduced by half, about 15 minutes. Remove from heat and stir in the Parmesan cheese and green onion.

To serve: Place 2 or 3 ravioli on each plate; top with a spoonful of the sauce.

Chicken Pyramid Dumplings

Once the simple wrapping and steaming techniques are mastered, these dumplings are quick to make for a crowd. This recipe provides a deliciously, light alternative to traditional Chinese potstickers.

MAKES ABOUT 40 DUMPLINGS

½ pound ground chicken or turkey

½ cup minced water chestnuts

⅓ cup chopped pine nuts

1 tablespoon minced fresh ginger

4 to 5 medium cloves garlic

½ cup minced fresh cilantro

2½ tablespoons low-sodium soy sauce

¼ cup dry sherry

⅓ cup minced green onions

1 egg, slightly beaten

1 teaspoon freshly ground coarse black pepper

⅛ teaspoon fennel seeds

40 (about 3½-inch) wonton wrappers

1 head cabbage or bok choy, shredded

Spicy Vinegar Dipping Sauce (page 279)

Make the Spicy Dipping Sauce a day ahead and refrigerate.

Thoroughly mix all the ingredients except the sauce, wonton wrappers, and cabbage in a large bowl.

Brush the edges of each wonton wrapper with a little cold water. Place 1 rounded teaspoon of filling in the center of the wrapper. Bring the 4 points together over the filling and gently press to adhere. Then press together the 4 seams to form a pyramid. (To freeze, place the dumplings on a baking sheet, without touching, and place in the freezer until firm. Transfer them to a freezer bag and freeze up to 1 month. Steam the frozen dumplings for 15 to 20 minutes.)

Put the dumplings in one layer on a lightly greased heatproof dish that is slightly smaller than the steamer. (Use a large steamer with 2 or 3 racks or steam in batches.) Bring the water in the steamer to a rolling boil. Put the plate of dumplings in the steamer on the rack and cover well. Reduce the heat to medium so that the dumplings steam gently.

Cook until the filling feels firm and the skin is translucent, 12 to 15 minutes. (The steamed dumplings may be held covered in a warm oven for 15 to 20 minutes. Add a cabbage or lettuce leaf to this holding tray to keep them moist.)

Serve the dumplings on a flat basket lined with the cabbage, accompanied by the dipping sauce.

TIP

All of the filling ingredients must be cut into fine uniform pieces.

Vietnamese-Inspired Spring Rolls

Even though these involve several steps, they are practical because they can be prepared ahead of time.

MAKES 8 SERVINGS; 16 ROLLS

Vietnamese Chili Sauce (Page 280)

FILLING

1 ounce cellophane noodles (bean thread vermicelli)

7 dried or fresh wood ear or shiitake mushroom

½ pound raw shrimp

½ pound lean pork

2 tablespoons peanut oil

3 cloves garlic, minced

⅓ cup dry sherry

2 tablespoon soy sauce

¼ cup chopped fresh cilantro leaves

3 tablespoons chopped fresh mint leaves

½ cup chopped green onions

½ cup chopped seeded cucumber

2 teaspoons fish sauce (nam pla)

½ teaspoon freshly ground coarse black pepper

16 large (about 8-inch-square) wonton skins

1 egg white, lightly beaten

4 to 5 cups peanut or vegetable oil

Shredded lettuce

Prepare the Vietnamese Chili Sauce up to 3 days in advance and refrigerate.

Prepare the filling: Cover the noodles with hot water. Let stand until completely soft, about 20 minutes. Drain and snip them into 1- to 2-inch pieces.

If using dried mushrooms, cover with boiling water and let rest until soft, about 15 minutes. Trim off any woody stems and finely slice the caps.

Peel and devein the shrimp and cut into small chunks. Slice the pork into matchstick-size pieces.

Heat the 2 tablespoons oil in a wok or sauté pan over medium-high heat. When almost smoking, add the garlic, shrimp, pork, and mushrooms. Sauté until the shrimp turns pink and the pork feels firm, 2 to 3 minutes. Add the sherry and soy sauce and cook 1 to 2 minutes. Remove from heat and let cool.

Combine all filling ingredients in a food processor and pulse until ground into a coarse, well-combined mixture.

To assemble the rolls: Place one wonton skin on the work surface with one corner toward you. Place about 2 tablespoons of filling mixture on the bottom third of the wrapper. Moisten the edges with a little of the egg white. Fold the bottom point over the filling, press it down to create a firm cylinder, then fold over the two sides and roll, pressing tightly. Make sure the final edge is moistened with egg white before pressing to seal. Repeat with remaining wrappers and filling. As the rolls are finished, place on a baking sheet, cover with plastic wrap, and refrigerate until cooking or up to 24 hours.

To cook: In a Dutch oven or electric frying pan, bring the oil to about 350F (175C). Add 4 or 5 rolls, depending on size of pan, and cook until golden, about 4 minutes. Turn them frequently while cooking to color evenly. Remove to paper towels and place in a 325F (165C) oven for up to 30 minutes, if not serving immediately.

To serve: For formal occasions, slice the rolls in half on the diagonal and serve each guest 4 halves. They are presented standing upright on shredded lettuce with a pool of sauce in the middle.

VARIATIONS
You may replace the pork with chicken or additional shrimp.

Vietnamese spring rolls are traditionally eaten as sort of an inside-out taco. Some mint and cilantro are sprinkled on a lettuce leaf, and a slice of the crispy roll goes in the middle. The lettuce is loosely wrapped around this crispy package and used as the diner-friendly holder for dipping in the spicy sauce. It makes a very accessible finger food for a buffet.

Spicy Honeyed Shrimp

These colorful shrimp skewers combine the flavors of one of my favorite Middle Eastern hot sauces, harissa, with soothing honey and refreshing pineapple. The sauce should be prepared and set aside in the refrigerator for at least 1 day or up to a week before using; the flavors improve with aging. The last minute preparation of the shrimp is minimal. Brilliant flavors and brilliant color make this perfect party food.

MAKES 8 SERVINGS; 16 SKEWERS

SPICY HONEY SAUCE

4 teaspoons ground coriander

1 tablespoon ground cumin

½ teaspoon turmeric

1 teaspoon cayenne pepper

6 serrano chiles

2 red bell peppers, roasted and peeled (page 315)

⅓ cup chopped onion

¼ cup extra-virgin olive oil

2 tablespoons cider vinegar

1 tablespoon minced garlic

¼ cup clover honey

¼ cup fresh lime or lemon juice

2 tablespoons grated lime or orange zest

2 teaspoons Kosher salt

1 to 1½ pounds medium raw shrimp

1 whole ripe pineapple, peeled and cut into chunks, or canned juice-packed pineapple chunks

2 to 3 tablespoons extra-virgin olive oil

½ cup thinly sliced green onion

¼ cup toasted sesame seeds

2 limes, cut into wedges

Prepare the sauce: Toast the coriander, cumin, turmeric, and cayenne pepper in a dry sauté pan over medium heat until aromatic, about 3 minutes. Set aside to cool.

Wearing rubber gloves, remove the ribs, seeds, and stem, from the serrano chiles.

In a food processor, pulse the bell peppers, onion, toasted spices, and olive oil into a smooth paste. Add remaining sauce ingredients and pulse to mix thoroughly. Makes 2 cups.

Prepare the Shrimp: Soak 16 (6-inch) bamboo skewers in water for at least 30 minutes before using. Preheat the grill or broiler to medium-high. Peel and devein the shrimp, leaving the tails intact.

Peel and cut the pineapple into 1-inch chunks.

Thread 1 or 2 shrimp onto each skewer, alternating with pineapple chunks. Brush with olive oil and season with salt and pepper. Grill over medium heat until just opaque, 2 to 3 minutes per side. Brush the shrimp and pineapple with sauce and cook about 1 minute longer on each side to color the glaze. The skewers can be served warm or at room temperature.

To serve: Liberally sprinkle with sesame seeds and green onions and accompany with the remaining sauce and lime wedges.

SERVING SUGGESTIONS

These are delicious accompanied by Mediterranean Bean Spread (page 163), a wedge of lemon, and toasted pita bread. Or, place the shrimp skewers on a bed of Aromatic Basmati Pilaf (page 261).

What makes this dish so special are the wonderful trimmings and the quality of the beef. Purchase a whole tenderloin with all the excess fat and sinew trimmed off by the butcher. The ease with which it is prepared is also wonderful. The whole tenderloin is seared either on the grill or under the broiler and sliced very thinly to serve at room temperature. Large Spanish capers, shavings of Parmigiano-Reggiano cheese, truffle oil, a creamy mustard sauce, and lemon all add up to a decadent little open-faced sandwich.

MAKES 8 TO 12 SERVINGS

Mustard-Horseradish Sauce (page 269)

1 pound trimmed prime-grade beef tenderloin

Extra-virgin olive oil

Kosher salt

Freshly ground coarse black pepper

1 bunch watercress or arugula

2 to 3 tablespoons truffle oil or best-quality extra-virgin olive oil

1 (3½-ounce) jar large capers, drained

3 to 4 ounces Parmigiano-Reggiano cheese, shaved

Lemon wedges

1 fresh baguette, sliced very thinly

Prepared the Mustard-Horseradish Sauce up to a day ahead and refrigerate.

Preheat the grill or broiler to high. Rub the beef with the olive oil, salt and pepper. Sear on all sides to rare (125F; 50C), 5 to 7 minutes. Remove from heat and refrigerate when cool. This can be done a day ahead of time.

Put the seared beef into the freezer and allow to almost freeze, about 2½ hours. Using a very sharp knife, slice the beef across the grain as thinly as possible. If you like you can put the slices between sheets of waxed paper and using a rolling pin or mallet gently pound them out even thinner. Keep the slices between sheets of waxed paper and well wrapped until just before serving to avoid any discoloration. (This should be done 5 or 6 hours before the party starts.)

To serve: Arrange the paper-thin slices of beef on a bed of watercress or arugula. Drizzle on the oil and dust liberally with pepper. Sprinkle with capers and the shaved cheese. Add a squeeze of fresh lemon juice at the last minute. Serve with the baguette slices.

SERVING SUGGESTIONS

Since I encourage people to assemble their own open-faced sandwich, I put out extra capers, shaved Parmigiano-Reggiano cheese, and the pepper mill as well as the Mustard-Horseradish Sauce. Accompany with a basket of sliced baguettes. A fine-grain brown bread is also great.

Lamb and Mint Pesto Borek

These are an aromatic delight as an hors d'oeuvre. They are also a very special accompaniment when served with a crisp green salad. The lamb can be replaced with ground turkey for those avoiding red meat.

MAKES 20 PIECES

FILLING
1 tablespoon oil or butter
1 cup minced onion
1 pound ground lamb
¼ teaspoon Kosher salt
¼ teaspoon freshly ground coarse black pepper

1 cup Pistachio Mint Pesto (page 277)
6 to 10 sheets phyllo dough
⅓ cup extra-virgin olive oil or melted butter
Paprika

Preheat the oven to 375F (190C).

Heat the oil in a sauté pan over medium-low heat. Add the onion and sauté until soft, about 5 minutes. Remove from pan and let cool. When cool, use a wooden spoon to mix the onion with the lamb, salt, and pepper. When thoroughly mixed, use the spoon to mix in the pesto.

To assemble: Lay 1 sheet of phyllo dough on a cutting board. Brush lightly with oil and top with a second sheet. Press them to adhere. Using a sharp knife, cut the dough into 8 (2-inch-wide) strips. Place 2 teaspoons of the filling at the end of each strip. Working with one strip at a time, fold the bottom edge up to meet the right edge to form a triangle and fold over like folding a flag, forming triangles. Brush the outside with oil and dust with paprika. Put the triangles on an ungreased baking sheet as they are completed. Repeat with remaining filling and pastry sheets.

Bake for 15 to 20 minutes, until crisp and golden. Place the triangles on paper towels to blot any excess oil and serve immediately.

Beef Saté

The skewers are fun on a buffet arranged on a platter lined with cilantro and shaved cucumber. Sprinkle liberally with chopped peanuts. Bowls of the sauce for dipping can be nestled in the middle of the platter or on the side.

For a more formal party, I frequently pass these on a tray. Make sure you give everyone a napkin so they can dispose of the skewer when they're through.

MAKES 8 TO 12 SERVINGS

Peanut Sauce (page 268)

2 pounds beef flank steak, pork loin, or boneless, skinless chicken chicken breast halves

MARINADE

3 tablespoons reduced-sodium soy sauce

1½ teaspoon ground cumin, toasted

6 cloves garlic, minced

2 tablespoons light brown sugar

¼ cup minced onion

1 tablespoon tamarind paste or lime juice

1 teaspoon ground coriander

3 tablespoons peanut oil

Prepare the Peanut Sauce one or two days ahead and refrigerate. Slice the beef across the grain into about ⅛-inch-thick strips.

Prepare the marinade: Combine all the ingredients in a large bowl and whisk well to dissolve the sugar.

Submerge the beef in the marinade and stir well to coat. Let the meat marinate for 1 to 2 hours in the refrigerator.

Meanwhile, soak the bamboo skewers in water for at least 30 minutes (this will keep them from burning during cooking).

Prepare the skewers: Thread 1 or more pieces of beef, depending on the size of the piece, on each skewer. Lay them flat on a tray and pour any remaining marinade over them.

Preheat the broiler or grill to medium. Grill skewers 1 to 2 minutes per side until cooked through. Serve immediately with warmed sauce for dipping. These skewers can be held in a 225F (105C) oven, wrapped in foil, for up to 25 minutes before serving.

SUGGESTION

Any leftover grilled beef is also delicious served cold on a salad of watercress, cucumber, red onion, and mint tossed in rice vinegar. I drizzle a little leftover Peanut Sauce on top for dressing.

Sesame Eggplant Salsa

This creamy eggplant dip was inspired by an appetizer I loved at the now-closed China Moon restaurant in San Francisco. The flavors are complex, surprising and delightfully balanced by the mellow Pita Crisps. I received raves every time my catering company introduced this at a party. It is best if made at least one day in advance.

MAKES 4 CUPS

Pita Crisps (page 167)

2 pounds eggplant

¾ **cup packed minced green onions**

2½ **tablespoons minced fresh ginger**

2 tablespoons minced garlic

1 small serrano or Thai chile, minced, or 1 teaspoon Chinese chili paste

3 tablespoon light brown sugar

2 teaspoon fresh lemon juice

1 tablespoon seasoned rice vinegar

2 tablespoon tamari or soy sauce

1 tablespoon canola oil

1½ **teaspoon dark sesame oil**

¾ **cup chopped, seeded and peeled tomatoes**

¾ **cup packed minced fresh cilantro, plus extra for garnish**

Sliced green onions

Prepare the Pita Crisps up to 3 days ahead.

Preheat the oven to 425F (220C).

Cut the stem ends off the eggplants and prick well all over with a knife. Place on a baking sheet and roast for 30 to 45 minutes depending on size. Turn at least once while roasting. The eggplant is done when a fork sinks easily into the thickest part. It should be completely soft. Remove from the oven and when cool enough to handle, scrape the creamy pulp from the skin into the food processor. Pulse quickly just until the eggplant is pureed.

Combine the minced green onions, ginger, garlic, and chile in a bowl.

Combine the brown sugar, lemon juice, vinegar, and tamari in a small bowl and whisk to blend.

Place a large sauté pan or wok over medium-high heat and swirl the canola oil around to coat the pan. Add the green onion mixture and sauté until softened without coloring, about 45 seconds. Add the sugar mixture and bring to a simmer, stirring rapidly. Reduce the heat and add the eggplant puree. Stir well to blend and heat through, 1 to 2 minutes, stirring constantly. Remove from the heat and stir in the sesame oil, tomatoes, and cilantro and fold to blend.

This may be served immediately, but it tastes better if made 1 or 2 days before and refrigerated. Bring it back to room temperature before serving. Garnish the top with the minced cilantro and sliced green onion and surround with the Pita Crisps.

Gravlax

This delicately cured salmon can be prepared using a variety of fresh herbs like dill, cilantro, fennel, or basil. They all produce a silky textured, easy-to-make, easy-to-serve luxurious hors d'oeuvre. The key to this recipe is the absolute freshest salmon.

MAKES 14 TO 18 SERVINGS

2 (1½-pounds) salmon fillets, with skin

½ cup sugar

½ cup Kosher salt

¼ cup ground white pepper

2 bunches fresh dill, chopped

TO SERVE

Dill-Mustard Sauce (page 269)

Dill sprigs

Dark bread slices

½ cup capers, drained

½ cup minced green onions

Run your fingers against the grain of the fillets to check for pinbones. Remove any remaining bones with tweezers. Wipe the flesh clean of any scales or trimmings.

In a flat pan or dish large enough to hold the salmon, spread a double thickness of cheese-cloth, leaving a large enough border to wrap up and over the 2 fillets.

Mix the sugar, salt, and pepper in a bowl.

Lay the first fillet, skin side down, on the cheesecloth. Sprinkle on half of the sugar mixture. Using your hand, rub it into the flesh. Sprinkle on the dill, packing it down so that all of it is used, covering the fillet from edge to edge.

Sprinkle the other fillet with the sugar mixture and rub it in. Place it on top of the dill layer, skin-side up, and press into place.

Wrap the cheesecloth up and over the sides and the end to create a tight package. Lay a piece of plastic wrap on top of this. Set a baking sheet flat on top of the salmon. Put 2 large cans of food or bricks flat on the baking sheet to evenly weigh down on the salmon.

Refrigerate for 4 days, turning the salmon package every 12 hours. Each time you turn the salmon, pour off and discard the liquid that will drain into the pan.

Prepare the Dill-Mustard Sauce up to a week in advance and refrigerate.

To serve: Use a dish towel or spatula to gently remove all of the spices and herbs from the salmon. To slice the gravlax you will need a very sharp knife to achieve the thinnest possible slices. Start at the tail end, cutting toward the tail at a very shallow angle.

Serve the slices on a platter decorated with dill sprigs accompanied by dark bread, the sauce, a bowl of capers, and a bowl of minced green onions. Let guests assemble their own open-faced sandwiches.

VARIATION

CILANTRO GRAVLAX
1 cup packed light brown sugar
¾ cup Kosher salt
¼ cup freshly ground coarse black pepper

2 bunches cilantro, minced
¼ cup extra-virgin olive oil
¼ cup gold tequila

Combine the brown sugar, salt, and pepper in a small bowl. Rub on the salmon. Arrange the cilantro on the first fillet and top with the second. Drizzle the oil and tequila over the salmon. Wrap and refrigerate as above.

Baba Ghannoush

This wonderful Middle Eastern dip goes together in minutes and will keep for days in the refrigerator. As is common with such simple recipes, there are many versions (see Variations below).

I serve the Baba Ghannoush as a dip with the Pita Crisps (page 167) or Syrian cracker bread. In Israel it is often served warm, drizzled over grilled fish.

MAKES 3 CUPS

2 pounds eggplant
1 tablespoon minced garlic
2 tablespoons fresh lemon juice
¼ cup tahini
1 teaspoon Kosher salt
¼ teaspoon cayenne pepper

GARNISH
⅓ cup minced fresh parsley
2 tablespoons extra-virgin olive oil
½ cup chopped pistachios, toasted (page 315)
Pinch paprika

Preheat the oven to 425F (220C). Cut the stem ends off the eggplants and prick well all over with a knife. Place on a baking sheet and roast for 30 to 45 minutes depending on size. Turn at least once while roasting. The eggplant is done when a fork sinks easily into the thickest part. It should be completely soft. Remove from the oven and let cool to room temperature.

In a food processor, puree the garlic, lemon juice, tahini, salt, and cayenne pepper to a smooth paste. Cut the eggplant in half and scoop the flesh into the food processor. Pulse until pureed.

To create a traditional presentation: Place the puree in a serving bowl. Arrange the chopped parsley around the edge of the bowl, drizzle the olive oil over the surface of the Baba Ghannoush, sprinkle the pistachios in the center, and finally dust with paprika for color.

VARIATIONS

Stir 1 cup chopped pitted kalamata or niçoise olives and 1 tablespoon zahtar (a Middle Eastern spice blend, containing sumac) into the puree and garnish as above.

Replace the tahini with plain yogurt and increased salt and garlic for a low-fat variation.

Sun-Dried Tomato and Pesto Torta

This is a real buffet centerpiece. Brilliant layers of red, white, and green alternate to create a beautiful and impressive hors d'oeuvre. I sold it, to great acclaim, through Neiman Marcus and many of California's gourmet markets. It is best made at least 24 hours ahead of time and can be frozen for up to 1 month. What more could you ask for—easy, impressive, delicious, and done ahead of time?

MAKES 1 LARGE TORTA; 15 SERVINGS

SUN-DRIED TOMATO LAYER

1 ⅓ cups sun-dried tomatoes, drained (see Tip on page 157)

⅓ cup tomato paste

⅓ cup cream cheese, softened

PESTO LAYER

1 ½ cups tightly packed fresh basil leaves (3 to 4 bunches)

¼ cup pine nuts

¼ cup chopped garlic

1 teaspoon fresh lemon juice

2 tablespoons extra-virgin olive oil

¼ cup freshly grated Parmesan cheese

⅓ cup cream cheese, softened

¼ teaspoon salt

¼ teaspoon ground white pepper

CREAM CHEESE LAYER

1 ½ (8-ounce) packages cream cheese, softened

4 ounces (1 stick) sweet butter, softened

¼ teaspoon Kosher salt

½ teaspoon ground white pepper

Basil or fresh greens for garnish

Line a large mixing bowl, charlotte mold, springform pan, or any other attractively shaped 2-quart container with one smooth sheet of plastic wrap with at least 3 to 4 inches of overhang. Since the torta retains the form of whatever it is made in, you can be very creative with your final presentation by choosing an unusual mold.

Prepare the tomato layer: Place the sun-dried tomatoes in the food processor and pulse to chop. Add the tomato paste and 2 tablespoons of the cream cheese and process to a fairly smooth consistency. Add the remaining cream cheese and process until well mixed. Some tomato bits are fine. Set aside.

Prepare the pesto layer: Rinse the basil leaves and remove the stems and any discolored leaves. Dry the leaves thoroughly. Put the basil leaves, pine nuts, garlic, lemon juice, and olive oil in the food processor. Pulse the processor to puree the basil and nuts completely. Add the remaining ingredients and pulse to mix thoroughly. Set aside.

Prepare the cream cheese layer: Put the cream cheese and butter in a mixing bowl and whip with an electric mixer on slow speed. When the butter has been completely incorporated into the cream cheese, beat in the salt and pepper.

To assemble: Put ½ cup of the tomato mixture in the bottom of your container. Tap the container gently on the counter to spread.

Put the pesto mixture into a pastry bag with a large round (½- to ¾-inch diameter) tip and gently pipe a solid layer in a tight spiral until you have made a layer approximately ½-inch thick. Repeat this process with the cream cheese mixture.

Tap the container gently on the counter as you fill to eliminate air pockets between the layers. Alternate layers of red, green, and white until you have filled the bowl. Smooth the top layer with a spatula and fold over the corners of the plastic wrap to cover. Wrap tightly with another sheet of plastic wrap and refrigerate for at least 24 hours or up to 1 week.

To serve: Select a serving platter large enough to hold the torta with at least a 6-inch border. Remove the plastic wrap. Fold back the inner wrap and use the corners as handles to gently loosen the firm torta from the sides of the container. When it is loosened, invert your serving platter on the container and then turn them right side up. Lift off the container and gently peel off the plastic wrap. Tuck clusters of fresh basil or other greens around the base of the torta.

If you are not going to serve it immediately, loosely drape fresh plastic wrap over the whole platter. You may serve any good cracker or sliced baguette with the torta.

TIP

If you use dry-packed sun-dried tomatoes, which frequently have a brighter flavor than oil packed, add them before measuring to a microwave-safe bowl. Cover with water and microwave on high for 60 seconds. Let the tomatoes rest in the water for about 15 minutes. Drain well, and they will be ready to use.

The Quesadilla Concept

There are as many delicious variations on quesadillas as you have leftovers in your refrigerator. Quesadillas can be completely assembled and frozen for up to two weeks before cooking. Flour tortillas are more traditional, but I prefer the heartier flavor of corn. Whichever tortilla you use, I find it simplest to work with a large size that can be cooked folded over, not stacked. Serve with Guacamole (page 282) or a salsa.

MAKES 8 SERVINGS

---

1 large (about 12-inch) flour tortilla

Filling of your choice (see below and next page)

To assemble the quesadilla: Spread an even layer of the cheese on one half of the tortilla. Top with layers of the additional ingredients. In general, the filling should be about ½-inch thick.

Fold over the tortilla and press. The stuffed quesadilla can be cooked in one of the following three methods.

1. Brush the outside with a light coating of oil and put directly on a medium-hot barbecue grill. Cook 3 to 4 minutes per side, turning carefully with a spatula, or until cheese melts.

2. Lightly oil a heavy-bottomed sauté pan or comal and sauté quesadilla on both sides, turning carefully with a spatula, until cheese melts.

3. Preheat the oven to 375F (190C). Coat the outside of the tortilla with a little oil or vegetable spray. Place on a baking sheet and bake about 5 minutes or until cheese melts.

Cut quesadilla into wedges and serve warm.

FILLINGS

Each recipe makes enough for 1 quesadilla.

BRIE-MANGO CHUTNEY FILLING

½ cup Brie, cut into small chunks

1 teaspoon mango chutney

2 tablespoons pine nuts

½ teaspoon minced poblano chile

MUSHROOM-WALNUT FILLING

⅓ cup shredded Cheddar cheese

3 tablespoons sautéed sliced mushrooms

1 tablespoon chopped walnuts

¼ cup queso anejo

Pinch each red chili flakes and cumin seeds

SHRIMP AND CREAM CHEESE FILLING

2 tablespoons cream cheese, softened

⅓ cup shredded Monterey Jack cheese

2 tablespoon minced green onion

1 tablespoon minced green chiles

3 tablespoon cooked, chopped shrimp and/or crab

CHEESE AND OLIVE FILLING

¼ cup queso cotija

¼ cup shredded Monterey Jack cheese

2 tablespoons chopped kalamata olives

3 cloves Whole Roast Garlic with Herbs (page 283)

2 tablespoons cooked corn

1 tablespoon minced fresh cilantro

POLENTA-CHEESE FILLING

1 tablespoon cream cheese, softened

¼ cup shredded Monterey jack cheese

⅓ cup prepared polenta (pages 178)

2 tablespoons *each* minced fresh cilantro and basil

1 tablespoon chopped poblano chile

Quick Grilled Pizza

Using a purchased dough makes this recipe quick and easy to prepare. The flavor developed by grilling the crust makes this a classy, brick oven–style pizza. The toppings can then be added and cooked to order, based on the guests' selections. Individual pizzas can be finished in the kitchen or on the grill in as little as 5 minutes per pie to be served crispy and delicious as an appetizer or entrée.

MAKES 8 TO 12 SERVINGS

4 (10-ounce) packages of pizza dough (see Note on page 160)

Olive oil

½ cup coarse cornmeal

Topping of choice (see Suggested Toppings on page 160)

Preheat the grill to medium-hot.

To form each pizza, either roll out the dough to the size suggested on the package with a rolling pin, or more traditionally, use the heel of your hand and your fingertips to flatten and stretch the dough into the desired size. Flip the dough and work the other side, dusting with flour as necessary. If the dough is too elastic to shape, let it rest for 15 minutes in the refrigerator and continue.

When the desired shape is achieved, brush the top with olive oil and set aside on a baking sheet lightly coated with cornmeal. Using a large spatula or pizza peel, place the pizza dough directly on the clean grill rack. Cook for about 2 minutes per side, checking for hot spots. Remove and dust with cornmeal to hold until topping and final cooking. (Grilled crusts can be wrapped when cool and refrigerated for up to 48 hours ahead of time.)

To finish: Preheat oven to 425F (220C) or preheat grill to medium-hot. Arrange desired topping, on the crust in the order the ingredients are listed. Bake on a cooling or roasting rack on a baking sheet for 5 to 7 minutes or place on a medium-hot grill for slightly less time.

SUGGESTED TOPPINGS
Each makes enough for 4 pizzas. Layer over the grilled crust in order listed.

SAUSAGE, EGGPLANT, AND SMOKED MOZZARELLA
1 large eggplant, sliced and grilled

1 pound spicy Italian sausage, crumbled, browned, and drained

1 cup sliced oil-packed, sun-dried tomatoes

2 tablespoons fennel seeds

2 cups (8 ounces) shredded smoked mozzarella

Drizzle of the olive oil from the tomatoes

ROSEMARY PESTO AND ASPARAGUS
1 cup Roasted Balsamic and Honey Onions (page 281)

1 pound grilled red bell peppers

4 ounces prosciutto, shredded

¾ cup Rosemary Pesto (page 277)

2 cups crumbled chevre

1 cup pine nuts

SPICY SHRIMP AND PEANUTS
Spicy Honeyed Shrimp (including pineapple; page 148)

1 cup chopped green onions

2 cups (8 ounces) shredded fontina cheese

½ cup toasted peanuts

¼ cup toasted sesame seeds

NOTE
Easy Pizza: Premade pizza dough, available in the freezer or refrigerator section of most grocery stores, is one of the timesaving products I enthusiastically recommend. If frozen, thaw in the refrigerator, then proceed. When grilled or baked, it forms the foundation for an exceptional quality fresh pizza or focaccia with very little work. You can be serving crispy, gooey pizza in 20 minutes, start to finish, if you use the refrigerated dough.

Cocktail Party Walnuts

These nuts were included in practically every cocktail menu I served. They are easy to make, addictively good, and clearly homemade. I generally serve them combined with the Savory Spiced Nuts (page 162).

MAKES ABOUT 2 CUPS

1 pound shelled, unsalted walnuts

1½ teaspoon Kosher salt

¼ cup sugar

1 teaspoon ground cardamom

1 teaspoon freshly ground coarse black pepper

¼ cup vegetable oil

1 tablespoon unsalted butter

Bring a saucepan of water to a boil and add the walnuts. Boil for 10 minutes. Drain and dry on paper towels.

Combine the salt, sugar, cardamom, and pepper in a bowl.

Heat the oil and butter in a large, heavy skillet over medium heat. Add the walnuts and toss to coat. Sprinkle with the spice mixture and toss to coat. Cook, tossing constantly, until the walnuts are a deep golden brown, 6 to 7 minutes.

Remove the pan from the heat. Using tongs or a slotted spoon, remove the walnuts from the oil and spread them out on a baking sheet lined with parchment paper so that they are not touching. When completely cool, store the nuts in an airtight container for up to 1 week.

Savory Spiced Nuts

Homemade spiced nuts are one of my favorite hospitality gestures. They're quick and easy to make, and they keep for weeks. Everyone loves a spiced nut with a cocktail; bring them out when you have nothing else but company in your kitchen.

MAKES 2 CUPS

½ teaspoon garlic powder

½ teaspoon ground ginger

½ teaspoon cayenne pepper

2 teaspoons garam masala

1 teaspoon sugar

1 tablespoon peanut or vegetable oil

2 teaspoons clarified unsalted butter (page 315)

2 cups unsalted, shelled pecans, cashews, macadamia, or blanched almonds

2 teaspoon fresh lime juice

1 teaspoon Kosher salt

Combine the garlic powder, ginger, cayenne pepper, garam masala, and sugar in a bowl.

Heat the oil and clarified butter in a large, heavy-bottomed sauté pan over medium heat. Add the nuts and toss to coat. Cook, stirring occasionally, until they begin to toast, about 4 minutes.

Sprinkle on the spice mixture and toss well to coat. Cook until the nuts brown, 3 to 4 minutes. Sprinkle on the lime juice and cook, stirring, until the nuts are dry, about 3 minutes.

Remove from the heat and sprinkle on the salt and toss to combine. Turn out the nuts on a baking sheet and spread to a single layer to cool completely. Store in a tightly covered container at room temperature for up to 2 weeks.

Fiesta Spread

I serve this southwestern cheese spread with tortilla chips, red pepper wedges, baguette slices, and jicama spears. It can be prepared and frozen up to 2 weeks before defrosting and serving. Surround it with clusters of cilantro sprigs.

MAKES 8 SERVINGS

1 (8-ounce) package cream cheese, softened

4 large cloves garlic, minced

1½ tablespoons diced roasted red bell pepper

2 tablespoons freshly grated Parmesan cheese

¼ cup minced fresh cilantro

2 tablespoons chopped fresh parsley

½ teaspoon pasilla chile powder

¼ teaspoon lemon pepper

¼ teaspoon red pepper flakes

¼ teaspoon ground cumin, toasted (page 315)

Combine all the ingredients in a food processor and pulse to combine. Cover and refrigerate at least 2 hours or up to 3 days before serving.

Mediterranean Bean Spread

This luscious, ready-in-a-minute spread or dip is my favorite as the centerpiece of a mezze platter including pita wedges, olives, grilled eggplant, sun-dried tomato relish, and cucumbers. It can also be served warm as a side dish with grilled fish or roast lamb.

MAKES 2 CUPS

Crispy Shallots (page 281)

10 large cloves garlic, unpeeled

1 (15-ounce can) garbanzo beans, drained, and rinsed (1½ cups)

1 (15-ounce can) white beans (cannellini), drained and rinsed (1½ cups)

½ cup fresh lemon juice

2 teaspoons ground cumin, toasted (page 315)

2 to 3 tablespoons extra-virgin olive oil

¼ cup minced fresh mint, basil, cilantro, or thyme

Kosher salt

Freshly ground coarse black pepper

Prepare the Crispy Shallots up to 3 days ahead.

Preheat the oven to 300F (150C). Place the garlic cloves on a baking sheet and roast for 15 to 20 minutes, until they begin to turn golden. Remove and let cool. Squeeze the cloves to press out the roasted garlic.

Combine the garlic, beans, lemon juice, and cumin in a food processor and puree until creamy. With motor running, slowly add the olive oil. Process to a smooth, thick puree. Add the fresh herb and pulse to leave some whole bits. Add salt and pepper to taste. Garnish with the shallots.

Blue Cheese Pâte

This simple, tasty spread can be used as a filling for pumpernickel tea sandwiches, a spread for crackers, or as a dip for crudité.

MAKES 2 CUPS

1 ½ teaspoons dried powdered rosemary (see Tip below)

1 teaspoon ground dried lemon peel (see Tip below)

¼ teaspoon ground white pepper

4 ounces blue cheese, softened

8 ounces chevre

1 (8-ounce) package cream cheese, softened

1 tablespoon minced green onion

¼ cup minced fresh parsley

1 cup diced walnuts or pistachios, toasted (optional; page 315)

In a food processor, pulse the rosemary, lemon peel, pepper, blue cheese, chevre and cream cheese, until blended. Mix as little as possible to achieve a homogeneous texture.

Remove the cheese mixture to a bowl and fold in the green onion and parsley. Cover and refrigerate until firm, at least 1 hour or up to 4 days.

SERVING SUGGESTIONS

- Serve in a tub surrounded by crackers or toasts.

- Coat red or green seedless grapes with the spread and then roll in chopped nuts.

- Pipe the spread into ripe apricot halves and garnish with a watercress leaf.

- Create a beautiful tea sandwich by cutting rounds from pumpernickel bread with a biscuit cutter. Fill the rounds with a lavish amount of the cheese spread and press together. Butter the edges of the rounds and roll in toasted chopped walnuts, pressing in place.

TIP

The rosemary and lemon peel should be ground extra fine in a spice grinder.

Skordalia with Crudités

I always think of skordalia as the Greek version of aïoli. Its strong flavors and creamy texture complement grilled chicken, poached fish, and in this case a simple crudité. It can be prepared up to 3 days in advance.

MAKES ABOUT 2 CUPS

SKORDALIA

1 large (about ¾ pound) russet potato

¾ cup walnuts, toasted (page 315)

¼ cup chopped garlic

2 teaspoons minced fresh oregano

¾ cup extra-virgin olive oil

⅓ cup fresh lemon juice

2 tablespoons cold water

⅓ cup minced fresh parsley

½ teaspoon Kosher salt

½ teaspoon freshly ground coarse black pepper

CRUDITÉS

2 bunches baby carrots with tops

2 bunches smallest multicolor radishes with tops

2 red or green bell pepper

Prepare the Skordalia: Peel and quarter the potato. Gently boil in enough lightly salted water to cover until tender, 12 to 15 minutes. Remove from the heat, drain, and let cool to room temperature.

In a food processor, pulse the walnuts, garlic, oregano, ¼ cup of the olive oil, and lemon juice until coarsely pureed. Add the cooked potato, remaining olive oil, and cold water and pulse just until the potato is creamy and well combined. Do not over process or the potato can become sticky.

Transfer to a large bowl and stir in the parsley, salt, and pepper. Taste and adjust seasoning if necessary. This can be served immediately or covered and refrigerated for up to 3 days.

Prepare the Crudités: Wash the carrots and radishes, including their tops, and cut off any roots. Pat dry. Remove the stems from the bell peppers. Cut them in half lengthwise and use the palm of your hand to flatten each half. Remove any seeds and cut the bell pepper into 1- to 2-inch squares. Wrap vegetables, and refrigerate up to 1 day.

To serve: Put the skordalia into an attractive bowl and surround with the colorful crudités.

Hors d'Oeuvre Twists

With a little imagination you can use ingredients you may already have on hand to create these delicious and whimsical cocktail snacks. They are also an attractive and popular addition to a bread basket for the dining table. To serve as an individual hors d'oeuvre I wrap them in paper-thin slices of Gravlax (page 153), prosciutto, or Carpaccio (page 149).

MAKES 32 TWISTS

---

1 (17¼-ounce) package frozen puff pastry (2 sheets)

2 fillings of choice (see page 167)

1 egg, lightly beaten

Sesame, fennel, or poppy seeds, or freshly grated Parmesan cheese

Preheat oven to 375F (190C). On a floured board, roll out 1 sheet of puff pastry to a 14 × 10-inch rectangle.

Cover pastry to within ¾ inch of the edge with an even coating of one of the fillings.

Using the longer side, fold over the left one-third of the sheet toward the middle. Press over filling. Fold over the right one-third to the left edge and press. Turn over, dust with flour and roll the rectangle out to a 10-inch square.

Cut into ½-inch-wide strips and twist holding both ends. Press the ends with your fingers to seal.

Brush each twist lightly with the egg, sprinkle with seeds or cheese, and pick them up with a spatula and transfer to a baking sheet. Press the ends down on the sheetpan to keep them from untwisting. Repeat with remaining pastry and filling. Cover with plastic wrap and refrigerate for 30 minutes.

Brush another baking sheet with butter. Place the twists about 2 inches apart on the buttered baking sheet. Bake for 18 minutes, until crisp and golden.

Serve hot or cool completely on a wire rack. Store in an airtight container at room temperature for 4 to 5 days. Re-crisp in a 350F (175C) oven, if needed.

FILLINGS
Each filling recipe makes enough for 1 sheet of puff pastry.

TAPENADE-FETA FILLING

⅓ cup tapenade mixed with ⅓ cup feta

MUSTARD-PARMESAN FILLING

½ cup freshly grated Parmesan cheese mixed with 2 tablespoons Dijon mustard

ONION-BLUE CHEESE FILLING

⅓ cup crumbled blue cheese mixed with ⅓ cup minced green onion

ROASTED GARLIC-CHEVRE FILLING

¼ cup minced roasted garlic mixed with ½ cup chevre and 1 tablespoon minced fresh sage or thyme

Pita Crisps

These wonderful homemade "crackers" add style to even a purchased dip or pâté. They are especially well paired with the Sesame Eggplant Salsa (page 152).

MAKES 30 TO 40 CRISPS

5 (6-inch) fresh pita

2 tablespoons extra-virgin olive oil

½ cup freshly shredded Parmesan cheese

¼ cup freshly grated Parmesan cheese

Freshly ground coarse black pepper

Preheat the oven to 325F (165C). Slice each pita in half and then cut each half into 6 to 8 pie-shaped wedges. If they come apart easily, separate the top and bottom of each wedge; the pieces will be crisper after baking.

Lay them out in one layer on a baking sheet. Brush the top of each piece liberally with olive oil. Sprinkle on the shredded cheese and press it lightly to adhere to the oil. Repeat with an even sprinkling of the grated cheese. Finish with a liberal grinding of black pepper.

Bake for 10 to 15 minutes, until golden and somewhat stiff. They will continue to crisp while cooling on the baking pan. When completely cool, pack them in a plastic bag and seal. They will keep for 2 to 3 days. They can be gently crisped for 5 to 10 minutes in a warm oven.

VARIATIONS

In addition to the Parmesan cheese, the wedges can be sprinkled with one of the following: fennel seeds, sesame seeds, cumin seeds, minced thyme, minced rosemary, or minced oregano.

Herb-Garlic Crostini

These spicy, garlic-laden little crisps are positively addictive. I have served them at hundreds of parties, and sold them through retail stores throughout the country to unequaled appreciation. They are a snap to make and keep well. Keep the extra topping in the refrigerator for up to 2 weeks before using.

MAKES ABOUT 40 CROSTINI

---

1 (1½-pound) sourdough baguette

TOPPING
¾ cup chopped garlic
1¼ cup extra-virgin olive oil
2 teaspoons dried basil

1½ cup freshly grated Parmesan cheese
¼ cup cream cheese, softened
2 teaspoons dried oregano
1 tablespoon plus 1 teaspoon red chili flakes

Preheat the oven to 325F (165C). Slice the baguette as thinly as possible. For crisper crostini, spread the slices out to dry for 1 to 2 hours before topping and baking.

To prepare the topping: Blend all ingredients in a food processor to an oatmeal texture. Makes 2¼ cups.

Brush the topping lavishly on baguette slices.

Place on an ungreased sheet pan. Bake 10 to 12 minutes, until crisp and golden. Let cool completely on a wire rack. Store in an airtight container at room temperature up to a week.

SERVING SUGGESTIONS

The crostini are excellent as an hors d'oeuvre on a tray with olives and nuts. They can also be topped with Sun-Dried Tomato and Pesto Torta (page 156), almost any pâté, or thin slices of French sausage.

Sangrita

This gorgeous Spanish cocktail is colored like a tropical sunset with the "kick of a rooster." To serve, add tequila and frozen cubes of orange juice with jalapeño slivers frozen in the middle

MAKES ABOUT 4 CUPS

1 cup fresh tomato juice

Juice of 3 limes

2½ cups fresh orange juice

2 good dashes of Tabasco sauce or ½ teaspoon cayenne pepper

1 teaspoon sugar

Tequila

Combine all ingredients in a blender and mix well. Refrigerate for at least 3 hours before serving or up to 2 days. Add 1 jigger of tequila per serving.

Bloody Mary Fantastico

My friend Evan, who diligently assisted in testing recipes, is also a great mixologist. This is her very zippy, secret Bloody Mary formula. It needs to be mixed at least 6 hours before serving to allow the horseradish to bloom. She serves this in glasses with the rims coated in celery salt (see page 171). To serve, add vodka and frozen cubes of lime juice with cilantro sprigs.

MAKES ABOUT 7 CUPS

1 (46-ounce) can V-8 vegetable juice

3 tablespoons grated fresh or drained prepared horseradish

1 teaspoon celery salt

3 tablespoons Worcestershire sauce

1 teaspoon Tabasco sauce, or to taste

3 tablespoons white wine

Juice of 2 limes

12 twists from a pepper mill

Vodka

Combine all ingredients, except Vodka, in a blender and mix well. Refrigerate for at least 6 hours before serving, or up to 2 days. Add 1 to 2 jiggers of vodka per serving.

Eggnog

Homemade eggnog was a holiday tradition in my family. It was one of those delicious treats that made the Christmas season so special, because we never enjoyed it any other time of year. Depending on your guests, you can decrease the amount of alcohol and still have a delicious punch. Freshly grated nutmeg is an absolute essential.

MAKES ABOUT 20 (½ CUP) SERVINGS

---

12 eggs, separated (see Note below)

1½ cups sugar

3 cups whole milk

1 teaspoon pure vanilla extract

2 cups dark rum

2 cups brandy

2 pints whipping cream

Pinch salt

Freshly grated nutmeg

Using an electric mixer, beat the egg yolks and sugar until thick and lemon yellow. Reduce the speed to low and whip in the milk, vanilla, rum, and brandy. Refrigerate for 2 to 3 hours.

Whip the cream until stiff. Whip the egg whites with a pinch of salt until stiff but not dry.

Fold the whipped cream into the egg yolk mixture. Fold in the egg whites. Cover and chill at least one hour.

Transfer to a punchbowl and sprinkle generously with grated nutmeg.

VARIATION

My mother used to float a big cloud of rum-scented whipped cream on top.

NOTE *Anyone with a compromised immune system, including children, the elderly, or anyone with a serious illness, should not eat raw eggs because of the possibility of salmonella poisoning. If you want to make a recipe that does not cook the eggs, look for the pasteurized eggs that are available in some markets.*

Traditional Margaritas

This grand cocktail is a very simple concoction with just a couple of personal choices to address. White or gold tequila? Triple sec or Grand Marnier? Blended or stirred? Salt or no salt? There is only one absolute as far as I'm concerned: don't blend this drink. The resulting slush is a watered-down travesty created for tourists.

Because this is such a concentrated cocktail (basically a little flavor plus the alcohol), I mix the tequila into the mix and nestle the pitcher into a bowl filled with ice. To serve, guests put chipped ice in their glasses, stir the contents of the pitcher, and pour it over the ice.

MAKES ABOUT 16 COCKTAILS

---

2 cups fresh lime juice, about 24 limes

3 cups (24 ounces) tequila

1 cup Triple sec or Grand Marnier

Coarse salt

Lime and orange slices

Combine all the ingredients except the garnish and salt in a large pitcher.

For serving, use a martini glass, a small wineglass, a champagne saucer, or special margarita glasses. To prepare the traditional salt-rimmed glass: moisten a clean sponge and put it flat on the counter. Put coarse ground salt (or special margarita salt) in a flat dish or saucer. Press the rim of the glass on the sponge; then press firmly into the saucer of salt.

Slip cut lime and orange slices over the lip of the glass.

Hot Buttered Rum

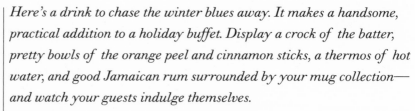

Here's a drink to chase the winter blues away. It makes a handsome, practical addition to a holiday buffet. Display a crock of the batter, pretty bowls of the orange peel and cinnamon sticks, a thermos of hot water, and good Jamaican rum surrounded by your mug collection—and watch your guests indulge themselves.

MAKES 3 CUPS OF BATTER; ABOUT 40 SERVINGS

1 pound dark brown sugar

½ pound unsalted butter, softened

½ teaspoon freshly grated nutmeg

½ teaspoon ground cinnamon

½ teaspoon ground cloves

TO SERVE

Orange peel strips

Cinnamon sticks

Hot water

Rum

In the food processor or mixer, process the brown sugar, butter, and spices until creamy. Cover and store in the refrigerator for up to 3 weeks.

To serve: Place a heaping tablespoon of the batter in a mug, along with a strip of orange peel and a cinnamon stick. And ¾ cup of boiling hot water, and a jigger of dark rum. Stir to blend and enjoy.

Mango Lassi

This is an exotically refreshing alternative to iced tea on a hot day. It's a great drink/condiment with spicy foods anytime!

MAKES 2 TO 3 CUPS

1 cup plain regular or nonfat yogurt

1 mango, peeled and diced

2 teaspoons grated fresh ginger

1 to 2 cups iced water

Pinch black pepper

Sugar to taste, depending on the sweetness of the mango

Blend the yogurt, mango, and ginger in a blender until pureed. Add enough iced water to achieve desired texture. Taste and add the pepper and sugar to taste. Serve immediately or refrigerate for up to 8 hours. Serve cold.

Worries go down better with soup than without.

—Yiddish proverb

Only the pure in heart can make a good soup.

—Ludwig van Beethoven

Homemade soup is the primordial comfort food—warm, soothing, the simmering essence of home and family. With a creative presentation soup is also elegant and exciting party fare. Use contrasting colored soups with complementary flavors, such as cream of garlic and roasted red pepper or a cool combination of strawberry and almond and swirl them discreetly together for a beautiful bowl.

Serving soup in two stages is another engaging idea. Begin by serving the soup with nothing but a delicate garnish displayed in the bottom of the bowls. For example, a scattering of fresh corn kernels, finely minced spinach, and basil, or enoki mushrooms and slivered scallops. Then bring the steaming pot of hot broth to the table and ladle it over these delicate ingredients, cooking them in just the flash of time they need to be perfection. I love this combination of drama and perfect cooking. Anne's Porcini Broth with Creamy Polenta and the Tortilla Soup both employ this idea.

Gazpacho with Green-Lipped Mussels

This unusual gazpacho is a light and healthy warm weather entrée full of robust vegetable flavors and packed with protein. I like to serve this soup in a glass bowl or goblet to show off the brilliant color combination of rosy tomatoes, dark green poblano chiles, and peach-toned mussels.

MAKES 8 TO 10 SERVINGS

MUSSELS

24 green-lipped mussels

2 cups white wine

1 onion, chopped

2 tablespoons chopped fresh dill

2 tablespoons chopped fresh cilantro

2 tablespoons chopped fresh parsley

8 black peppercorns

SOUP

2 cups tomato juice

6 tablespoons red wine or sherry vinegar

¼ cup fresh lemon juice

½ teaspoon cayenne pepper

¼ cup pepper vodka

¼ cup extra-virgin olive oil

2 cucumbers, peeled, seeded, and coarsely chopped

3 cloves garlic, chopped

2 shallots, chopped

1 medium onion, sliced

2 poblano chiles or red bell peppers, diced

⅓ cup minced fresh dill

⅓ cup minced fresh cilantro

6 large tomatoes, seeded and chopped

1 teaspoon Kosher salt

Freshly ground coarse black pepper

2 avocados, diced

GARNISH

6 radishes, finely sliced

Dill sprigs or celery stalks

Prepare the mussels: Scrub the mussels and wash thoroughly under cold running water. Discard any mussels that don't close when tapped.

In a large saucepan, combine the wine, onion, herbs, and peppercorns. Bring to a boil, reduce heat, and simmer 3 minutes. Add the mussels, cover, and cook over high heat 3 to 4 minutes, until mussels open, shaking the pan occasionally.

Remove the mussels with a slotted spoon to a large bowl. When cool enough to handle, use a spoon to remove the meat from each shell. Depending on size, cut the mussels into 2 or 3 large chunks. Cover and refrigerate.

Prepare the soup: Combine the tomato juice, vinegar, lemon juice, cayenne pepper, vodka, and olive oil in a large bowl and whisk to combine well.

Combine the cucumbers, garlic, shallots, onion, and chiles with a little of the tomato juice mixture in a blender or food processor and pulse to finely chop. Reserve half of the chopped mixture and puree the remaining half.

Add the chopped and pureed vegetable mixtures to the remaining tomato juice mixture, and stir to combine. Stir in the herbs, tomatoes, and salt and black pepper to taste. Taste and add more cayenne if needed. The soup can be made to this point and refrigerated the day before serving.

To serve: Stir in the avocado and reserved mussels. Pour into bola grande (large) wineglasses, float radish slices in each serving and garnish with a dill sprig or celery stalk.

VARIATION: GAZPACHO WITH SHRIMP
Substitute 24 large, raw unshelled shrimp for the mussels. Cook as for the mussels until the shrimp turn pink. Cool and peel.

Onion Soup with Garlic Flans

  ⑤

The little garlic cloud floating in this classic onion soup is a delightful surprise. It adds a cheesy richness to the soup without the traditional heavy cheese crust.

MAKES 12 CUPS, ABOUT 8 ENTRÉE SERVINGS

1 stick (½ cup) unsalted butter

6 large onions (9 to 10 cups), finely sliced

2 tablespoons sugar

1 teaspoon Kosher salt

1 teaspoon freshly ground coarse black pepper

12 cups (3 quarts) beef stock, preferably low sodium

¼ cup Madeira

1 cup vermouth

Garlic Flans (page 264)

In a large stockpot, melt the butter over low heat until foamy. Add the onions and toss to coat. Cover and let simmer to wilt the onions, 15 to 20 minutes, stirring occasionally.

Toss the sugar with the onions, increase the heat to medium, and cook, uncovered, until onions are caramelized and a deep brown, stirring occasionally, 30 to 35 minutes. During the last 10 minutes of cooking, stir the onions almost constantly to avoid sticking. Add the salt and pepper. Stir to blend and stir in half of the beef stock. Bring to a simmer and simmer 15 minutes.

Add the remaining stock, Madeira, and vermouth. Cover and simmer gently for 30 to 40 minutes to develop the full flavor. Taste for salt and pepper.

Meanwhile, prepare the Garlic Flans.

To serve: Place 2 to 3 Garlic Flans in each bowl. Ladle soup over the flans.

Paisley-Patterned Summer Soup

Beautiful, all done ahead, and delicious on a warm summer night, it's the perfect choice to precede a grilled seafood entrée.

MAKES 8 SERVINGS

CANTALOUPE COCKTAIL

2 cups chopped cantaloupe

1 cup chopped fresh or frozen peach

1½ cups dry white wine

2 tablespoons amaretto

STRAWBERRY GINGER CREAM

2 cups (about 1 pound) fresh strawberries, cleaned

½ cup rosé, zinfandel, or other light-bodied red wine

¼ teaspoon ground ginger

1 teaspoon freshly ground coarse black pepper

1 tablespoon Triple Sec or Grand Marnier

½ cup whipping cream or plain yogurt

TOPPING

1 cup whipping cream

¼ teaspoon ground ginger

Strawberry fans

Prepare the Cantaloupe Cocktail: Puree all the ingredients in a blender. Pour into a pitcher, cover, and refrigerate until chilled. Makes 4 cups.

Prepare the Strawberry Ginger Cream: Puree all the ingredients in a blender. Pour into a pitcher, cover, and refrigerate until chilled. Makes 3 cups.

Prepare the Topping: Whip the cream until soft peaks form. Beat in the ginger.

To serve: Pour a heaping ⅓ cup of the Strawberry Ginger Cream into each bowl. Artistically drizzle ½ cup of the Cantaloupe Cocktail across the strawberry portion. Garnish with a strawberry fan and a dollop of ginger whipped cream.

Poblano Cheese Soup

I was never really attracted to the idea of cheese soup, because it sounded too heavy and glutinous for a party. This is quite the opposite, light, sprightly, zesty, yet cheesy. Make an even lighter variation by replacing half of the Cheddar cheese with queso cotija.

MAKES 4 ENTRÉES OR 8 FIRST-COURSE SERVINGS

2 large dried ancho chiles

2 teaspoons balsamic vinegar

2 to 3 tablespoons unsalted butter

¾ cup minced onion

¼ cup minced carrot

2 (about 1¼ cups) poblano chiles, seeded and minced

¼ cup chopped celery

3 cloves garlic, minced

3 tablespoons all-purpose flour

4 cups chicken broth

2 cups Mexican beer

¼ cup chopped fresh cilantro

4 cups (1 pound) shredded sharp Cheddar cheese

Kosher salt

Freshly ground coarse black pepper

GARNISH

4 corn tortillas

Vegetable oil, for frying

Kosher salt

Cayenne pepper

½ cup whipping cream

¼ teaspoon sugar

½ cup chopped fresh cilantro

In a bowl, cover the ancho chiles with boiling water and the balsamic vinegar; set aside. Let stand until rehydrated, about 30 minutes. Remove the stems and seeds and mince the flesh.

Melt the butter in a Dutch oven over medium-low heat. Add the onion carrot, and poblano chile. Sauté, stirring occasionally, until onion begins to caramelize, 7 to 10 minutes. Add the celery, ancho chiles, and garlic and sauté 3 to 4 minutes. Stir in the flour and cook, stirring constantly, until brown, 2 to 3 minutes.

Slowly whisk in the chicken broth and beer and bring to a boil, whisking constantly until the soup thickens slightly, about 7 minutes. Reduce the heat to low and simmer for 30 minutes.

Stir the cilantro into the soup. Whisk in the cheese, a handful at a time, and cook until it melts. When the cheese is completely incorporated, the soup is the consistency of a thin cream soup.

Prepare the garnish: Slice the tortillas into ¼-inch matchstick-size pieces. Heat 2 inches of oil in a deep skillet over medium-high heat. Add the tortillas and fry until crisp. Drain on paper towels. Dust the tortillas with the salt and cayenne pepper. Whip the cream and sugar until soft peaks form. Fold in the cilantro.

Bring the soup back almost to a boil and add salt and pepper to taste. Serve immediately with a dollop of cilantro whipped cream and tortilla strips scattered across the top.

Anne's Porcini Broth with Creamy Polenta

The porcini broth is better if made and refrigerated the day before serving. The porcini flavor continues to infuse the broth. Anne Dreyer, the caterer who created this recipe, usually serves this to her clients as a first course, with some chives sprinkled on top. I think it is so luscious it deserves to be served in a larger bowl as an entrée.

MAKES 4 OR 5 SERVINGS

PORCINI BROTH

3 tablespoons chopped dried porcini mushrooms

6 cups homemade, or reduced-sodium, canned chicken broth

3 tablespoon unsalted butter

1 small shallot, minced

½ cup sliced crimini mushrooms

1 teaspoon veal demi-glace (optional; see Note on page 179)

½ cup Madeira

Freshly ground coarse black pepper

CREAMY POLENTA

1 tablespoon unsalted butter

½ small onion, diced

1 clove garlic, minced

½ cup coarse cornmeal

2 cups homemade, or reduced-sodium, canned chicken broth

1 cup milk or light cream

¼ cup minced fresh chives, plus extra for garnishing

3 tablespoons freshly grated Parmesan cheese

Prepare the broth: Combine the porcini mushrooms and 2 cups of the chicken broth in a saucepan and simmer gently for 10 minutes. Remove from heat, cover, and let rest for 20 minutes.

Strain the mushrooms and broth through cheesecloth or a paper towel in a strainer into a bowl. Reserve the broth. Lift the mushrooms from the strainer and rinse thoroughly under running water to remove any remaining grit.

Melt 2 tablespoons of the butter until foamy in a sauté pan over medium heat, add the shallot and the porcini and crimini mushrooms and sauté until the shallot is golden, 4 to 5 minutes.

Pour the mushroom broth into a saucepan. Add the mushroom mixture, remaining 2 cups chicken broth, and the demi-glace if using. Simmer over medium heat for 10 minutes.

Add the Madeira and pepper and simmer 1 to 2 minutes. Remove from heat and refrigerate 6 hours or overnight.

Prepare the polenta: Melt the butter until foamy in a medium saucepan over medium heat. Add the onion and garlic and cook until beginning to turn golden, 3 to 4 minutes. Stir in the cornmeal. Add the chicken broth, milk, chives, and Parmesan cheese. Cook, stirring constantly, until the polenta becomes as thick as gruel, about 10 minutes. Remove from heat and set aside.

To serve: Reheat the broth over low heat. Spoon about ¼ cup of polenta into each bowl. Ladle over the porcini broth and sprinkle on a few chives. Serve immediately.

NOTE *Demi-glace Gold Stock is available by mail, 800-860-9385.*

Salty Stock

Any stock that is going to be boiled down, or reduced in volume, to make a sauce or soup should be absolutely, or nearly, free of salt. As the stock reduces and intensifies, even a small amount of salt can become overpowering. Salt and season when you have finished the reduction. Be especially careful with canned broths; many of them are very high in sodium.

Tortilla Soup

Growing up in Southern California, I was introduced to this dish as a youngster, and I've loved it ever since. The recipe looks deceptively long, but there are just a series of simple steps that can be completed simultaneously. Poach the chicken in the microwave while the vegetables roast in the oven, and you fry the tortilla strips and chiles on the stovetop. It can all be completed in advance! Then it's on to the fun, guest-participation assembly of each unique bowl of soup.

I suggest this kind of entertaining for several reasons: It's easily prepared in advance, the presentation is unusual and attractive, and guests each get to create their own dish.

MAKES 4 TO 8 SERVINGS

1 dried ancho chile

About 1¼ pounds skinless, boneless chicken breasts

9 cups chicken broth

2 bay leaves

1 sprig cilantro

1½ medium onions, quartered

3 large tomatoes

5 to 6 cloves garlic, peeled

4 tablespoons extra-virgin olive oil

1 tablespoon dried oregano

Juice of 2 to 3 limes

Kosher salt

Freshly ground coarse black pepper

TOPPINGS

1¼ to 1½ cups peanut oil or fresh lard, for frying

16 corn tortillas

4 pasilla chiles

1 to 1½ cups (4 to 6 ounces) shredded Monterey Jack cheese or queso cotija

2 avocados, cubed

1 bunch cilantro, chopped

1 to 1½ cups crema fresca or sour cream

Lime wedges

Gold tequila

Stem and seed the ancho chile and roast in a hot, dry pan until aromatic, 2 to 3 minutes. Be careful not to scorch.

Place the chicken breasts, 1 cup of the broth, the bay leaves, and cilantro in a microwave-safe container. Cover loosely with plastic wrap and microwave on high for 5 to 7 minutes, until tender.

Add the toasted ancho chile to the chicken and liquid, re-cover, and set aside to cool. When cool, remove the bay leaves and shred the chicken into a second bowl. Reserve the broth and chile.

Preheat the broiler. Toss the onions, tomatoes, and garlic with the olive oil to coat. Place the tomatoes and onion on a sheet pan, and broil for 5 minutes. Add the garlic to the pan and broil for 10 to 15 minutes, until vegetables are well colored.

When cool enough to handle, slip the skins off the tomatoes. Add the tomatoes to a blender with the garlic, onions, reserved chicken broth from chicken, including the ancho chile, and oregano. Blend until pureed.

For topping: Cut the tortillas into ¼- to ½-inch-wide strips. Heat 1 cup of the peanut oil in a large Dutch oven over medium heat. Add the tortilla strips, in batches so as not to overcrowd the pan. Toss to coat with the oil and fry until crisp and beginning to brown, 5 to 6 minutes. Add more oil as needed. Remove the tortilla strips with tongs and drain on paper towels.

Remove stems and seeds from the pasilla chiles and use scissors to snip into strips or rings. Add 2 tablespoons of the olive oil to the Dutch oven if necessary and increase the heat to medium-high. Add the pasilla chiles and sauté until they begin to crisp, about 1 minute. Remove to paper towels to drain.

Add the remaining 2 tablespoons olive oil to the Dutch oven over medium heat and heat until hot. Add the pureed vegetables, reduce heat, and sauté until thickened and darker in color, about 10 minutes, stirring occasionally to avoid sticking.

Add the remaining 8 cups of chicken broth and bring to a boil. Reduce the heat to low, cover, and simmer for 10 minutes. (Everything can be completed up to this stage as much as a day in advance and refrigerated.) Add the lime juice and salt and pepper to taste.

To serve: Put some shredded chicken, 4 or 5 tortilla strips, and a cilantro sprig in each bowl. Ladle the broth over the chicken. Use bowls of the toppings to create a centerpiece on the buffet or dining table.

Roasted Eggplant Soup

The smokiness imbued by long charring on the grill gives this simple soup a rich flavor. The addition of a colorful, spicy sauce, swirled on each serving, creates a flavor complex enough to be satisfying as a light lunch.

MAKES 8 CUPS

2½ pounds eggplant

3 tablespoons extra-virgin olive oil

1½ cups diced onions

½ cup minced shallots

4 cloves garlic

6 cups chicken broth

1½ tablespoons minced fresh oregano

1 teaspoon minced fresh thyme

¼ teaspoon ground cinnamon

1¼ teaspoons Kosher salt

White pepper

Poblano Cream Sauce (page 279) or Harissa (page 272)

Preheat the grill to hot. Slice the stem ends off the eggplants, prick all over, and roast over on the hot grill until completely soft, turning to char evenly, about 25 minutes. Remove the eggplants from the grill to a deep bowl to capture the escaping juices as the eggplants cool. When cool enough to handle, remove the charred skin and scoop the pulp into a measuring cup. You need 3 cups of pulp; include the juice from the bowl.

Heat the olive oil in a heavy-bottomed stockpot over medium-low heat. Add the onions and shallots and sauté until the onions are soft, about 10 minutes. Add the garlic and sauté until the onions and garlic are golden, about 5 minutes.

Add the eggplant pulp and stir well to blend. Sauté until thickened, about 10 minutes. Add the broth, herbs, cinnamon, salt, and pepper and simmer for 30 minutes.

Meanwhile, prepare the Poblano Cream Sauce. (If serving the Harissa, it should be made a day ahead.)

Use an immersion blender or a food processor to puree the soup.

Ladle hot soup into bowls. Garnish with a drizzle of Poblano Cream Sauce or Harissa.

Salads and Salad Dressings

What garlic is to salad, insanity is to art.

—Augustus Saint-Gaudens, *Reminiscences*

Seeking out the freshest seasonal produce available is a fundamental catering strategy. Begin with top-quality ingredients to ensure that even a simple recipe will produce spectacular results. As with computers, the only way to get good results out is to put good stuff in. This is especially true of a salad—where the ingredients are usually served au naturel. If it is available, I encourage you to pay a little extra for the generally superior flavor of organic produce.

Salad Tips

- **Wash and dry salad greens several hours or up to one day before using. Layer in a plastic bag with paper towels, seal well, and refrigerate. They will become crisp and taste super fresh.**

- **To brighten up even a simple green salad, toss in a handful of chopped fresh herbs.**

- **It's always best to let guests dress their own salads.**

- **Instead of using the common salad bowl, line a large basket, flower pot, wine crate, or top hat with plastic wrap and a sturdy green leaf such as kale or romaine. Your salad bowl is now ready to receive its contents.**

- **The addition of homemade croutons or Herb-Garlic Crostini (page 168) turns a plain salad into something special.**

- **Invest in really good balsamic, sherry, and fruit vinegars and fine olive and walnut oils; great vinaigrettes will become the standard at your table.**

- **Today's "warm" salads are an easy, appealing solution to a one-course meal, and offer lots of room for creativity. Caesar salad with grilled *anything* is the most common example of this combination of a first course and entreé. If you would like to try this idea, add poached or grilled chicken to the Wilted Spinach Salad with Chevre or lamb to the Armenian Parsley and Walnut Salad.**

Roasted Beet Salad with Gorgonzola

Sweet roasted beets, tangy cheese, and glazed walnuts are combined in a salad with character. This could easily be a vegetarian entreé. The vibrant colors of this simple dish and the rich, caramelized flavor of the vegetables and the nuts create an entertaining home run. The salad can be prepared a day ahead, and assembled just before serving.

MAKES 8 SALAD SERVINGS

GORGONZOLA VINAIGRETTE

3 tablespoons fresh orange juice

2 tablespoons red wine or raspberry vinegar

2 teaspoons sugar

1 teaspoon grated orange zest

½ cup crumbled Gorgonzola cheese

¼ cup extra-virgin olive oil

Kosher salt

Freshly ground coarse black pepper

SALAD

2½ pounds fresh beets

24 shallots or cipolline onions

2 to 3 tablespoons olive oil

½ teaspoon Kosher salt

3 large strips orange peel

4 cups slivered fennel

3 bunches watercress

½ bunch chives, cut into 2-inch lengths

½ cup Cocktail Party Walnuts (page 161)

Prepare the vinaigrette: Add all the vinaigrette ingredients, except for the oil and ¼ cup of the cheese, to a blender. Blend until combined. With the motor running, slowly add in the oil and blend until the dressing thickens (emulsifies). Pour the dressing into a bowl and whisk in the remaining ¼ cup of cheese. Cover and refrigerate for up to 2 days.

Prepare the salad: Preheat the oven to 375F (190C). Wash the beets and trim off any roots or stems. If larger than the size of a golf ball, cut the beets in half. Leave shallots or cipolline in one piece, but cut a cross in each end and remove the papery skins. In a large bowl, toss the beets and onions with the olive oil and Kosher salt to coat.

Enclose the beets and strips of orange peel in a foil pouch and place the pouch directly on the oven rack. Spread the onions out on a heavy sheet pan, and roast along with the beets for about 45 minutes, turning every 10 to 15 minutes. Let the beets roast for an additional 15 minutes after you remove the onions, until easily pierced with a knife. Remove beets from oven and carefully open the pouch to allow the steam to escape.

When cool enough to handle, slip the peel off the beets. Cut the onions into half and cut the beets into the same size pieces if necessary.

Meanwhile, trim the stem end and any tough outer leaves from the fennel bulb; reserve any feathery fronds for garnish. Using a mandoline or very sharp knife, slice across the bulb into paper-thin slices; set aside.

Wash the watercress, remove the large stems, and dry well.

To serve: Toss the beets and shallots separately with the dressing to coat. Serve warm on a mixture of the fennel and watercress. Decorate the top with a sprinkling of chives (when available the blossoms are a beautiful addition) and the walnuts.

VARIATION

To serve cold: Allow the vegetables to cool completely then refrigerate for up to 24 hours. Toss the beets and shallots separately with the dressing and bring to room temperature before serving. Present the shallots on a bed of watercress or arugula with the beets piled around the edge. Garnish with additional Gorgonzola cheese and walnuts.

Mushroom Salad

This delicate salad is the perfect starter for a meal with a rich entreé. It needs to be tossed with the dressing immediately before serving. Poached shrimp or scallops, cut in slivers, are excellent in this salad.

MAKES 8 TO 10 SALAD SERVINGS

1½ pounds crimini or button mushrooms	2 large tomatoes, peeled and diced
1 lemon, halved	Lemon Goddess Dressing (page 197)
2 ripe avocados	1 bunch chives, cut into 2-inch lengths
3 cups shredded endive (about 3 heads)	½ cup pine nuts or slivered almonds, toasted (page 315)
1 cup sliced green onions	

Wash the mushrooms and remove any woody stems. Finely slice the caps. Squeeze a little lemon juice over the mushrooms; set aside.

Peel the avocados and dice. Squeeze on a little lemon juice and toss to coat.

Combine the mushrooms, avocados, endive, green onions, and tomatoes; toss gently to combine. Drizzle with the dressing to taste and toss gently so as not to crush the avocado or tomato.

Garnish each serving with chives and nuts.

Curried Shrimp Salad

This main-dish salad can be prepared well ahead of time. Its hearty texture and slightly exotic flavors appeal to men and women equally. The colorful presentation makes it a perfect addition to a buffet. Shredded cooked chicken can be substituted for the shrimp.

MAKES 8 MAIN-COURSE SERVINGS

CURRY DRESSING

¼ cup peanut oil

2 tablespoons Dijon mustard

3 tablespoons clover or orange blossom honey

¾ cup mayonnaise

2 teaspoons curry powder, toasted (page 315)

1 tablespoon fresh lemon juice or tamarind pulp

¼ teaspoon white pepper

3 tablespoons unsweetened shredded coconut

3 tablespoons reduced-sodium chicken broth

1 lemon, sliced

½ bunch fresh parsley

4 whole peppercorns

1 onion, quartered

1 fresh sage or bay leaf

2 pounds raw medium shrimp in shells (25 to 40 per pound)

8 slices ripe pineapple

1 tablespoon peanut oil

1 tablespoon sugar

1 head cabbage, shredded

2 cups diced red bell pepper

1 cup thinly sliced green onions

2¼ cups corn kernels, roasted (see page 253), or canned, drained whole-kernel corn

1 head romaine lettuce, torn into bite-size pieces

1 cup salted, dry-roasted peanuts

1 bunch cilantro, chopped

Prepare the dressing: Combine all the dressing ingredients in a food processor or blender. Process until smooth and creamy; it will be quite thick. (The dressing can be refrigerated for up to 4 days before using.)

Cook the shrimp: Add 3 to 4 quarts of water, the lemon, parsley, peppercorns, onion, and sage to a large stockpot; bring to a rolling boil over high heat. Reduce the heat and simmer for 7 to 10 minutes. Add the shrimp and simmer until pink, about 4 minutes. Drain the shrimp and stop the cooking and set color by tossing ice cubes on top. When cool, peel and devein the shrimp. Set aside. Refrigerate up to 12 hours if needed.

Preheat grill or broiler. Brush the pineapple slices with the peanut oil, sprinkle with sugar, and grill or broil until golden. Set aside to cool.

To serve: Mix the cabbage, bell pepper, green onions, and corn together in a large bowl. Add the dressing and toss to coat.

Arrange a bed of lettuce on 8 individual plates or one large plate. Top with the dressed cabbage mixture. Attractively arrange the shrimp in a circle. Garnish with the peanuts, pineapple, and a sprinkle of cilantro. Serve immediately.

VARIATION

Shredded, poached chicken breasts (see page 192) make an excellent replacement for the shrimp.

Cilantro Slaw

Originally I made this slaw as part of the Fish Tacos (page 220). However, it is so good on its own I started serving it with other dishes. Light, piquant, and unusual, it's great with everything from fried chicken to ribs.

MAKES 4 TO 5 SALAD SERVINGS

½ cup mayonnaise

2 tablespoons cider vinegar

1 teaspoon sugar

2 teaspoons minced garlic

3 cups finely shredded cabbage

½ cup finely shredded green onions

1 cup finely sliced red bell pepper

½ teaspoon cumin seeds, toasted (page 315)

⅓ cup minced fresh cilantro

Kosher salt

Freshly ground coarse black pepper

Whisk the mayonnaise, vinegar, sugar, and garlic in a bowl until combined.

Toss the cabbage, green onion, and bell pepper in a large bowl.

Pour the mayonnaise mixture over the cabbage mixture, sprinkle with the cumin seeds and cilantro, and toss to coat. Add salt and pepper to taste, and serve. (The slaw can be prepared and refrigerated up to 24 hours in advance.)

Wilted Spinach Salad with Chevre

The salad can be mostly prepared ahead of time and refrigerated. Just bring it out at dinnertime, heat the dressing and walnut cups, and toss with a flourish. When you break into the walnut cups, the warm cheese melts to coat the greens and herbs. Serve the Herb-Garlic Crostini (page 168) on the side.

MAKES 8 SALAD SERVINGS

SHERRY VINAIGRETTE

½ cup sherry vinegar

1 teaspoon Dijon mustard

2 tablespoon finely minced shallot

¾ cup extra-virgin olive oil

WALNUT CUPS

1½ cups walnuts, toasted (page 315)

Pinch Kosher salt

3 tablespoons all-purpose flour

1 egg white

SALAD

1½ pounds (about 8 cups) fresh spinach, cleaned

2 cups watercress

¾ cup chopped fresh mint

2 teaspoons minced garlic

3 tablespoons minced fresh oregano

2 cups (about 8 ounces) chevre, softened

8 walnut halves

Freshly ground coarse black pepper

Prepare Sherry Vinaigrette: In a small microwave-safe bowl, whisk together the vinegar and mustard. Add the shallot. While whisking slowly, pour in the olive oil and whisk until the dressing thickens slightly. Set aside.

Prepare Walnut Cups: Preheat the oven to 350F (175c). Combine the walnuts and salt in a food processor and pulse to finely grind the walnuts. Add the flour and egg white and process until well mixed. Place about 1 tablespoon of mixture into each greased mini muffin cup and press on bottom and sides to form cups. Bake for 12 to 15 minutes, until golden. Remove and let cool completely on a wire rack.

Prepare the salad: Wash the spinach well in running water to remove any mud and silt. Remove the stems and dry the leaves in layers of paper towels or with a salad spinner. Rinse and drip dry the watercress and mint. If not using immediately, layer the greens in a plastic bag with paper towels and refrigerate. (Cooling for a few hours actually improves the texture and flavor of the greens.)

To serve: Preheat the oven to 375F (190C). Put 1 to 2 tablespoons of chevre in each walnut cup. Drizzle with a little of the vinaigrette and top each one with a walnut half. Put the assembled cups on a heavy baking sheet.

In a large salad bowl, toss the spinach, watercress, mint, garlic, and oregano to combine.

Bake the filled walnut cups for about 4 minutes, until bubbling.

Put the vinaigrette in a loosely covered container in the microwave and heat on high for 1½ minutes, until bubbling hot. Uncover carefully and whisk again to blend.

Put one-eighth of the mixed greens on each salad plate. Top with one of the warm walnut cups and immediately drizzle the hot dressing over each plate. Season with pepper and serve immediately.

VARIATION

To make this into a substantial or entreé course, add 1 to 1½ cups shredded, poached chicken breasts (see page 192).

Queen Elizabeth's Salad

The salad is named for the guest of honor at the party where it was first served. The presentation is typical of a formal composed salad, but it's not difficult and is quite lovely, and delicious.

MAKES 8 SALAD SERVINGS

1 cup Raspberry Vinaigrette (page 195)

3 ruby grapefruits

3 Haas avocados

½ lemon

16 beautiful snow peas

½ cup enoki mushrooms

3 heads butter lettuce, torn into bite-size pieces

1 cup pine nuts, toasted (page 315)

½ cup fresh raspberries

Prepare the Raspberry Vinaigrette; set aside.

Peel the grapefruits, removing all white pith. Use a sharp or serrated knife to slip between the membranes and remove the segments. Set aside.

Peel the avocados and slice into thin wedges; drizzle with a little lemon juice to avoid discoloration.

Remove the strings and ends from the snow peas. Make a diagonal cut across the stem end of each snow pea. Use a knife tip or your finger to gently open the pod.

To serve: Take a cluster of 3 or 4 enoki mushrooms, trim the ends, and insert into the snow pea "vases." Arrange 1 cup of lettuce on one side of the plate. On the other side of the plate create a fan with alternating slices of the avocado and grapefruit. At the top of the plate, place 2 of the snow pea vases. Sprinkle the lettuce with the pine nuts and raspberries; drizzle everything with the dressing. Serve immediately.

Winter Fiesta Salad

A seasonal recipe if there ever was one—I always think of it for Christmas buffets because of the brilliant red pomegranate seeds and the green spinach. This tangy dressing is also excellent on a cold bean salad.

MAKES 8 SALAD SERVINGS

TANGY CITRUS DRESSING

3 tablespoons fresh lime or lemon juice

¼ cup chopped fresh cilantro

⅓ cup extra-virgin olive oil

1 clove garlic, peeled

¼ teaspoon Kosher salt

¼ teaspoon ground pasilla chile or cayenne pepper

Freshly ground coarse black pepper

SALAD

2 bunches fresh spinach

2 navel oranges or tangerines, peeled, seeded, and sliced

1 Bermuda onion, very thinly sliced

1 large jicama, peeled and cut into spears

Seeds from 1 pomegranate

½ cup walnuts, toasted (page 315)

Prepare the dressing: Combine all the ingredients in a blender and puree. Add salt and peppers to taste. (This can be made the day before and refrigerated.)

Prepare the salad: Remove roots and any thick stems from the spinach and rinse thoroughly in cold running water to remove any mud and silt. Spin or drain spinach to dry completely.

On either 8 individual plates or a buffet platter, arrange the salad as follows: Arrange a bed of spinach, artfully arrange the orange slices, onion rings, and jicama spears on the spinach, and sprinkle with the pomegranate seeds and walnuts. Drizzle the dressing to taste over everything.

California Chicken Salad

This simple, light recipe is so completely satisfying that you may find yourself making it all summer long. It was always one of our most requested salad entreés. The pink, green, and white salad glazed with the raspberry dressing is as beautiful as it is tasty.

MAKES 8 MAIN-COURSE SERVINGS

2½ pounds boneless, skinless chicken breasts

½ cup low-sodium chicken broth

½ teaspoon dried thyme

3 pink grapefruits

4 quarts (about 1 pound) torn butter lettuce

3 large avocados

½ cup pine nuts, toasted (page 315)

2 bunches watercress, large stems removed

Raspberry Vinaigrette (page 195)

Place the chicken breasts, broth, and thyme in a microwave-safe container. Cover loosely with plastic wrap and microwave on high for 8 minutes, until tender. Let stand in broth until cool. Remove chicken from liquid and shred by hand into large chunks.

Peel and segment the grapefruits, cutting off all of the bitter white pith. Reserve the juice.

Rinse and dry the lettuce. If you are making this ahead of time, place the lettuce in a large plastic bag, layer with a few paper towels, and place in the vegetable drawer of your refrigerator. (Salad can be completed to this point up to 24 hours before serving.)

Peel and slice the avocados. Drizzle the reserved grapefruit juice over the avocados to stop discoloration. Tear the lettuce into bite-size pieces and place in one large bowl or divide among 8 plates. Arrange the chicken, grapefruit, and avocado slices on top of the lettuce. Sprinkle with the pine nuts and garnish with the watercress.

Drizzle salad with the vinaigrette to taste or serve it on the side.

Panzanella Salad

This hearty salad is simple, inexpensive, beautiful, and delicious. It's a great opportunity for a novice host to present a rustic homemade treat. If you have day-old sourdough, French, or Italian bread on hand, this is the perfect way to use it up. If you don't have any old bread, make this salad anyway, because it's delicious.

MAKES 8 SALAD SERVINGS

5 tablespoons extra-virgin olive oil

1 tablespoon fresh lemon juice

2 tablespoons minced garlic

4 cups cubed day-old sourdough bread (see Note below)

3 cups diced, peeled, and seeded tomatoes

½ cup minced yellow onion

½ cup pitted kalamata or niçoise olives

3 tablespoons freshly grated Parmesan cheese

⅓ cup chopped fresh Italian parsley

½ cup chopped fresh basil

3 tablespoons red wine vinegar

¼ cup pine nuts, toasted (page 315)

Freshly ground coarse black pepper

Red pepper flakes (optional)

Preheat oven to 375F (175C). Combine 3 tablespoons of the olive oil, lemon juice, and garlic in a mini food processor. Pulse until pureed. Toss cubed bread in the oil mixture to coat. Place the bread on a sheet pan. Bake until crisped, 7 to 10 minutes.

Combine the bread, tomatoes, onion, olives, Parmesan cheese, parsley, and basil in large salad bowl. Toss to mix.

Drizzle on the vinegar and remaining 2 tablespoons olive oil and toss to coat. Sprinkle with pine nuts and season with black pepper and red pepper flakes, if using, to taste.

Serve immediately or the bread will become soggy. (The individual components can all be prepared several hours ahead of time and tossed together at party time.)

NOTE **If you only have fresh bread, cut it into cubes and dry out in a preheated 375F (190C) oven for 4 to 5 minutes. Cool to room temperature, then use in the recipe.**

Armenian Parsley and Walnut Salad

Great on a buffet, this is easy and appealing as an appetizer. The earthy flavors of this salad are best chilled but not cold. It can be held up to 24 hours before serving. This simple recipe is the place to use the best olive oil and freshly squeezed lemon juice; it really shows. Serve with Pita Crisps (page 167) and Mediterranean Lamb Roast (page 222).

MAKES 8 SALAD SERVINGS

---

2 bunches fresh parsley

1 cup pitted kalamata, Greek, or niçoise olives (about 1¼ cups with pits)

1 cup walnuts, toasted (page 315)

1 bunch green onions

2 large tomatoes, peeled and seeded

⅓ cup good-quality extra-virgin olive oil

⅓ cup fresh lemon juice

½ teaspoon cumin powder

½ teaspoon red pepper flakes

Kosher salt

Freshly ground coarse black pepper

Remove the stems from the parsley and mince either by hand or with quick pulses in a food processor. The parsley should be finely chopped, but if you use a food processor be careful not to puree it. The parsley should form a fluffy base for the other textures.

Chop the olives, walnuts, and green onions by hand into a rough dice. Dice the prepared tomatoes and drain.

Combine all of the chopped ingredients in a large wooden bowl. Add the olive oil, lemon juice, cumin, and red pepper flakes and toss to combine. Add salt and pepper to taste.

Raspberry Vinaigrette

This delicate dressing is especially good on baby greens, steamed beets or carrots, and any salad with chevre. Fresh raspberries are best, but the frozen variety, packaged without the addition of sugar, is acceptable, if well drained before adding.

MAKES 8 SERVINGS

¼ cup raspberry vinegar

1 teaspoon balsamic vinegar

¼ teaspoon pure vanilla extract

1½ teaspoons sugar

½ teaspoon Kosher salt

¼ teaspoon ground white pepper

1 tablespoon minced fresh thyme

1 tablespoon finely minced shallots

⅓ cup canola oil

⅓ cup extra-virgin olive oil

⅓ cup raspberries

Add the vinegars, vanilla, sugar, salt, pepper, thyme, and shallots to a medium bowl and whisk to combine.

While whisking, slowly add the oils and whisk until the dressing thickens. Add the raspberries and whisk briefly to blend without breaking them completely apart.

This can be used immediately, but it is best prepared at least 2 hours ahead. (The dressing, covered, can be refrigerated for up to 1 week.)

Asian Peanut Dressing

This is one of a category of "warmed dressings" I have created, which improve with a quick heating of the key ingredients to release flavors. Not only is this my favorite Chinese chicken salad dressing, it is a tasty sauce for warm noodle dishes including vegetables or pork.

MAKES ABOUT 2 CUPS

---

3 to 4 tablespoons smooth, unsalted peanut butter

2 tablespoons dark sesame oil

¼ cup canola oil

1 tablespoon sugar

1½ to 2 tablespoons soy sauce

1 tablespoon Chinese chili sauce (Lee Kum Kee or Guilin)

½ cup minced green onion (white part only)

1 tablespoon hoisin sauce

¼ cup chicken broth

3 tablespoons seasoned rice vinegar

⅓ cup dry sherry

¼ cup red wine vinegar

1½ tablespoons minced fresh ginger

1 teaspoon minced garlic

Combine the peanut butter, sesame oil, canola oil, sugar, soy sauce, chili sauce, green onion, and hoisin sauce in a large bowl.

Combine the chicken broth, rice vinegar, sherry and red wine vinegar in a microwave-safe container. Add the ginger and garlic and stir to mix. Cover with a paper towel and heat in the microwave on high for 25 to 30 seconds, until hot. Immediately pour the hot liquid over the peanut butter mixture and stir well to melt and blend.

Set aside until cool or cover and refrigerate for later use. (The flavor is better the next day and the dressing will keep for up to 2 weeks.)

Lemon Goddess Dressing

The lightest of citrus dressings, with a creamy texture from the almond puree. This technique of using powdered nuts for thickening is a healthful trick for those avoiding dairy products.

MAKES 2¼ CUPS

6 tablespoons chopped blanched almonds

6 tablespoons water

½ cup plus 2 tablespoons fresh lemon juice

2 tablespoons honey

½ tablespoon minced fresh basil

¼ teaspoon minced fresh dill

¼ teaspoon freshly ground coarse black pepper

1 teaspoon grated lemon zest

½ teaspoon Kosher salt

1 cup canola or vegetable oil

¼ cup plain yogurt (optional)

Put the almonds and water into a blender and blend on high until pureed. Add the remaining ingredients, except for the oil, and blend until combined. With the motor running, slowly pour in oil and run until the dressing is thick and creamy. Add the yogurt if you want a thicker consistency.

Balsamic Vinaigrette

This is delicious on grilled vegetables or warm salads.

MAKES ABOUT 3 CUPS

⅓ cup balsamic vinegar

2 tablespoons fresh lemon juice

1 teaspoon freshly ground coarse black pepper

2 cups extra-virgin olive oil

2 large tomatoes, peeled and seeded

4 cloves minced garlic

2 teaspoons chopped fresh thyme

Place the vinegar, lemon juice, and pepper in a blender or food processor. Pulse just to blend. Add the olive oil ⅓ cup at a time, pulsing to combine. When all of the oil has been incorporated, and the mixture has thickened, add the tomatoes, garlic, and thyme and pulse until combined. (The dressing is best if made the day before using, covered, and refrigerated; it will keep for up to 1 week.)

We all have hometown appetites. Every other person is a bundle of longing for the simplicities of good taste once enjoyed on the farm or in the hometown (he or she) left behind.

—Eulogy for Clementine Paddleford

Popular opinion about what is appropriate to serve as a main course has evolved in the last twenty years. *Everything* is in. If it's served with care and made from excellent ingredients, you're in style. Great big, hearty cuts of meat and a martini have returned to favor. At the same time, there are many more parties where a vegetarian entrée is served. Another trend at hip restaurants and parties is comfort food. Old-fashioned homegrown recipes that mom might have prepared—especially if she was from the Midwest—provide a gentle respite from rigid nouvelle cuisine.

As Americans have become more worldly, a menu constructed of several small courses from diverse cuisines has also become popular. Experiencing a variety of flavors and textures within the scope of a single meal appeals to the armchair traveler in us all. Many of the main dish recipes in this section can easily be served in a reduced portion as a part of this kind of grazing menu. Combine them with selections from the appetizer and side dish sections to round out the menu. When I serve a meal in this way, I usually prepare four to five small courses in place of the appetizer and main course.

Single-dish entrées like a warming bowl of Quick Risotto Reggiano with Asparagus or the Tortilla Soup (page 180) are welcomed as sophisticated, elegant light suppers, perfect for a summer evening get-together.

My goal for every party is to figure out what each group of guests would really enjoy and give it to them. Contrasts of texture, flavor, color, and style of presentation create an element of surprise which is essential in my overall menu. However, the main course should be a home run. This is the framework on which the rest of the meal is balanced.

The Theater of the Meal

THE FIRST COURSE

Introduction: The appetizer

"Hark, friend appetite. Let me introduce your senses to the pleasures to come."

THE ENTRÉE

The meat of the matter: The plot is revealed.

Hearty appetites are nourished, a satisfaction of curiosity and longing.

THE DESSERT

Denouement: The happy ending.

Everything turns out all right in the end. Sweet dreams!

For a very formal occasion there may be more than three acts, but the principle and balance remains the same: tantalize, satisfy, and reward.

Alicia's Pollo Entomatado

My friend Sebastian, who is from the Cuernavaca area of Mexico, provided this recipe from his mother's collection. The bounteous quantity of tomatillos gives the chicken a lemon tang. The serrano chile is optional, but I like the flavor it adds. This dish is perfect made ahead of time and reheated for a casual party.

MAKES 8 SERVINGS

---

2 (4½-pound) roasting chickens, cut into serving pieces or 6 to 7 pounds of your favorite chicken pieces

2 cups chicken broth

16 cloves garlic, chopped

2 large yellow onion, chopped

3 pounds fresh tomatillos

About 8 tablespoons vegetable oil

½ teaspoon minced, dried thyme

1 teaspoon minced, dried marjoram

4 bay leaves

1½ teaspoons minced dried oregano

1½ teaspoons Kosher salt

½ teaspoon freshly ground coarse black pepper

1 fresh serrano chile, minced (optional)

GARNISH

1 cup sour cream or crema fresca

2 tablespoons pepitas (shelled pumpkin seeds) or walnuts

2 tablespoons chopped fresh cilantro

Place the chicken pieces in a large stockpot with the chicken broth and enough water to cover. Add 6 cloves of the garlic and 1 of the onions. Cover the pot and simmer over medium-low heat until the chicken is just cooked, about 20 minutes.

Using a slotted spoon, remove the chicken pieces from the broth. Set the broth aside to cool. Skim the fat from the surface of the reserved broth before using.

Remove the papery outer skin from the tomatillos and rinse. Dice the tomatillos. Heat 3 tablespoons of the oil in a large nonstick sauté pan over medium heat. Add the remaining garlic and onion. Sauté until the onion is soft and golden, 4 to 5 minutes. Add the tomatillos and sauté until the tomatillos are soft, about 10 minutes. Add the herbs, serrano chile if using, and 2½ cups of the reserved chicken broth. Reduce the heat, cover, and simmer for 20 minutes. Add salt and pepper and remove from the heat.

Heat 2 to 3 tablespoons of vegetable oil in a flameproof casserole or a Dutch oven over medium-high heat. Add the chicken pieces, in batches, and sauté all sides until golden. When all of the chicken has been browned, pour off any excess oil. Return the chicken pieces to the casserole and pour the tomatillo sauce over the chicken. Cover the pan and simmer over low heat for 15 minutes. (The dish can be prepared a day ahead of time to this point and refrigerated. Reheat covered in a 325F (165C) oven for about 20 minutes or until warmed through.)

To serve, top chicken with sour cream and sprinkle with pepitas and cilantro.

SERVING SUGGESTION
Serve with corn tortillas, spicy rice, and grilled red and yellow peppers.

Chicken Piccata

Often simplest dishes are the best. When I'm tired and want a delicious meal, this recipe is one of my favorites. It's a great solution for last-minute company, too. I serve this nestled on a bed of the Creamy Chard with Feta (page 243).

MAKES 8 SERVINGS

8 boneless, skinless chicken breast halves

Kosher salt

Freshly ground coarse black pepper

¾ cup all-purpose flour

6 tablespoons unsalted butter

¼ cup sliced shallots

½ cup dry white wine

¼ cup chicken broth

1 tablespoon plus 1 teaspoon fresh lemon juice

¼ cup chopped fresh parsley or cilantro

3 tablespoons capers

1 tablespoon grated lemon zest

Pound the chicken breasts between two sheets of waxed paper or plastic wrap until very thin and even in thickness. The pieces should be about 5 inches across. Salt and pepper both sides of each piece.

Put the flour in a plastic bag and toss the chicken breasts, one at a time, to coat well. Remove and shake off any excess flour.

Heat the butter in a large sauté pan over medium heat until foamy. Add the shallots and chicken, in batches. Sauté until golden, 3 to 4 minutes per side, turning once. Keep chicken in a warm oven, tented with foil.

Deglaze the pan with the wine and chicken broth, stirring up the browned bits from the pan. Increase the heat to high and boil until reduced by half. Stir in the lemon juice and immediately drizzle the sauce over the chicken. Sprinkle generously with the parsley, capers, and lemon zest.

Chicken Breasts Stuffed with Prosciutto and Pesto

These neat little rolls are a perfect picnic basket addition. If sliced before packing, they can even be eaten with your fingers. This dish can be completed the day before needed, up to the step where the chicken goes in the oven. Just take the stuffed chicken out of the refrigerator about 45 minutes ahead of time to warm up before you put them in to bake.

MAKES 8 SERVINGS

ROSEMARY PESTO
⅓ cup freshly grated Parmesan cheese
⅓ cup rosemary leaves
1 tablespoon fresh lemon juice
½ cup pine nuts, toasted (page 315)
4 cloves garlic, crushed
2 tablespoons extra-virgin olive oil

¼ cup unsalted butter
1 teaspoon balsamic vinegar
8 boneless, skinless chicken breast halves

6 ounces thinly sliced mozzarella cheese
Kosher salt
Freshly ground coarse black pepper
3 ounces paper-thin slices prosciutto
½ cup dry vermouth
¼ cup chicken broth
⅓ cup minced fresh parsley
Rosemary sprigs
Lemon curls

Prepare the pesto: Place the Parmesan cheese and rosemary in a food processor and pulse to puree. Add the remaining ingredients and process until pureed.

To assemble the rolls: Preheat the oven to 350F (175C). Put the butter and vinegar into a microwave-safe bowl and melt in the microwave on high for 45 seconds. Set aside.

Pound the chicken breasts between 2 sheets of waxed paper or plastic wrap until very thin and even in thickness. The pieces should be about 5 inches across. If the tenders come loose, save them for another recipe.

Cut the mozzarella into strips that are no more than 2 inches long and ⅛ inch thick.

Lay the chicken on your work surface, and salt and pepper. Cover the surface of the chicken with one layer of prosciutto and sprinkle with 2 teaspoons of the pesto. Place a mozzarella strip crosswise across the center, lengthwise of the breast. Starting at the point end of the breast, roll up tightly, tucking in the sides to form an envelope, sealing in the filling. Using kitchen twine, tie once or twice around the middle and once lengthwise to create a package.

Place the rolls, seam side down, in a shallow 8-inch-square baking pan. Brush the tops with the butter mixture and sprinkle with pepper. Pour the vermouth and chicken broth around the rolls. Bake, basting frequently with remaining butter mixture and pan juices, about 30 minutes, until firm and golden.

Remove from the oven and take the rolls out of the pan with a slotted spoon. Cover with foil and set aside. Remove any melted cheese from the cooking liquid. Bring the cooking liquid to a boil over medium-high heat to reduce slightly, 2 to 3 minutes. Stir in the parsley and set aside.

To serve: Remove the twine from the chicken rolls. Arrange the chicken rolls on a platter decorated with rosemary and lemon curls and drizzle with the reduced cooking juices. For individual plates, slice the rolls crosswise in thirds to reveal the layers, and place on individual dinner plates with a drizzle of sauce and rosemary.

Chicken with Artichokes and Olives

This is a great do-ahead recipe for a party. The entire dish can be completed the day before and just reheated to serve. To present this dish on a buffet, cut the chicken into chunks that can be eaten without a knife. Top the chicken with ⅓ of the sauce and garnish with olives and minced chives. Put the rest of the sauce in a bowl on the side to be added as guests serve themselves.

MAKES 8 SERVINGS

1½ cups beef stock

3 cups chicken broth

2½ pounds boneless, skinless chicken breast halves

5 tablespoons balsamic vinegar

8 large artichokes or 2 (14½-ounce) cans water-packed artichoke hearts, drained

1½ tablespoons unsalted butter

¼ cup minced shallots

5 tablespoons Dijon mustard

4½ ounces pitted kalamata or nicoise olives

3 tablespoons chopped fresh tarragon

GARNISH

2 tablespoons grated lemon zest

4 tablespoons minced fresh chives

Combine the beef stock and chicken broth in a heavy saucepan over high heat and bring to a rolling boil. Boil until reduced to about 2 cups and set aside.

Remove any fat from the chicken breasts and place breasts in a shallow bowl or plate. Drizzle with 2 tablespoons of the balsamic vinegar and rub in. Cover and refrigerate for 1 to 2 hours.

To prepare fresh artichokes: Using a large knife or cleaver, trim the stem and the top half from each artichoke. Using a sharp paring knife, peel away the outside leaves until you have only the heart (center) remaining. Pull or cut out the hairy choke that is attached to the heart.

Place the artichoke hearts in a microwave-safe dish and pour ¼ cup chicken broth around them. Cover with plastic wrap and cook for 10 minutes on high. To test for doneness, pierce the center of a stem with a knife tip; the artichokes are done if the knife slips in easily. Cut each artichoke heart into quarters and set aside.

Heat the butter in a medium sauté pan over medium heat. Add the shallots and sauté until the shallots are clear, 5 to 7 minutes. Add the reduced stock, mustard, and the remaining vinegar and simmer gently for 5 to 10 minutes, whisking well. Add the artichokes, olives, and tarragon and simmer gently 5 minutes. Set the sauce aside or refrigerate.

Preheat the grill to medium-high. Dust one side of the chicken breasts well with pepper. Place chicken, peppered side up, on the hot grill. Cook for about 8 minutes; turn when the chicken has colored and is no longer sticking to the grill. Grill for 3 to 5 minutes, until cooked through. Do not overcook; the flesh should give slightly when pressed.

Gently warm the sauce in the microwave or over low heat if needed. Meanwhile, slice the chicken breasts diagonally into 2 to 3 wedges. Top each chicken breast with a generous ladling of the sauce. Garnish with a sprinkling of lemon zest and chopped chives.

SERVING SUGGESTIONS
This is best served over kasha or fettuccine tossed with lemon zest and chopped parsley.

Cuban Chicken

This can be served immediately after cooking, but it improves if made the day before and reheated at party time. This is one of my personal favorites for casual entertaining at home. I serve it with wild rice topped with green onion rings and radish slices. A basket of warm French bread is essential for dipping in the fruity juices.

MAKES 8 SERVINGS

½ cup fresh orange juice

¼ cup fresh lime juice

¼ cup minced garlic

1 jalapeño chile, minced

2 tablespoons grated orange zest

Kosher salt

Freshly ground coarse black pepper

4 pounds skinless chicken breast halves and thighs

⅓ cup peanut oil

4 cups chopped onions (about 2 large)

1½ cups chopped red bell pepper (about 1 large)

1½ cups chopped russet potatoes or orange sweet potatoes (sometimes called garnet yams)

1 cup tomato sauce

1 cup dry white wine

⅓ cup capers, drained

½ cup seedless raisins

½ cup pitted Spanish green olives

1 tablespoon grated lime zest

GARNISH

½ cup minced fresh parsley

Combine the orange and lime juices, garlic, chile, 1 tablespoon of the orange zest, and 1½ teaspoon salt in a large bowl. Add the chicken pieces, toss to coat, and marinate at least 2 hours or overnight in the refrigerator.

Remove the chicken from the marinade and pat dry on paper towels. Reserve the marinade.

Season the chicken pieces with salt and pepper. Heat the peanut oil in a heavy Dutch oven over medium heat. Add the chicken, in batches, and brown on both sides. Leave space around the pieces so that the chicken can brown without burning. Remove the chicken pieces to a platter as they are finished.

When all of the chicken has been browned, add the onions, bell pepper, and potatoes to the Dutch oven and sauté until the onions are translucent, 5 to 7 minutes.

Return the chicken to the pan. Add the tomato sauce, wine, capers, raisins, olives, and reserved marinade. Reduce heat to low, cover the pan, and simmer gently for 30 to 40 minutes. Season to taste and cut into the largest piece of chicken to check for doneness.

When the chicken is done, remove from the heat. Stir in the remaining orange zest and the lime zest. Let rest, covered, for 5 to 10 minutes.

Using the lid to hold back the solid pieces, pour off the cooking liquid into a small saucepan; strain if necessary. Boil the cooking liquid over medium-high heat until reduced to about 1½ cups. Pour over the chicken in the pan. Transfer the chicken mixture to a serving platter or ladle out individual portions on dinner plates. Garnish with the parsley.

Tandoori-Flavored Chicken

This recipe uses your oven or grill to replicate the delicious textures and flavor created in a traditional tandoor oven. The marinade and technique work equally well on lamb or chicken. To serve as an entrée, the whole bone-in chicken pieces are used, while the lamb is boned and threaded on skewers before grilling. Whether as an appetizer or entrée the Mint-Cilantro Raita (page 285) is a beautiful, refreshing accompaniment.

MAKES 8 SERVINGS

4 pounds skinless chicken breasts and thighs
⅓ cup fresh lemon juice
1½ teaspoons salt

MARINADE
1 tablespoon minced fresh ginger
1 tablespoon minced fresh garlic
1 teaspoon minced jalapeño chile

½ cup minced yellow onion
¾ cup regular or nonfat plain yogurt
1 tablespoon garam masala, toasted (page 316)
½ teaspoon paprika

¼ cup peanut oil

Cut diagonal slashes across the meaty side of the chicken breasts and thighs, cutting to the bone. Place the chicken in a nonreactive bowl. Drizzle with the lemon juice. Sprinkle with the salt and rub in well. Let rest for 1 hour.

To prepare the marinade: Combine the ginger, garlic, chile, and onion in a blender or food processor and pulse until pureed. Add the yogurt, garam masala, and paprika and process until blended.

Pour the yogurt mixture over the chicken and toss to coat evenly. Cover and marinate chicken in the refrigerator for at least 12 hours, and up to 24 hours.

To cook on the grill: Preheat the grill to hot 500F (260C). Brush both sides of the chicken with the peanut oil and place on the grill, slashed side up. Grill for 10 minutes. Turn, and brush again with the oil. Grill for 10 minutes more, turn, and reapply oil. Grill until browned [internal temperature should be 160F (70C)], about 25 minutes total cooking time.

To cook in the oven: Preheat the oven to 500F (260C). Place the chicken in one layer on a well-oiled roasting rack in a shallow baking pan. Brush the tops with oil and bake, without turning, for 20 to 25 minutes, until the chicken begins to crisp and become dark brown. The chicken can be held in a warm oven, covered in foil, for 15 for 20 minutes if necessary.

SERVING SUGGESTIONS

Serve on a bed of Deberah's Quick Orange Rice (page 259) with lime wedges on the side. Grilled or roasted onion halves are a classic vegetable side dish.

VARIATION: TANDOORI-FLAVORED LAMB

Substitute 4 pounds boned leg of lamb for the chicken. Cut the lamb into 2-inch chunks. Place the lamb in a nonreactive bowl. Drizzle with the lemon juice. Sprinkle with the salt, and rub in well. Let rest for 1 hour.

Pour the marinade over the lamb. Cover and refrigerate for 24 to 36 hours. Remove lamb from the marinade and drain off the excess. Thread the lamb on skewers, leaving space between each piece so that they can brown. Brush both sides of the lamb with the peanut oil and place on the grill. Grill for 10 minutes, turn the skewers, and brush again with the oil. Grill for 10 minutes more, turn, and reapply oil. Grill until done [internal temperature should be 145F (65C) for medium], about 25 minutes total cooking time.

To cook in the oven: Preheat the oven to 500F (260C). Place the lamb in one layer on a well-oiled roasting rack in a shallow baking pan. Brush the tops with oil and bake, turning once, for 20 to 25 minutes, until the edges of the meat begin to crisp and become dark brown.

Pepes
(Balinese Dumplings)

I first saw Pepes prepared in the village of Munduk on Bali. A large, rough mortar and pestle and a cleaver were the only pieces of equipment used in this simple, traditional preparation. The Pepes were cooked on a griddle over an open fire. I have also steamed them with succulent results. This recipe is an interpretation of that Balinese classic by Joe Schultz of India Joze. Pepes could be either a first course, an entrée, or part of an exotic buffet.

MAKES 12 TO 14; 6 MAIN-DISH SERVINGS

---

1 pound chicken thighs

1 ½ pounds boneless, skinless chicken breast halves

6 unsalted macadamia nuts

1 ½ tablespoons chopped fresh ginger or kencur (see Note on page 209)

1 ½ teaspoons Kosher salt, or to taste

¼ cup chopped garlic

¼ cup chopped shallots

2 ½ tablespoons chopped red serrano chile

1 teaspoon fresh lime juice

½ red bell pepper

¾ teaspoon white pepper

1 tablespoon peanut oil

Fresh banana leaves (see Note on page 209)

20 dried daun salam leaves (use if available, there is no substitute)

Jejeruk (pages 274) or other sauce

Remove the skin and bone from the chicken thighs. Chop the thighs and breasts very finely, using a cleaver or a food processor with careful on/off pulses. If you overprocess you'll wind up with chicken puree. Rinse the chopped chicken in cool water and squeeze firmly to drain.

In a mortar and pestle or blender, crush the macadamia nuts, ginger and salt. Add the garlic, shallots, serrano chile, and lime juice and grind to a paste. Transfer to a bowl. Add the chicken, bell, pepper, white pepper, and peanut oil and stir to mix well. Fry or microwave a tablespoon of the mix to test for seasoning and adjust; the mixture should be spicy.

Tear the banana leaves into 8-inch squares. Place 3 tablespoons of filling in a rectangle in the middle of each piece. Lay 1 or 2 daun salam leaves on the filling. Fold over one long side of the leaf and roll into a tight package, like a burrito. Secure the ends with wooden picks.

Preheat a grill. Cook the chicken packages over medium-low heat until firm and are cooked through, about 10 minutes total cooking time. Turn every 2 minutes.

Serve in the banana leaves with Jejeruk on the side.

NOTE

Fresh banana leaves can be ordered at most Latin American and Asian markets. (There are several mail-order sources in The Gourmet Network, page 317.) Heavy-duty foil can be substituted for the banana leaves. The pepes can also be wrapped in soaked corn husks (as for tamales) and steamed.

Ginger Roast Duck Breasts

My friend Ted Gray, corporate chef at Newport Meat, worked on this recipe for months to find a perfect, simple preparation for duck breasts for his chef clientele. The result is a recipe simple enough to encourage any home cook to consider duck for the next dinner party.

MAKES 4 SERVINGS

2 shallots

3 cloves garlic

3 sprigs parsley

2 sprigs rosemary

1 sprig thyme

1 sprig oregano

3 basil leaves

2 teaspoons chopped fresh ginger

1/2 teaspoon freshly ground coarse black pepper

1/2 teaspoon white pepper

1 tablespoon Kosher salt

2 pounds boneless duck breasts (Muscovy or domestic duck)

2 tablespoons extra-virgin olive oil

3/4 cup chicken broth

1 tablespoon unsalted butter

GARNISH

1/2 cup fresh raspberries

1 bunch watercress

Chop the shallots, garlic, herbs, and ginger together to a very fine texture. Combine with the peppers and salt.

Score the duck fat lightly in a crisscross pattern cutting just the fat without going through to the meat. Rub the duck, on both sides, with the olive oil and then with the herb mixture. Place the duck in a plastic bag, seal well, and refrigerate overnight.

Preheat the oven to 400F (205C). Use a paper towel to wipe most of the herb mixture off the duck. Sauté the duck, fat side down, in a heavy-bottomed sauté pan over medium-high heat for 4 to 5 minutes. Reduce heat to medium and cook until fat is golden brown, 4 to 5 minutes.

Turn the duck over and place in the oven for about 10 minutes, for medium rare. Watch the duck very carefully at this stage, since over cooking will make the duck tough.

Remove the duck from the pan and let rest for 4 to 5 minutes while preparing the sauce. Discard the fat in the pan. Place the pan over medium heat and deglaze with the chicken broth. Use a wooden spoon to stir up the sticky brown bits on the bottom of the pan. Let boil until reduced by half. Remove the sauce from heat and whisk in the butter. Strain the sauce.

To Serve: Slice each duck breast on the diagonal. Serve each guest 3 or 4 slices, fanned on the plate. Top with about 1 tablespoon of the sauce. Garnish with raspberries and a sprig of watercress.

Turkey Tonnato

This is a delicious cold buffet or picnic entrée. And it is easy, can be done ahead, and inexpensive! I think these flavors are wonderful on a cold plate with grilled Polenta wedges and a roasted red pepper salad. For a buffet party presentation, surround the tonnato with marinated roasted red bell peppers and mushrooms.

MAKES 8 SERVINGS

2 cloves garlic, cut into slivers

1 (3½-pound) boneless turkey breast

1 to 2 tablespoons olive oil

Kosher salt

Finely ground white pepper

Freshly ground coarse black pepper

1 onion

3 stalks celery

1 cup chicken broth

Tonnato Sauce (page 271)

4 cups endive, mâche, arugula, spinach, or a combination

2 tablespoons minced fresh Italian parsley

½ cup pitted niçoise olives

Preheat the oven to 350F (175C). Insert slivers of garlic into the turkey breast. Roll the turkey into a neat loaf and tie with kitchen twine. Rub 1 to 2 tablespoons of olive oil all over the roast and liberally dust with white and black pepper and salt.

Roughly chop the onion and celery and put in roasting pan with ½ cup of the chicken broth. Lay the seasoned turkey on top of the vegetables. Loosely tent with foil. Add more stock as necessary to cover the vegetables and keep them from burning. Bake for about 45 minutes, until an instant-read thermometer registers an internal temperature of 160F (70C).

Remove the turkey and let cool in pan. Discard the onion and celery, wrap the turkey in plastic wrap and refrigerate at least 4 hours or up to 2 days.

To serve: Arrange the greens on a platter. Slice the turkey into about ⅛-inch-thick pieces, and arrange on top of the greens. Drizzle with the sauce. Sprinkle with the parsley and olives.

Glazed Thanksgiving Turkey

This is just one of a hundred versions of a beautiful, traditional Thanksgiving roast turkey. This is turkey the way my mother and grandmother made it. The only challenge in this preparation is handling a big bird, and the long cooking time. Have the butcher remove the wishbone for easier carving.

MAKES 12 SERVINGS, PLUS LEFTOVERS

1 (12- to 14-pound) turkey
Grandma Morgan's Thanksgiving Stuffing (page 265)
Kosher salt
Freshly ground coarse black pepper
½ cup unsalted butter
¼ cup fresh orange juice
¼ cup Madeira
1 tablespoon minced fresh thyme
1 (14½-ounce) can chicken broth

4 bay leaves
4 stalks celery, roughly chopped
1 large onion, chopped
3 carrots, roughly chopped
10 cloves garlic (leave papery skin on)

GRAVY
2 cups white wine
½ cup Madeira

Completely defrost the turkey in the refrigerator, if necessary.

Preheat the oven to 325F (165C). If the stuffing was refrigerated, bring to room temperature before putting into the turkey.

Remove any giblets from the turkey. Discard any excess fat from the neck or chest cavity and rinse the cavities thoroughly with cool water and pat dry. Salt and pepper thoroughly.

Combine the butter, orange juice, Madeira, thyme, 1 teaspoon salt, and ½ teaspoon pepper in a microwave-safe bowl. Microwave on high until melted, about 60 seconds.

To fill the neck cavity with stuffing, place the turkey breast side down. Fill this area very loosely, pull the skin flap up and over and secure to the backbone with a skewer. Turn the turkey over to fill the rear cavity. Stuff turkey lightly with the stuffing; do not pack it. (This size turkey will hold about 7 cups of stuffing.) If there is skin to pull together to cover the stuffing, secure it with skewers. If this skin has been trimmed off, cover the exposed stuffing with foil.

Set the stuffed turkey breast-side up on a roasting rack in a 3- to 4-inch-deep roasting pan. Add 1 cup of the broth and 1 cup of water into the roasting pan. Brush the turkey liberally with the melted butter mixture.

Roast on the middle rack of the oven for 20 minutes per pound, basting every 30 minutes with the butter mixture. If any areas start to darken too quickly, cover lightly with foil. After about 2 hours of cooking, add the chopped vegetables, bay leaves and garlic to the roasting pan, placing them under and around the turkey. Continue to baste with drippings of the butter mixture. If the pan dries out, add additional broth or water. Roast for a total of about 4 hours. The turkey is done when an instant-read thermometer inserted in the thickest part of the thigh reads 160 to 165F (70C). The drumsticks should move loosely in their sockets.

Remove the turkey to a carving board and tent loosely with foil. The turkey should rest at least 30 minutes before carving. (This gives you plenty of time to make the pan gravy.)

To make the gravy: Use a slotted spoon to remove cooked vegetables from the roasting pan to a bowl; set aside to cool slightly. Discard the bay leaves. Puree the vegetables in a food processor or blender.

Tip the roasting pan to collect the liquids in one corner. Spoon off all visible fat. Put the roasting pan on the stovetop, across 2 burners on medium heat. When the pan starts to sizzle, add white wine to deglaze the pan; use a wooden spoon to stir up and dissolve the brown sticky bits on the pan. When all of these cooking solids are melted into the wine, stir in ½ cup or more of the roasted vegetable puree. Simmer, stirring constantly, until thickened, 4 to 5 minutes. Add the Madeira and taste for salt and pepper. If too thin, add a little more vegetable puree and simmer for 5 to 7 minutes.

Carve the turkey and serve with the gravy.

Grilled Scallops with Bacon

If you can't get fresh (not previously frozen) sea scallops, forego this dish. It's a delicious and beautiful entrée that can be prepared in no more than 45 minutes from beginning to serving.

If large, fresh oysters are available, they are a wonderful alternative to the scallops.

MAKES 8 SERVINGS; 16 SKEWERS

MARINADE
½ cup canola oil

½ cup dry sherry or vermouth

2 tablespoons soy sauce

1 tablespoon honey

2 cloves minced garlic

1 tablespoon curry powder

1 teaspoon minced fresh ginger

2 pounds fresh large sea scallops

1 large russet potato, peeled and cubed

16 slices bacon (about ½ pound)

Caribbean Rice (page 260)

To prepare the marinade: Combine all the ingredients in a large bowl.

Cut the scallops in half from top to bottom so that they are about 1-inch chunks. Add the scallops and potato to the marinade, stir to coat and let marinate for 30 minutes.

If using bamboo skewers, soak them in cold water for 30 minutes.

Bring 1 quart of water to a boil. Drop in the bacon slices and boil for 90 seconds. Remove and drain in a colander. Rinse in cold water; set aside.

Preheat grill to medium-high (until you can hold your hand 4 to 5 inches off the grill for no more than 4 to 5 seconds).

Start each skewer with a potato and run the skewer through one end of a bacon slice, slip on a scallop, bring the bacon back around, and repeat, using 3 scallops per skewer. End with a potato "stopper." Brush all over with marinade.

Using tongs, place the skewers on the grill. Turn from side to side every 2 minutes to evenly color the scallops and bacon. Grill for a total of 5 to 7 minutes, until the scallops are opaque and the bacon crisp.

Serve 2 skewers per person with the Caribbean Rice.

SERVING SUGGESTION

This same dazzling entrée can be made in miniature as a wonderful hors d'oeuvre or in a small portion as a first course.

Baked Sea Bass with Caribbean Salsa

The preparation for this exuberantly flavored main course will probably take no more than half an hour. The salsa (without the banana) and the pesto can be prepared the day before. All you have to do during the party is bake the fish and serve it.

Any firm, fresh fish that is available in your market in ¾- to 1-inch-thick fillets or steaks can be substituted for the sea bass. Large shrimp, peeled and deveined before coating, are also delicious; they will cook in only 5 to 7 minutes.

MAKES 8 SERVINGS

PEPITA PESTO

2 tablespoons minced garlic

⅓ cup fresh orange juice

¾ cup pepitas (shelled pumpkin seeds)

¼ teaspoon Kosher salt

¼ teaspoon freshly ground coarse black pepper

1 tablespoon extra-virgin olive oil

1½ teaspoons cumin seeds

1 cup fine bread crumbs

3 pounds ¾- to 1-inch-thick Chilean sea bass fillets

3 tablespoons unsalted butter, melted

Caribbean Salsa (page 287)

¼ cup pepitas (shelled pumpkin seeds), toasted (see Note, page 315)

¼ cup chopped fresh cilantro

½ cup pink grapefruit segments

Preheat the oven to 425F (220C).

To prepare the pesto: Combine the garlic, orange juice, pepitas, salt, pepper, olive oil, and cumin seeds in a food processor. Pulse until pureed. Transfer to a large bowl and mix in the bread crumbs with a fork.

To prepare the fish: Rinse the fish and pat dry with paper towels. Cut into 8 equal portions. Pour 2 tablespoons of the butter over the fillets and rub in. Press each piece of fish into the plate of pesto to make a crust.

Butter a large shallow baking pan and line it with parchment paper; butter the paper. Place the coated fillets on the parchment paper.

Bake 12 to 14 minutes for 1-inch-thick fillets, until the fish is firm and opaque but not dry.

To serve: Pool the Caribbean Salsa on each plate, and center a piece of fish on the salsa. Garnish with toasted pepitas, cilantro, and grapefruit segments.

Frogmore Stew

Versions of this traditional one-pot meal are served all over the low country of South Carolina for Sunday dinners and backyard picnics. While it does need to be cooked and served immediately, the simple preparations can all be completed before guests arrive. This is one of my favorite dishes for impromptu summer entertaining.

Frogmore Stew is a complete meal except for a crispy salad, like my Cilantro Slaw (page 187), and big slabs of garlic bread. It's not traditional, but I sometimes add a couple of pounds of littleneck clams or green-lipped mussels.

MAKES 8 SERVINGS

---

2 pounds spicy smoked sausage, such as andouille or chaurice

2 pounds raw, large shrimp in shells (16 to 20 per pound)

6 ears of corn

1 lemon

1 red onion

4 quarts water or warm dark beer

1 package crab boil, such as Zatarain's

1 teaspoon Kosher salt

1½ pounds fingerling or new potatoes

Herb Butter (page 271)

Freshly ground coarse black pepper

Lemon slices

Cut the sausage into 2- to 3-inch chunks. Peel and devein the shrimp, leaving the tails on. Cut the corn ears crosswise into half and then into quarters. Cut the lemon and onion into thin slices.

In a large (about 12-quart) stockpot, bring the water, crab boil, and salt to a boil over high heat. Reduce the heat and simmer for 15 minutes. Add the sausage and onion and simmer over low heat for 10 minutes. Add the potatoes and simmer for 10 to 12 minutes. Add the shrimp, corn, and lemon and simmer until shrimp are bright pink for 3 to 5 minutes.

To Serve: Remove the stew from the heat. Using a slotted spoon or tongs, transfer all the ingredients except the broth to a large bowl or deep platter. Toss with the Herb Butter and dust liberally with black pepper. Serve with lemon slices and lots of napkins.

Bridget's Cajun Jambalaya

This is another flavorful, Southern one-pot meal taught to me by my friend Bridget Payne. Bridget grew up in Lake Charles, Louisiana, hunting and fishing on the bayou with her father and brothers. This is her grandfather's jambalaya recipe passed on by Bridget's father to her. The recipe can easily be doubled to serve as the main course for a crowd. Bridget serves this with skillet corn bread and Dixie beer.

MAKES 8 TO 10 SERVINGS

---

1 (4½-pound) chicken

5 cups water

2 teaspoons Demi-Glace Gold Stock base (see Note on page 217)

1 large onion, finely chopped

1½ bunch green onions

⅓ cup chopped fresh cilantro

1 stalk celery, diced

¼ cup diced green bell pepper

1 teaspoon minced garlic

Kosher salt

Freshly ground coarse black pepper

2 to 3 teaspoons cayenne pepper

1 pound fully cooked spicy Louisiana sausage, such as hot links or andouille

1 to 2 cups chicken broth

¼ cup vegetable oil

3 bay leaves

2½ cups long-grain white rice

Combine the chicken, water, and bouillon in a large stockpot over medium-low heat. Cover and simmer until the chicken is cooked, about 30 minutes. Remove from heat and let the chicken cool, in the liquid, in the refrigerator.

Combine the onion, green onions, cilantro, celery, bell pepper, and garlic in a large baking pan and liberally season with Kosher salt, black pepper, and cayenne pepper; set aside.

Discard some of the fat from the surface of the cooled chicken liquid. Remove the chicken from the pot, reserving the liquid, and pull the meat from the bones in chunks. Discard the skin and bones. Set the cooking liquid and meat aside.

Slice the sausage into ¼-inch rounds. Add 2 tablespoons oil to a heavy (preferably cast iron) skillet over medium-high heat. Sauté the sausage until browned. Remove from the remaining skillet with a slotted spoon. Add the diced vegetables and remaining 2 tablespoons oil, reduce the heat to medium, and sauté until well browned. Remove from heat.

Measure the reserved cooking liquid and add enough canned broth to equal 5 cups. Combine the broth, chicken, browned sausage, bay leaves, and vegetables in the stockpot and taste for seasoning. Bring to a boil, reduce the heat to low, and add the rice. Stir to mix and cover. Cook until rice is tender and has absorbed the liquids, 20 to 25 minutes.

Serve hot. (The jambalaya can be refrigerated for up to 2 days and reheated in the oven or microwave before serving.)

NOTE

Demi-Glace Gold Stock base is available by mail, 800-860-9385. Substitute bouillon granules.

Garlic Shrimp Sauté

The sauce for this dish was one that I manufactured; it was my all-time, bestselling product. Even though you create the sauce, it is still one of the quickest entertaining entrées in my repertoire.

MAKES 8 SERVINGS

2½ pounds large raw shrimp in shells (16 to 20 per pound)

⅓ cup minced garlic (about 8 cloves)

½ cup extra-virgin olive oil

⅓ cup clarified butter (see page 315)

1 teaspoon dried basil

2 teaspoons red pepper flakes

⅓ cup fresh lemon or lime juice

Kosher salt

Freshly ground coarse black pepper

1 to 2 tablespoons dry white wine

½ cup chopped fresh parsley, plus extra for serving

½ cup freshly grated Parmesan cheese, plus extra for serving

Cooked fettuccine or soft polenta from the porcini broth (page 233)

Peel and devein the shrimp, leaving the tails attached.

Combine the garlic, olive oil, butter, basil, and red pepper flakes in a large bowl. Add the shrimp and toss to coat. Cover and refrigerate for 3 to 4 hours.

Bring a large cast-iron sauté pan to almost smoking hot over medium-high heat. Add half of the shrimp and half of the marinade. Add half of the lemon or lime juice and a sprinkle of salt and pepper. Sauté the shrimp, stirring with a slotted spoon or tongs, until rosy pink and firm to the touch, 3 to 5 minutes.

Remove shrimp to a bowl and keep warm. Cook the remaining shrimp with the remaining marinade and lemon juice. Remove shrimp from sauté pan and add to shrimp in the bowl.

Add the wine to the hot pan, stir, and cook 1 minute to deglaze. Return all the shrimp to the pan and stir to combine. Remove pan from the heat. Sprinkle the parsley and Parmesan cheese over the shrimp and toss to mix.

Serve over fettuccine and top with lavish sprinkles of Parmesan cheese, parsley, and freshly ground coarse black pepper.

Sea Bass Stew with Pasta

This is a quick, and beautiful entrée on a buffet. To display on a platter, toss the pasta with half of the stew, and then arrange the remaining stew on top, decorate with chopped parsley, freshly ground coarse black pepper, and lemon twists. Serve immediately after assembling.

MAKES 8 SERVINGS

1 1/2 pounds Chilean sea bass

3/4 cup pitted kalamata or niçoise olives

3 tablespoons extra-virgin olive oil

1 cup minced yellow onion

2 tablespoon minced garlic

1 3/4 pounds tomatoes—peeled, seeded, and chopped (2 1/3 cups)

3/4 teaspoons Kosher salt

2 teaspoons fresh minced oregano

1/2 teaspoon red pepper flakes

freshly ground coarse black pepper

1/2 cup dry vermouth

2 tablespoons fresh lemon juice

2/3 cup shredded fresh basil (about 1 bunch)

PASTA AND BEAN MELANGE

3/4 pound capellini pasta

Pinch salt

2 cups canned cannellini beans [about 1 1/2 (15-ounce) cans]

GARNISH

1/4 cup chopped fresh Italian parsley

8 to 10 lemon peel twists (see page 315)

To prepare the stew: Cut the fish into 1-inch cubes. Roughly chop the olives. Combine the fish and olives in a bowl and set aside.

Heat the olive oil in large heavy bottom sauté pan or Dutch oven over medium heat. Add the onion and garlic and sauté, until softened, 7 to 8 minutes.

Add the tomatoes, salt, oregano, red pepper flakes, black pepper, vermouth, and lemon juice and simmer over medium-low heat for 5 to 7 minutes to warm through.

Add the fish chunks and olives to the tomato mixture and simmer for 6 to 7 minutes. Add the basil and simmer for about 1 minute. Remove from heat and cover.

To prepare the Pasta and Bean Melange: Add pasta to a large pot of rapidly boiling salted water. Stir well, reduce the heat to medium and cook at a rolling boil until pasta is tender, 2 to 3 minutes.

Drain and rinse the beans and put into a large pasta bowl.

Drain the pasta and add to the beans. Toss lightly to mix without breaking up the beans.

To serve: Serve each guest 1 cup of the Pasta and Bean Melange. Top with 1 cup of the stew. Garnish with chopped Italian parsley and lemon peel twists. Serve immediately.

Skewered Lamb Ruffles with Almond Mint Pesto

In this simple recipe, inspired by the flavors of Greece, tender strips of lamb are grilled or broiled on a skewer and served with a fresh and savory pesto. This dish works equally well served hot from the grill as an entrée or at room temperature as easy finger food for a cocktail party or picnic.

MAKES 8 SERVINGS; 16 SKEWERS

1½ to 2 pounds boneless lamb
⅓ cup extra-virgin olive oil
Kosher salt

Freshly ground coarse black pepper
Pistachio Mint Pesto (page 277), made with almonds

If using bamboo skewers, soak them in water for at least 30 minutes to prevent burning.

Preheat the broiler or grill to high.

Thinly slice the lamb into 4 × 1-inch strips. Lightly brush the lamb with the olive oil and season with salt and pepper. Thread the lamb on to the skewers, creating a ruffle.

Place under the broiler or on the grill and cook for 1 to 2 minutes on each side until medium rare, or to desired doneness. Serve with the pesto as a dipping sauce.

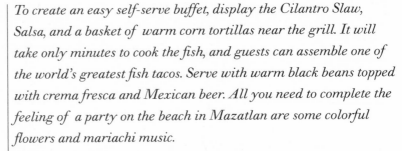

Fish Tacos with Citrus Salsa

To create an easy self-serve buffet, display the Cilantro Slaw, Salsa, and a basket of warm corn tortillas near the grill. It will take only minutes to cook the fish, and guests can assemble one of the world's greatest fish tacos. Serve with warm black beans topped with crema fresca and Mexican beer. All you need to complete the feeling of a party on the beach in Mazatlan are some colorful flowers and mariachi music.

MAKES 8 SERVINGS

Cilantro Slaw (page 187), drained

Citrus Salsa (page 287), drained

2 tablespoons vegetable oil

2 tablespoons fresh lemon juice

Kosher salt

Freshly ground coarse black pepper

2 pounds fresh sea bass, swordfish, or shark fillets

2 dozen yellow or blue corn tortillas

Prepare the Cilantro Slaw and Citrus Salsa and refrigerate.

Preheat a grill to medium-high. Combine the oil, lemon juice, salt, and pepper in a large bowl. Add the fish and toss to coat. Grill the fish, turning once, until crispy, about 8 minutes total cooking time. Cover with foil until you are ready to assemble the tacos.

Meanwhile, wrap the tortillas, in groups of 12, in foil and place in a 375F (190C) oven for about 10 minutes, until warm. Or, for a crisper texture, place individual tortillas directly on the warm grill and toast on both sides.

To assemble: Let each guest crumble some fish across a tortilla, top with 1 to 2 tablespoons of slaw and 1 tablespoon of salsa. Roll up to enclose the filling.

Rack of Lamb with Tapenade

Once you have prepared the Tapenade, which can be done up to a week in advance, assembling and cooking this impressive, festive dish is a zip. If it is available at your market, Colorado-raised lamb is markedly preferable. Because Colorado lamb is corn fed, as opposed to the grass-fed lambs from New Zealand and Australia, the racks are meatier and more flavorful.

This is nicely complemented by the Pear and Potato Gratin with Horseradish (page 255).

MAKES 8 SERVINGS

Kosher salt

Freshly ground coarse black pepper

4 (8-bone) racks of lamb, French trimmed by the butcher

¾ cup Tapenade (page 276)

10 to 12 tablespoons coarse cornmeal or unseasoned bread crumbs

Preheat the oven to 400F (205C). Salt and pepper the underside of each rack. Spread about 3 tablespoons of the tapenade over the meaty top of each rack.

Sprinkle each rack with 2 to 3 tablespoons of the cornmeal to cover the tapenade and press in.

Place the lamb on a baking sheet or shallow roasting pan, tapenade side up leaving space between each rack. Roast for 25 to 30 minutes for medium rare, until an instant-read thermometer registers an internal temperature of 135F (55C) to 140F (60C).

Let the lamb rest for at least 10 minutes before cutting into serving portions of 3 to 4 ribs per person.

Mediterranean Lamb Roast

Preparation of this meltingly tender roast relies more on a flamboyant approach than on complicated cooking techniques. You should serve your guests the same variety of red wine that you use in the marinade. The roast is equally successful served cold, sliced on a buffet.

MAKES 8 SERVINGS

---

3 cups hearty red wine

½ cup extra-virgin olive oil

1 leg of lamb, boned and butterflied by the butcher (about 4 pounds boned)

1 (3-ounce) can anchovies in olive oil

10 to 12 cloves garlic

2 bunches fresh rosemary branches

Kosher salt

Freshly ground coarse black pepper

AU JUS

½ cup beef stock

¼ cup pitted and diced kalamata or niçoise olives

Combine the wine and olive oil in a large roasting pan.

Trim off all excess fat and any tendons from the lamb. Submerge the lamb in the wine mixture and marinate at room temperature for 1 hour or 4 to 6 hours in the refrigerator. Remove the lamb from the marinade, reserving the marinade, and pat lamb dry for easier handling. Refrigerate the marinade.

Drain the oil from the anchovies.

Slice any large garlic cloves and pull the rosemary branches into individual stems. Spread out the boned leg of lamb on the work surface. Salt and pepper the lamb thoroughly on both sides.

Insert all of the garlic, anchovy fillets, and rosemary stems into every nook and cranny left by the butcher's boning process. If there are not enough cavities, use a paring knife to make small slits. Try to balance the dispersion of these three intense flavors throughout the lamb.

Now, reassemble the lamb into some semblance of the roast you picked up from the butcher, using kitchen twine. Don't worry about being too neat, there will be twigs and bits sticking out. But, you want to tuck in any small or thin pieces of meat, which might cook too quickly.

(The lamb can be prepared to this point up to 24 hours in advance if it is wrapped well in plastic wrap and refrigerated. It must be brought back to room temperature before cooking.)

To cook: Preheat the oven to 450F (230C). Mix the marinade well and pour ½ cup over the roast and massage it in with your hands. Place the lamb on a rack in a shallow roasting pan and roast for 15 minutes. Reduce the heat to 350F (175C) and roast for about 1½ hours, until an instant-read thermometer registers an internal temperature 140F (60C) for rare or 150F (165C) for medium. Baste with the reserved marinade about every 20 minutes.

Remove the lamb from the roasting pan to a cutting board. Let stand at least 10 minutes before slicing. (It can rest, tented with foil, for up to 30 minutes.)

To prepare the au jus: Put the roasting pan on the stovetop, across 2 burners on medium-high heat. Pour any unused marinade into the hot roasting pan to deglaze the juices and solid particles on the bottom. If you need additional liquid, use the beef stock. Add the chopped olives. Simmer for 2 to 3 minutes. Reserve the sauce in the warm oven to pour on the lamb when it is served.

To serve: Completely remove the kitchen twine. Slice the lamb, against the grain, into about ½-inch-thick slices. The anchovies will have disappeared into the meat, but you will see pretty cross sections of the garlic and rosemary. Serve about 1 tablespoon of the aromatic sauce on each slice.

Party Prime Rib

Chef Gray's unusual preparation of prime rib requires about 4½ hours to produce a moist, tender roast. Measuring the internal temperature is imperative for prime rib; don't attempt this recipe without an instant-read or other good meat thermometer. The 1½-hour resting period that he recommends allows the juices to redistribute and the meat to relax, resulting in a very tender roast. It also allows you to use the oven for preparing other elements of the meal.

MAKES 14 SERVINGS

---

1 (15- to 17-pound) prime rib beef roast, bone-in

Extra-virgin olive oil

Kosher salt

Freshly ground coarse black pepper

Garlic powder

2 cloves garlic, cut into slivers

⅓ cup Dijon mustard

1½ cups diced carrots

1½ cups diced celery

2 onions, diced

8 cloves garlic, peeled

Freshly grated or prepared horseradish

JUS LIÉ

1 cup plus 3 tablespoons red wine

1 cup beef broth

2 tablespoons cornstarch

1 tablespoon unsalted butter

Pat the roast dry with paper towels, then rub olive oil all over. Season liberally with salt, black pepper, and garlic powder. Insert garlic cloves about ½-inch deep throughout the roast. Rub the entire roast with a thin coating of Dijon mustard. Let the roast rest at room temperature for at least 30 minutes before roasting.

Preheat the oven to 425F (220C). Place the roast, fat side down, on a meat rack in a large roasting pan. Roast for about 30 minutes, until browned. Turn roast over and cook 25 to 30 minutes, until fully browned on top.

Add the diced vegetables and peeled garlic to the bottom of the pan and reduce the heat to 250F (120C). Roast about 2 hours, until the meat reaches an internal temperature of 110F (42C), for rare or 115F (45C) for medium rare.

Remove the roast from the oven, loosely tent with foil, and let rest for 1½ hours. Remove the cooked vegetables from the roasting pan and reserve.

To finish: Preheat the oven to 400F (205C). Trim away the excess fat and place the roast, fat side up, in the roasting pan. Cook for about 15 minutes. Remove from pan and let rest 15 minutes before slicing. (During this rest, the internal temperature will rise to about 125 to 130F (50F), which is perfect for rare or to 130 to 135° (55C) for medium rare.)

Meanwhile, to prepare the Jus Lié: Spoon all visible fat from the pan juices. Place the pan on the stovetop, over 2 burners on medium-high. When the pan starts to sizzle, deglaze by adding the 1 cup wine and the beef broth. Use a wooden spoon to get up the browned bits from the bottom of the pan. Add the reserved vegetables and let simmer until reduced by one-third, about 2 minutes. Skim off any scum that rises to the surface.

In a small cup, stir the cornstarch into the remaining 3 tablespoons red wine. Remove the sauce from the heat. Whisk in the cornstarch mixture. Whisk to mix well, return to the heat, and simmer 2 to 3 minutes.

Pour the sauce through a strainer, pressing the vegetables to release their flavor. Stir in the butter. Serve immediately with the sliced roast. Don't forget the horseradish!

Solange Family Brisket with Prunes

When my husband's family emigrated to Palestine they grew from an acorn into an oak tree. So, Solange, which meant acorn in Russian, became Aloni, from the oak tree, in Hebrew. This brisket is a result of my husband's family traditions combined with my endless recipe fussing.

MAKES 8 TO 10 SERVINGS

---

1 (4-pound) center-cut beef brisket

¼ cup extra-virgin olive oil

1 pound (about 3 large) yellow onions, sliced

½ teaspoon sugar

2 cups sliced cremini mushrooms (about 5 ounces)

2 cups beef stock

2½ cups cabernet

1½ teaspoons Kosher salt

1 teaspoon freshly ground coarse black pepper

10 cloves garlic, peeled

1 cup pitted prunes, cut into halves

1 tablespoon chopped fresh thyme

2 cups rough cut carrot

Preheat the oven to 325F (165C). Trim all excess fat from the brisket, leaving about ¼ inch.

Heat the olive oil in a large heavy-bottomed sauté pan or Dutch oven over medium-high. Add the onions and sauté until soft, about 10 minutes. Add the sugar and toss to combine. Add the mushrooms and sauté until mushrooms begin to color, 5 to 7 minutes. Remove the onions and mushrooms to a bowl. Pour in the beef stock and wine and stir to deglaze. Scrape up any browned or sticky bits and turn off the heat.

Salt and pepper the brisket all over. Add to the pan with the wine. Add the onions and mushrooms with any liquid, garlic cloves, prunes, and thyme.

Cover and cook for 1½ hours. Add the carrots. Cover and cook 1½ to 2 hours more, until the meat is fork tender.

Remove the pan from the oven and let rest for 10 minutes. Remove the brisket and vegetables to a large bowl or platter and cover. Spoon off the fat from the surface of the liquid.

To serve: Slice the brisket, across the grain, into ¼-inch-thick slices. Top with the warm cooking juices and the vegetables.

SERVING SUGGESTIONS

To create a gourmet cold cut spread: Prepare the brisket a day ahead of your party. Follow all recipe directions through degreasing the sauce and refrigerate.

To serve: Remove the brisket from the juice to a cutting board. Strain the juice and vegetables through a sieve, pressing to extract as much of the vegetable flavors as possible. Slice the brisket, across the grain, into ¼-inch-thick slices, and display on a platter. A bowl of the warmed sauce on the side makes it special.

TIP
Check your oven thermostat with an oven thermometer if you haven't done so recently. An inaccurate thermostat could be disastrous since you don't check this dish for hours.

Roast Tenderloin of Beef with Gorgonzola

This is so easy it's almost a spur of the moment recipe. As long as the beef is excellent, you have a slam dunk. Leftovers from this roast are great as part of a cold luncheon plate on those days when you don't want to heat up the house preparing a company meal.

MAKES 8 SERVINGS

1 (4-pound) tenderloin of beef, USDA prime
¼ cup minced fresh thyme
¼ cup extra-virgin olive oil
½ cup chopped garlic
1 cup hearty red wine

3 tablespoons crushed black peppercorns
¾ cup beef stock
1 cup chopped watercress
⅔ cup crumbled Gorgonzola or Stilton cheese

Ask the butcher to roll and tie up the roast into a compact shape. It is not necessary to remove absolutely all of the fat, which is the current grocery store trend, as some fat adds flavor during roasting.

In a food processor, pulse the thyme, olive oil, garlic, and ½ cup of the red wine into a paste. Rub the paste, reserving 1 tablespoon, evenly over the surface of the roast. Let the roast rest at room temperature for 1 hour.

Preheat the oven to 450F (230C).

Sprinkle the peppercorns evenly over the surface of the roast and press into place.

Put the roast into an ungreased, shallow roasting pan. Roast for 15 minutes and reduce the heat to 350F (175C). Roast for 20 to 25 minutes more for rare in the center [120 to 125F

(50C) internal temperature], basting with the pan juices. Remove the roast from the oven.

Place the roast on a cutting board, tent with foil, and let stand for at least 10 minutes before carving. If convenient for the rest of your schedule, a 20-minute rest is best.

Place the pan on the stovetop, over 2 burners on medium. When the pan starts to sizzle, deglaze by adding the beef stock and remaining red wine to loosen all of the brown bits in the bottom of the pan. Simmer for 10 minutes or until reduced to about ½ cup. Stir in the reserved 1 tablespoon of paste and simmer for 3 minutes more. Remove from heat.

Carve the roast into about ½-inch-thick slices. Serve 2 slices per guest on a bed of watercress. Top each portion with about 1½ tablespoons cheese and glaze with 1 tablespoon of sauce.

SERVING SUGGESTION

To serve cold, start each plate with a bed of watercress, radish, and endive dressed with vinaigrette. Alternate 2 or 3 slices of the tenderloin with ripe tomato slices across one side of the plate. Crumble Gorgonzola over it all, and offer baskets of warm Pita Crisps (page 167). Yowee!

Chef Gray's Shanghai Roast

My friend Ted Gray is a CIA graduate, who currently serves as corporate chef and vice president of Newport Meat Company, one of the finest meat purveyors in the country. Having grown up in the Midwest, he is really a meat man at heart anyway. His recipes bring out the best in a good piece of meat.

MAKES 8 TO 10 SERVINGS

MARINADE

½ cup hoisin sauce

½ cup applesauce

½ cup Asian garlic-chili sauce

½ cup tomato ketchup

2 cloves garlic, minced

1 tablespoon minced fresh ginger

2 chopped green onions

¼ cup dry sherry

¼ cup rice wine vinegar

¼ cup honey

½ tablespoon sesame oil

2 teaspoons soy sauce

2 (about 1½ pounds) trimmed beef tri-tip

Kosher salt

Freshly ground coarse black pepper

Combine all the marinade ingredients in a bowl large enough to hold the meat; mix thoroughly.

Pat the meat dry with paper towels. Season well with salt and pepper. Place the meat in the marinade, turn to coat, cover, and refrigerate for 24 hours or if time allows up to 48 hours.

Preheat a grill to high. Remove the meat from the marinade, reserving the marinade. Place the meat directly on the grill rack and cook about 15 minutes per side for medium rare, basting frequently with the marinade.

Let the meat rest in a large pan 10 to 15 minutes before thinly slicing against the grain. Serve with the drippings from the pan.

SERVING SUGGESTIONS

Serve with Classic Mashed Potatoes (page 256) and Chinese beer.

Chain Gang Chili

The best Super Bowl party, down-and-dirty, moving-day, all-beef chili. The combination of chiles gives it a complex, rounded chile flavor. I serve beans and the other garnishes on the side for guests to add at their own discretion—a small rijsttafel of chili.

MAKES 8 SERVINGS

3 large dried pasilla chiles

1 dried California chile

1 to 2 (12-ounce) bottles dark beer or ale

1 tablespoon chopped chipotle chile in adobo

1 (3-pound) beef brisket

Kosher salt

Freshly ground coarse pepper

3 to 4 tablespoons extra-virgin olive oil

4 large Spanish onions, thinly sliced

16 large cloves garlic, minced

1 cup diced carrot

1½ tablespoons ground cumin

¼ cup chile powder

1 (16-ounce) can tomato sauce

1 (14½-ounce) can beef broth

Cayenne pepper

Place the pasilla and California chiles in a microwave-safe bowl, cover with cold water, and heat in the microwave on high for 2 minutes. Set aside to soak for at least 20 minutes. When the chiles are nice and soft, remove the stems and seeds and place the chiles in a food processor or blender with ¼ cup of the soaking liquid, ¼ cup of the beer, and the chipotle chile. Puree to a smooth consistency.

Cut the beef into ¾-inch cubes. Thoroughly salt and pepper the beef. Heat 1 tablespoon of the oil in a large, heavy-bottomed sauté pan over medium heat. Add the beef cubes, in batches, and sauté until browned, about 15 minutes; set aside.

Heat 2 tablespoons of the oil in a large Dutch oven over medium heat. Add the onions, garlic, and carrot and sauté until the onions are soft and tender, about 10 minutes. Add the chile puree, cumin, and chile powder and sauté for 5 minutes, stirring frequently so that it does not scorch. Add a little beer if necessary. The mixture will become a thick, aromatic paste. Add the beef into the Dutch oven and stir well to coat.

Add the beer remaining in the first bottle, tomato sauce, and beef broth. Cover and simmer for 1½ hours over low heat and taste for seasoning. Add salt, black pepper, and cayenne, if necessary. Add more beer or water if the chili is too dry. Simmer until the meat is tender, 30 minutes more.

Serve with *frijoles de la olla* (canned pinto beans, drained and reheated in chicken broth with 1 teaspoon of cumin and two tablespoons of chopped fresh cilantro), Crispy Shallots (page 281), chopped cilantro and green onions tossed together, shredded Monterey Jack cheese and crispy tortilla strips. Stand back. Everyone will have seconds and bowl-scraping thirds.

Barbecued Pork Ribs

This very simple recipe is perfect for a Fourth of July picnic or any casual party. Everything can be prepared well in advance and the resulting ribs are a classic. They are messy to eat, so provide finger bowls or towels so your guests can relax and devour the ribs with the enthusiasm they deserve.

MAKES 8 SERVINGS

Dry Rub (page 276)

2 recipes Barbecue Sauce (page 273), reserving half for serving

5 to 6 pounds pork baby back ribs (about 3 racks)

¼ cup toasted sesame seeds

¼ cup sliced green onions

Prepare the Dry Rub and Barbecue Sauce.

Liberally sprinkle the rub on both sides of the ribs. Rub in and let rest for 1 hour.

Preheat the oven to 325F (165C). Wrap individual racks in heavy foil and place in a roasting pan. Bake for about 1 hour, until the meat is very tender. Remove the pan from the oven, open the foil, drain off the liquids, and brush the racks liberally with the sauce.

Increase the oven temperature to 375F (190C). Return the ribs to the pan, meaty side up, and cook for 10 to 15 minutes, until the sauce is bubbling. Slather on the sauce again and return to the oven for 15 minutes more.

To serve: Cut into individual ribs or into 3- to 4-rib sections. Sprinkle liberally with the sesame seeds and chopped green onions. Serve extra sauce on the side.

SERVING SUGGESTIONS

I usually serve my Cilantro Slaw (page 187), baked beans, and Herb-Roasted Corn on the Cob (page 253) to accompany these succulent ribs. Provide lots of napkins and moistened hand wipes or finger bowls.

Mustard Steak

The epitome of less is more. A clean, hot grill, USDA prime meat, a couple of simple pantry additions, and you can have one of the world's greatest steaks in minutes. When grilling steaks, try to purchase ones of consistent thickness so they cook evenly. I usually throw some fat slices of Vidalia or Maui onions on the grill with the steaks to arrange on top when they're served.

This mustard paste is also successful on chicken breasts and thighs for the grill or oven.

MAKES 8 SERVINGS

---

40 cloves garlic (about 10 tablespoons)

1 tablespoon Kosher salt

½ cup Dijon or Pommery mustard

1½ teaspoons coarsely ground black pepper

8 (6- to 8-ounce) beef filet mignon or New York strip steaks

2 tablespoons extra-virgin olive oil

Preheat a grill or broiler to medium-high.

Finely mince the garlic by hand on your cutting board. Sprinkle the salt over the minced garlic and dragging/pressing the side of your knife blade across this mixture, grind the garlic into a paste.

Scrape the garlic paste into a small bowl. Add the mustard and pepper and mash to blend.

Brush a little less than half the mustard mixture thinly on both sides of each steak. Drizzle the olive oil on both sides of the steak on top of the mustard mixture and gently spread without removing the mustard.

Grill or broil the steaks for 7 to 8 minutes on the first side. Turn the steaks and spread 1 to 2 tablespoons of the remaining mustard mixture on the top of each steak. Grill for 6 to 7 minutes for medium rare; the meat will feel soft with a little resistance.

TIP

Cleaning the grill: Take a whole lemon and rub its skin vigorously across an already wire-brushed grill rack. This is the easiest way that I know to make the grill "stick free."

SERVING SUGGESTIONS

Serve with Seeded Roast Roots (page 250) and a robust red wine.

Salsiccia all'Uva

This unusual, rustic dish from my friend Susan Kaufman's Serafina restaurant in Seattle, can be mostly prepared in advance. Prepare the sausage sauté (without the grapes) and the polenta ahead of time. To serve, reheat the sausage with the grapes in a 350F (175C) oven. The polenta can also be reheated in the oven.

MAKES 8 SERVINGS

SAUSAGE SAUTÉ

Roasted Balsamic and Honey Onions (page 281)

12 (8-ounce) sweet Italian sausages

6 cups green seedless grapes (pick off stems and wash)

2 cups chicken broth

2 tablespoons minced fresh rosemary

2 tablespoons balsamic vinegar

POLENTA

6 cups chicken broth

2 cups milk

2 cups finely ground polenta or 3 cups coarse cornmeal

1 teaspoon Kosher salt

1 teaspoon freshly ground coarse black pepper

8 tablespoons Gorgonzola cheese

Prepare the Roasted Balsamic and Honey Onions.

Prepare the Sausage Sauté: Slice the sausages in half, on the diagonal. In a large skillet over medium-high heat, brown the sausages. Add the grapes and toss to combine. Reduce the heat to low and add the prepared onions and chicken broth. Simmer until the sausages are cooked, 8 to 10 minutes. Add the rosemary and balsamic vinegar. The grapes should be soft but should not lose their shape.

Prepare the Polenta: In a 3-quart saucepan over medium heat, bring the chicken broth and milk to a boil. Reduce the heat to low. In a stream that you can see through, pour in the polenta or cornmeal, stirring constantly. **(CAUTION: Polenta can splatter, so use a long-handled spoon).** Cook, stirring, until the polenta becomes very thick and starts to pull away from the sides of the saucepan, 10 to 12 minutes. The polenta should be smooth and creamy. If there are any dry lumps, break them up with a whisk and continue. Stir in the salt and pepper. (The polenta can be made one day ahead to this stage and put in a cake pan to cool.)

If you are serving the polenta immediately, it can be spooned onto the plates.

To serve: Divide the polenta among the dinner plates. Sprinkle with the Gorgonzola cheese. Spoon the sausage and grapes over the polenta.

Smoked Salmon and Asparagus Strata

Smoked salmon combines with the herbs and the chevre to give this dish an almost indescribable lusciousness. Herbaceous, slightly smokey, and light as a cloud. I loved this the very first time I made it. It can be assembled the day before the party and then baked, or reheated if already baked, in a low oven. It is beautiful to serve as the golden custard, pink salmon, and bright green asparagus reveal themselves.

MAKES 6 TO 8 BRUNCH SERVINGS

---

1 pound fresh asparagus

1 loaf challah or other egg bread

1 tablespoon unsalted butter

1/2 cup chopped shallots

5 eggs, plus 1 yolk

1 3/4 cups milk

2 cups whipping cream

1 teaspoon Kosher salt

1/2 teaspoon ground white pepper

6 ounces smoked salmon, thinly sliced

1 cup freshly grated Parmesan cheese

2 tablespoons chopped fresh chives

1 1/2 teaspoons chopped fresh dill

1 1/2 teaspoons chopped fresh thyme

Pinch cayenne pepper

1 (5 1/2-ounce) package fresh chevre

1/2 cup grated Gruyère cheese

Preheat the oven to 350F (175C). Butter a 2½- to 3-quart baking dish.

Snap off the woody ends of the asparagus and blanch the tips for 1 to 3 minutes, depending on thickness, in rapidly boiling water. Remove with a strainer and immediately plunge into a bowl of ice water to stop the cooking, set aside to drain. Slice the asparagus lengthwise into halves, and then into 1-inch lengths.

Slice the bread into enough 1-inch-thick pieces to form 2 layers in the baking dish and toast lightly, in the oven or toaster; set aside.

Melt the butter until foamy in a sauté pan over low heat. Add the shallots and sauté until golden, 2 minutes. Remove from heat and set aside.

In a large bowl, combine the eggs, milk, cream, salt, cayenne and white pepper.

Cover the bottom of the baking dish with one layer of the toasted bread. Evenly cover with half of the salmon, half of the asparagus, half of the Parmesan cheese, half of the shallots, half of each of the herbs, and all of the chevre. Cover with the remaining slices of bread, remaining salmon, asparagus, herbs, and shallots. Sprinkle on the remaining Parmesan cheese and the Gruyère cheese. Pour over the egg mixture to within one inch of the top of the dish. Depending on the shape of the baking dish, there may be extra liquid. Let rest, covered, for at least 4 hours or overnight in the refrigerator.

Bake the dish, uncovered, until bubbling and set and a knife inserted in the middle will come out clean, 35 to 40 minutes. Remove from the oven and let rest 10 minutes before serving.

Pappardelle with Feta and Olives

I love the look of these wide, green-flecked ribbons of pasta. If you are going to take the time to make your own fresh pasta I think it's impressive to make an unusual shape like this which clearly states: This is homemade; you can't buy anything like this. *In this recipe, the focus is on the fresh pasta, and not on the sauce.*

MAKES 8 SERVINGS

Basic Pasta Dough (page 313), with 4 teaspoons minced fresh thyme added

½ cup extra-virgin olive oil

2 large sweet onions, thinly sliced

2 teaspoons minced garlic

1 cup pitted, chopped kalamata or niçoise olives

8 ounces feta or chevre, crumbled

½ cup chopped fresh parsley

2 teaspoons minced fresh thyme

½ cup sliced fresh figs, when available

Prepare the pasta dough. When rolling out the dough, stop at setting 6. If you roll the dough out thinner, it will tear around the herb pieces.

Fold up each sheet of dough like ribbon candy to form a flat package. Slice across this package to create 1-inch-wide strips. (At this point, the dough can be frozen for up to 2 weeks. Do not thaw before cooking.)

Heat the olive oil in a large saucepan over medium heat. Add the onions and cook until soft and golden, 5 to 6 minutes. Add the garlic and cook until aromatic, 1 to 2 minutes, and remove from the heat. If the garlic starts to become too dark, pour it into a bowl to cool it off.

Meanwhile, cook the noodles in a large pan of vigorously boiling water until tender, 3 to 5 minutes.

Pour hot water into the serving bowl to warm it. Drain. Drain the noodles and put them in the warmed bowl. Sprinkle with the olives, cheese, parsley, and thyme. Drizzle the garlic oil over everything and use tongs to toss well. Garnish with the figs, if available. Serve immediately.

 **Mushroom Strudel**

I love this strudel because it can be made well in advance and frozen until needed. Its rich texture and flavors make it a satisfying, elegant luncheon with just a crisp green salad and a glass of sherry.

You can use any combination of cremini (Italian brown), morel, or porcini mushrooms that you are lucky enough to find in your market.

MAKES 8 ENTRÉE OR 12 APPETIZER SERVINGS (3 STRUDELS)

½ ounce dried porcini or morels

1½ pounds cremini mushrooms (about 8 cups sliced)

½ cup freshly shredded Parmesan cheese

¾ cup shredded Gruyère cheese

¾ teaspoon freshly grated nutmeg

½ cup chopped fresh Italian parsley

6 tablespoons unsalted butter

1 cup minced shallots or white onion

1½ tablespoons minced garlic

1 tablespoon dry sherry

1 cup walnuts

3 eggs

½ cup whipping cream

1 teaspoon Kosher salt

¾ teaspoon white pepper

1 tablespoon minced fresh thyme

About 24 sheets phyllo dough

3 tablespoons vegetable oil

¾ cup fine bread crumbs

Put the dried mushrooms into a small bowl and cover with warm water to rehydrate. Let sit about 30 minutes. Wash and slice the fresh and soaked, dried mushrooms. Combine the cheeses, nutmeg, and parsley in a bowl.

Melt 4 tablespoons of the butter in a large sauté pan over medium heat until foamy. Add the shallots and garlic and sauté until the shallots are clear, 2 to 3 minutes. Add the fresh and dried mushrooms and sauté until the mushrooms have started to brown and most of the liquid has evaporated from the pan, about 15 minutes. Add the sherry and simmer for 2 minutes. Remove the mushroom mixture to a large bowl and set aside to cool.

Add the remaining 2 tablespoons of butter to the sauté pan. Add the walnuts and sauté, stirring frequently, until toasted, about 3 minutes. Remove from the heat and set aside to cool.

Beat the eggs and cream together lightly with a fork. Add the salt, pepper, and thyme. In a large bowl, combine all ingredients and mix well. Set aside if making the strudels immediately or refrigerate until you are ready to use it.

Preheat the oven to 400F (205C). Line a large baking sheet with parchment paper.

Cover the working surface with a sheet of plastic wrap slightly larger than the phyllo sheets. Lay out one sheet lengthwise, brush it well with the oil, being sure to cover out to the edges.

Lightly sprinkle with some of the bread crumbs. Lay on the next sheet and repeat with the oil and bread crumbs until you have 6 to 7 layers of phyllo sheets.

Divide the filling in thirds; each will equal about 2 cups. On the closest side of the phyllo rectangle, spoon the filling into a log shape, stopping about 2 inches from either edge of the phyllo. Use the plastic wrap to help lift the bottom edge of the pastry to roll it over the filling. Fold over both ends and continue to roll up tightly. Brush the outside with oil. Sprinkle lightly with grated nutmeg. Repeat with remaining filling to create 2 more strudels. (The strudels can be well wrapped and frozen for up to 2 weeks before baking. To bake, place the frozen strudels on a baking sheet. Bake in a preheated oven; the baking time will be slightly longer.)

Place the strudels, seam side down, on the baking sheet. Make 3 to 4 shallow cuts across the top to facilitate cutting when serving.

Bake for about 30 minutes or until golden. Let rest at least 10 minutes before slicing. Serve warm.

VARIATION: CHICKEN LIVER AND MUSHROOM STRUDEL

The addition of sautéed chicken livers gives this dish a lush richness that nicely complements the mushrooms and crispy pastry. Replace the walnuts with ½ cup chicken livers. Add the sherry to the chicken livers instead of to the mushrooms.

After cooking the mushrooms, add 2 tablespoons of butter to the sauté pan and increase the heat to medium-high. Add the chicken livers and a dash of salt and pepper. Sauté, stirring frequently, until cooked through, 5 to 6 minutes. Add the sherry to pan and simmer until the liquid is thick and syrupy.

Remove from the heat and set aside to cool. When cool, chop the livers very finely, incorporating the pan juices. Add to the remaining ingredients.

NOTE:

Fresh phyllo dough is available from the Fillo Factory in New Jersey at 800-OK-FILLO. (See the Gourmet Network, page 317.) If you enjoy making phyllo preparations, their dough is worth the trouble of ordering it. It is much easier to handle than the frozen products available in most national supermarkets.

Quick Risotto Reggiano with Asparagus

This wonderfully easy, luscious risotto was inspired by the risotto technique in Barbara Kafka's Microwave Gourmet. *The already simple preparation (for risotto) can be made even more party-friendly by completing all but the last step before guests arrive. This is the only practical way to include risotto in a party menu.*

MAKES 8 SERVINGS

2 tablespoons unsalted butter

2 tablespoons extra-virgin olive oil

⅓ cup minced shallots

1¼ cups arborio rice

3 cups chicken broth

2 tablespoons chopped dried mushroom (porcini, morel, or shiitake)

⅓ cup dry vermouth

½ pound thin asparagus, cut into 1-inch lengths

1 teaspoon minced fresh thyme

⅓ cup freshly grated Parmigiano-Reggiano cheese

2 tablespoons minced chives

Kosher salt

Freshly ground coarse black pepper

Heat the butter and the oil in a microwave-safe, 3-quart casserole dish, uncovered, for 2 minutes. Add the shallots and cook, uncovered, for 2 minutes. Add the rice and stir to coat with the oil. Cook for 2½ minutes.

Add the broth, dried mushroom, and vermouth and cook uncovered for 11 minutes. Stir well and cook 6 minutes more. Mix in the asparagus and thyme and cook for 5 minutes.

Remove from the microwave and let stand, uncovered, for 5 minutes. Stir in the cheese and chives, add salt and pepper as desired, and serve immediately.

(To make ahead for a party, prepare through cooking with the broth and set aside. When you are ready to serve dinner, add the asparagus and thyme and finish the preparation. Serve immediately.)

Vegetable-Coconut Curry

As far as I'm concerned anything with coconut milk is appealing. This light and easy curry, with lots of aromatic spices, is no exception. Vegetable-Coconut Curry is an exciting solution to a satisfying vegetarian main dish. It can be completed up to one day in advance and gently reheated to serve.

MAKES 8 SERVINGS

1 large russet potato or sweet potato, peeled and cut into small dice

¼ cup clarified butter (page 315)

¼ cup peanut oil

½ teaspoon mustard seeds

½ teaspoon cardamom seeds

4 minced cloves garlic

2 tablespoon minced fresh ginger

1 cup chopped shallots

¼ cup curry powder (see Note on page 240)

½ cup vegetable broth or water

1 red bell pepper, finely sliced

1 cup julienned carrot

½ pound haricot vert or other tender green beans, cut into 2-inch lengths

2 cups cauliflower florets

1 cup chopped fresh pineapple

1 (13½ ounce) can coconut milk

1 (13½ ounce) can reduced-fat coconut milk

2 to 3 serrano chiles, seeded and minced

1 tablespoon Kosher salt

½ cup fresh or frozen green peas

1 cup sliced seedless grapes

½ cup chopped fresh cilantro

Place the potato in a microwave-safe container and cook for 2 minutes. Set aside to cool.

In a heavy 5- to 6-quart pan, heat the clarified butter and peanut oil over medium heat until a light haze forms over it. Add the mustard and cardamom seeds, garlic, and ginger and sauté for 2 minutes. Add the shallots and sauté until soft and golden brown, 12 to 15 minutes. Stir in the curry powder and sauté for 2 to 3 minutes until aromatic. Add the vegetable broth and stir to mix well.

Add the bell pepper, carrot, potato, green beans, cauliflower, and pineapple and toss to coat with the spices. Add the coconut milk, chiles, and salt. Bring to a boil. Cover, reduce heat, and simmer about 15 minutes. If the mixture becomes dry, add water a tablespoon at a time.

Add the peas and grapes and simmer until heated through, 2 to 3 minutes. Garnish with the cilantro.

Serve on cooked basmati rice, topped with chopped fresh cilantro. You could also complement this curry by offering guests toasted almonds or peanuts and a fruit chutney or mango pickle on the side.

NOTE

It is important to use a good quality curry powder, such as Sun brand.

Eggplant Involtini

This richly satisfying, vegetarian dish can be prepared ahead of time except for the final addition of the capers. If you can find extra large capers, usually from Spain, they make a beautiful finishing touch. When fried, they crisp and pop open like little flowers.

MAKES 8 MAIN-DISH SERVINGS OR 24 APPETIZER SERVINGS

EGGPLANT

3 large eggplants

Kosher salt

About ½ cup extra-virgin olive oil

1 cup shaved Parmesan cheese

SAUCE

2 tablespoons extra-virgin olive oil

½ cup sliced shallots

2 tablespoons minced garlic

2 teaspoons dried oregano

1 (28-ounce) can plum tomatoes, drained

1 tablespoon tomato paste

½ teaspoon freshly ground coarse black pepper

1 cup minced fresh basil

FILLING

10 ounces (2½ cups) shredded mozzarella cheese

6 ounces (¾ cup) ricotta cheese

¼ cup dried currants, raisins, or dried cherries

⅔ cup finely chopped fresh mint

½ cup chopped walnuts, toasted (page 315)

GARNISH (OPTIONAL)

2 tablespoons large capers, drained and rinsed

3 tablespoons extra-virgin olive oil

Prepare the eggplants: Cut the eggplants lengthwise into ¼-inch-thick slices; you should have about 24 slices. Sprinkle both sides with salt and layer them in a colander for 1 hour to drain.

Meanwhile, prepare the sauce: Heat the olive oil in a sauté pan over medium heat. Add the shallots, garlic, and oregano. Sauté until the shallots are soft and yellow, 4 to 5 minutes. Add the tomatoes, tomato paste, and pepper and simmer until thickened, 7 to 8 minutes.

Remove from the heat and stir in the basil. Taste for salt and pepper. The sauce can be prepared ahead up to this point and refrigerated for up to 3 days.

Remove the eggplant from the colander, thoroughly rinse off all salt with cold water and press with paper towels to remove any remaining moisture.

Preheat the oven to 325F (165C). Heat 1 tablespoon of the olive oil to almost smoking in a large, heavy-bottomed sauté pan over medium-high heat. Add the eggplant slices, in batches, in one layer and sauté until brown, about 3 minutes. Turn and brown second side, adding additional oil as necessary. Remove to paper towels to drain and continue with next batch.

Prepare the filling: Combine all the ingredients in a medium bowl and mash together with a fork to mix.

Assemble the Involtini: Put 1 tablespoon of filling on the end of each eggplant slice and roll up into a tube. Place rolls, ends down, close together in a shallow, ungreased 13 × 9-inch baking pan. The eggplant rolls can be prepared ahead up to 1 day, tightly wrapped, and refrigerated. (If refrigerated, bring eggplant and sauce to room temperature before combining and baking.)

Ladle the sauce over the eggplant rolls to cover. Bake for 15 minutes. Add the Parmesan cheese, increase the temperature to 400F (205C) and bake for 10 minutes or until bubbling.

Serve 3 rolls per person for an entrée or 1 for an appetizer.

To make the garnish, if using: Completely dry capers on paper towels. Heat the olive oil in a small sauté pan over high heat. Toss the capers into the hot oil and cook until they begin to swell and crisp, about 1 minute. Sprinkle the capers over each serving.

In France old Crainequebille sold leeks from a cart, leeks called "the asparagus
of the poor." Now asparagus sells for the asking, almost, in California markets;
and broccoli, that strong age-old green, leaps from its lowly pot to the Ritz's
copper saucepan.

Who determines, and for what strange reasons, the social status of a veg-
etable?

—M. F. K. Fisher

An innovative cook is frequently revealed in his or her selection of what to serve "on the side." Our current generation of inventive, internationally influenced chefs have proven that an entrée plate doesn't need to be composed of a piece of meat or fish, a starch, and a vegetable—that three-compartment, TV-dinner look. Nestle a grilled chicken breast or rosy, sliced lamb on the colorful White Beans with Proscuitto and Sage for a complete and satisfying winter meal. Complement Ginger Roast Duck Breasts, (page 209) with a mixed grill of hearty portobello mushrooms, delicate Japanese eggplant, and asparagus for a simple, elegant supper. So long as the flavors marry well and the colors are harmonious, there are no hard and fast rules when planning side dishes.

Some of my current favorites to round out the entrée plate are roasted, caramelized vegetables—especially root vegetables such as Seeded Roast Roots. I also find endless ways to use delicious, forgiving polenta—soft and creamy with cheese melted through it, firm and grilled in triangles or stuffed into multicolored peppers and roasted as in Polenta-Stuffed Peppers.

Creamy Chard with Feta

I loved chard, even before all of the hoopla about its health benefits, and this recipe produces a luscious version of the rustic green. The recipe also works well with fresh spinach.

MAKES 8 SERVINGS

6 cups chopped chard (thick stems removed), about 2 bunches

3 tablespoons unsalted butter

¾ cup chopped onion

3 tablespoon all-purpose flour

1 (14½-ounce) can chicken broth

¼ teaspoon ground white pepper

½ cup crumbled feta cheese

Freshly grated nutmeg

Bring a large pot of salted water to a boil. Drop in the chard and simmer gently until tender, 4 to 5 minutes.

Drain into a colander and rinse under cold water. Squeeze out excess water.

In a large sauté pan, melt the butter until foamy. Add the onion and cook until clear. Sprinkle on the flour and cook, stirring, until it thickens into a paste (*roux*), about 2 minutes. Slowly whisk in the broth. Simmer, stirring, until thickened, 2 to 3 minutes.

Add the chard and white pepper and stir to mix. Cook to heat through and blend, 2 to 3 minutes.

Remove from heat, stir in the feta cheese and top with the nutmeg.

Serve immediately.

VARIATION

For a buffet: Preheat the oven to 375F (190C). Mix ½ cup freshly grated Parmesan cheese and ¼ cup bread crumbs. Put completed chard into a buttered casserole dish. Top with the bread crumb mixture and dot with butter. Sprinkle with freshly grated nutmeg. Bake until browned and bubbly, about 25 minutes.

Curried Carrot Mousse

The curry helps this aromatic dish retain a brilliant carroty orange color. It holds very well on a buffet in a chafing dish. It also reheats well if made ahead of time. In any case, garnish with the golden shallots.

MAKES 8 SERVINGS

½ recipe Crispy Shallots (page 281)

6 cups peeled, chopped carrots

1 cup chicken broth

¼ cup unsalted butter

½ cup chopped shallots

½ cup chopped onion

1 tablespoon minced fresh ginger

3 tablespoons dry sherry

⅛ teaspoon freshly grated nutmeg

½ teaspoon curry powder

1 teaspoon Kosher salt

½ teaspoon freshly grated coarse black pepper

⅔ cup heavy cream

Prepare the Crispy Shallots up to 3 days ahead and store in an airtight container. If made ahead, warm in a 300F (150C) oven before using.

Combine the carrots, chicken broth, and enough water to cover in a saucepan. Cover and simmer over medium heat until carrots are tender, 20 to 25 minutes. Remove from the heat and let cool in the liquid. Drain the carrots, reserving the cooking liquid.

Melt the butter in a saucepan over medium heat. Add the shallots and onion and sauté until the onion is clear, about 3 minutes. Add the ginger and sauté until aromatic, 1 to 2 minutes.

Add the sherry and let simmer 2 minutes. Add the carrots, nutmeg, curry powder, salt, and pepper. Simmer 5 minutes. Add ⅓ to ½ cup of the reserved cooking liquid and the cream. Use an immersion blender to puree or when cool enough to handle, puree the carrot mixture in a food processor.

Serve immediately and garnish with the Crispy Shallots.

Green on Green

A combination of bright green vegetables dressed with luscious green Artichoke Pesto brightens any table. Lightly steam a combination of at least three of either the sugar snap peas, asparagus, snow peas, shelled peas, or green beans plus the green onions.

MAKES 6 TO 8 SERVINGS

1 pound sugar snap peas, sliced on the diagonal

1 pound asparagus, trimmed

½ pound snow peas, trimmed

¾ pound shelled fresh green peas

1 pound small green beans, cut on the diagonal into 2-inch lengths

1 bunch green onions, trimmed and cut in 2-inch lengths

½ to ¾ cup Artichoke Pesto (page 276)

1 bunch chives, cut into 3-inch lengths, chive blossoms, or nasturtiums, for garnish

Choose 3 of the vegetables plus the green onions. Steam each vegetable separately until crisp-tender. Combine in a large bowl and drizzle on the Artichoke Pesto; toss to combine. Top each serving with some chive pieces.

Potato Latkes

This potato latke (pancake) recipe comes from my husband's mother. She died before we could meet but her reputation as a formidable Jewish cook, along with a number of her recipes, has survived intact.

MAKES 8 SERVINGS

About 2 pounds russet potatoes

1 egg plus 1 yolk, beaten

½ teaspoon Kosher salt

Freshly ground coarse black pepper

2 to 3 tablespoons matzo meal

1½ cups peanut or vegetable oil for frying

Sour cream and caviar or applesauce, to serve

Wash the potatoes (and peel if desired, I don't) and cut into chunks. Put the potatoes in a large bowl of cold water to draw out the starch and let stand 20 to 30 minutes.

Use the grater on your food processor if you have one. Drain the potatoes, pat dry, and put through the food tube of the food processor to create a fine shred. You can also grate the potatoes by hand with the large openings on a regular box grater/shredder.

Transfer the potatoes to a colander and let drain for about 10 minutes to remove the excess potato liquor. Transfer the grated potatoes to a large bowl, add the egg, salt, and pepper, and toss with a fork to mix. Sprinkle the matzo meal over the potatoes, a spoonful at a time. Mix to incorporate, until the mixture is dry enough to hold together.

Heat the oil in a heavy cast-iron skillet over high heat or in an electric frying pan to about 350F (175C). The oil should be at least 1½ inches deep. Use a slotted spoon and a fork, or two forks, pressing together, to drain about 1 tablespoon of the mixture at a time and immediately slip into the hot oil. Don't overcrowd the pan. Use tongs or a spatula to turn the latkes over to brown evenly, about 2 minutes per side. Transfer to a baking sheet lined with paper towels. The pancakes can be served immediately or held in a warm 325F (165C) oven, layered with paper towels, for up to 45 minutes.

Serve warm with a dollop of sour cream and caviar.

SERVING SUGGESTIONS

Once I became enamored of these latkes, I couldn't resist meddling (as my husband described it) with the basic recipe to create variations; see the recipe for Sweet Potato, Chives, and Orange Latkes (page 247). A combination of these different flavors, each made in a silver-dollar size, with a variety of toppings makes wonderful hors d'oeuvres to display on a buffet or tray pass.

Sweet Potato, Chives, and Orange Latkes

The natural sweetness of the sweet potato is enhanced by the frying process and complemented by the orange and nutmeg.

MAKES 8 SERVINGS

3 cups grated orange sweet potatoes (sometimes called garnet yams)

⅓ cup chopped fresh chives

1 teaspoon minced garlic

1 tablespoon chopped fresh thyme

2 tablespoons grated orange zest

2 good pinches freshly grated nutmeg

1 egg and 1 egg yolk, slightly beaten

½ teaspoon Kosher salt

½ teaspoon freshly ground coarse black pepper

3 tablespoons fine cornmeal

1½ cups peanut or vegetable oil

½ cup sour cream

1 tablespoon honey

Thyme leaves, to garnish

Add the sweet potatoes, chives, garlic, thyme, orange zest, and nutmeg to a large bowl. Add the beaten egg mixture, salt, and pepper and toss with a fork to mix. Sprinkle the cornmeal over the sweet potato mixture, a spoonful at a time. Mix to incorporate until the mixture is dry enough to hold together.

Heat the oil and cook the latkes as directed on page 246.

Cook as for Potato Latkes (page 246).

Combine the sour cream and honey. Serve the latkes with a dollop of the sour cream mixture and garnish with a thyme leaf.

Leek and Mushroom Tarte

This crisp rectangular tarte is beautiful, elegant, and earthy. It makes an excellent first course before a light meal. It is also appealing on a buffet as a vegetable side dish.

MAKES 4 APPETIZER OR 8 SIDE DISH SERVINGS

---

1 (17 ½-ounce) frozen package puff pastry, thawed

2 eggs

4 tablespoons unsalted butter

½ cup minced shallots

3 tablespoons minced garlic

1 ½ cups sliced cremini mushrooms

1 tablespoon Madeira

4 leeks, thinly sliced

½ cup chicken broth

1 ½ teaspoons minced fresh rosemary

1 tablespoon grated lemon zest

Kosher salt

Freshly ground coarse black pepper

½ cup freshly grated Parmesan cheese mixed with 2 tablespoons dry bread crumbs

Preheat the oven to 400F (205C). Roll each sheet of pastry out to a 12 × 10-inch rectangle. Cut 4 (1-inch-wide) strips from 1 sheet. Brush the edges of the remaining sheet with cold water and lay on the strips to form a rim. Trim as necessary at the corners. Press to adhere.

Beat 1 egg lightly with a fork. Brush the whole sheet and frame with the egg wash. Prick the bottom of the pastry with a fork. Place on an ungreased baking sheet. Bake until golden and puffed, about 7 minutes. Set aside to cool.

Melt 2 tablespoons of the butter in a sauté pan over medium heat. Add the shallots and garlic and sauté until soft, about 5 minutes. Add the mushrooms and sauté until all moisture is released, about 10 minutes. Deglaze pan with the Madeira. Remove from the heat.

Melt the remaining butter in a sauté pan over medium heat. Add the leeks and sauté until soft, about 10 minutes. Add the chicken broth and simmer until liquid is mostly evaporated. Stir in the rosemary, lemon zest, salt, and pepper. Remove from the heat.

Lightly beat the remaining egg in a bowl and add the mushroom and leek mixtures. Toss to mix.

Pour the egg mixture into the prebaked crust and spread to cover the bottom. Sprinkle with the Parmesan cheese mixture. Bake for 15 minutes, until filling is set. Cut into pieces and serve immediately.

Polenta-Stuffed Peppers

I like to prepare this with a combination of green poblano chiles and red, yellow, and orange bell peppers. Especially on a fall buffet, the contrasting colors make a beautiful presentation. I also serve this as an entrée.

MAKES 8 TO 10 SERVINGS

---

4 red or yellow bell peppers, large poblano chiles, or a combination

1 tablespoon unsalted butter

½ cup minced onion

1½ tablespoons minced garlic

1 cup coarse cornmeal or polenta

3½ cups chicken broth

½ cup heavy cream

¾ cup fresh or canned, drained corn kernels

⅓ cup chopped fresh basil

⅓ cup chopped fresh cilantro

¾ teaspoons Kosher salt

½ cup freshly grated Parmesan cheese

½ cup shredded Gruyère cheese

Cut the tops off the bell peppers and remove the seeds and ribs. Slice each chile in half from stem end to blossom end. Arrange in a shallow, buttered baking dish.

Melt the butter in a saucepan over medium heat. Add the onion and garlic and cook until the onion softens, 3 to 4 minutes. Add the cornmeal and stir to mix. Slowly pour in the chicken broth, stirring to combine. Add the cream, corn, basil, cilantro, salt, and ¼ cup of the Parmesan cheese. Cook, stirring constantly with a wooden spoon, until the polenta becomes as thick as gruel, about 10 minutes. Remove from heat.

Meanwhile, preheat the oven to 375F (190C). Fill the bell peppers with the polenta. Sprinkle with the remaining Parmesan cheese and the Gruyère cheese. Bake for 20 to 25 minutes, until golden and bubbling. Serve hot. (The peppers can be stuffed and baked the preceding day. To serve, bring to room temperature and reheat at 350F (175C) for about 12 minutes.)

Seeded Roast Roots

This wonderfully simple recipe produces a delicious, satisfying, and slightly exotic version of the ubiquitous potato. This can be held warm in the oven or on a buffet with no problem.

MAKES 8 SERVINGS

3 pounds russet potatoes

1 pound orange sweet potatoes (sometimes called garnet yams)

3 medium red onions

3 heads garlic

¼ cup extra-virgin olive oil

2 tablespoons fresh lemon juice

¾ teaspoon ground cumin

¼ teaspoon cayenne pepper

3½ tablespoons sesame seeds

1½ tablespoons mustard seeds

1½ tablespoons cumin seeds

1 teaspoon Kosher salt

Freshly ground coarse black pepper

Preheat the oven to 425F (220C). Oil 2 sheet pans. Cut the unpeeled potatoes into 1-inch chunks. Peel the onion, but leave the root. Cut the onion into 1-inch wedges through the root end. Separate the garlic into cloves.

Mix the olive oil, lemon juice, cumin, and cayenne in a large bowl. Add the potatoes and onion and toss to coat.

Using a slotted spoon, transfer the vegetables to the oiled pans; do not crowd the vegetables or they will not brown well. Reserve the remaining oil mixture. Toss the unpeeled garlic in the reserved oil mixture.

Roast the potatoes and onion for 30 minutes, turning occasionally, then scatter the oiled garlic over the vegetables. Roast for 20 to 25 minutes more, until all the vegetables are golden.

Heat a small sauté pan over medium-high heat. Add the seeds and move them rapidly around the pan until they begin to "pop," about 1 minute. Remove from heat. Combine the seeds and the salt.

Remove the vegetables from the oven and use your fingers to slip the skins off the garlic cloves. Sprinkle everything with the salt and seeds mixture and season with black pepper. Serve immediately.

Spinach in Black Bean Sauce

This simple preparation has always been a favorite of my clients, served with the Barbecued Pork Ribs (page 231).

MAKES 8 SERVINGS

4 bunches fresh spinach

¼ cup peanut oil

1 cup finely sliced red bell pepper

¼ cup minced garlic

3 tablespoons black bean sauce

2 tablespoons fresh lemon juice

4 teaspoons dark sesame oil

¼ cup minced green onions

½ teaspoon white pepper

2 tablespoons toasted sesame seeds

Remove any thick stems from the spinach and wash well. Thoroughly dry the spinach in a salad spinner or on paper towels.

Put the peanut oil in a wok or large sauté pan over high heat and heat almost to smoking. Add the bell peppers and garlic and stir-fry, until peppers are softened, without burning the garlic, 2 to 3 minutes.

Add the spinach, in batches, to the hot pan and toss rapidly, using 2 large spoons or tongs, until wilted, about 1 minute.

Reduce the heat to medium and stir in the black bean sauce, lemon juice, sesame oil, green onions, and white pepper.

Heat through, 1 to 2 minutes and serve topped with the sesame seeds. (This can be prepared ahead of time and refrigerated for up to 1 day. To serve, gently reheat on the stovetop or in the microwave, then top with the sesame seeds.)

White Beans with Prosciutto and Sage

Excellent as a first course for a Mediterranean lamb supper or an easy-to-pack side dish for a picnic menu. This dish is equally good served warm or at room temperature.

MAKES 8 SERVINGS

1 (1-pound) package dried Great Northern white beans (see Variation on page 253)

1⅓ cups chicken broth

1 bay leaf

2 medium leeks

2 ounces thinly sliced prosciutto

3 tablespoons minced fresh garlic

¼ cup extra-virgin olive oil

2 tablespoons chopped fresh sage

½ teaspoon dried rosemary

2 tablespoons fresh lemon juice

Kosher salt

Freshly ground coarse black pepper

GARNISH

2 bunches of sage

½ cup diced red bell pepper

Sort through the beans for rocks and discolored beans. Follow the cooking directions on the package, but replace 1 cup of water with 1 cup of chicken broth and add the bay leaf. Simmer, uncovered, until tender but not falling apart, about 1½ hours. Drain the beans in a colander and rinse with cold water. Put beans in a large bowl.

Trim off the root and all but 1 inch of the dark green end from the leeks. Slice an X lengthwise in each leek, from the root end to within 1 inch of the dark green end. Loosen the layers, submerge in a bowl of cold water, and slosh vigorously to rinse out the silt that lodges between the layers.

Put the rinsed leeks in a microwave-safe dish with the remaining ⅓ cup of chicken broth. Cover with plastic wrap and cook on high 4 to 5 minutes, until tender when pierced with a knife tip. Drain the leeks and reserve the chicken stock.

Cut the prosciutto lengthwise into very narrow ribbons.

Cut the leeks into ⅛-inch-thick rounds. Sauté the garlic and leeks in the olive oil in a sauté pan over low heat, until the garlic is soft and clear, 3 to 4 minutes. Add the chopped sage, rosemary, and the reserved chicken broth and simmer until reduced slightly, 3 to 4 minutes. Remove from the heat and stir in the prosciutto and lemon juice. Add the leek mixture to the beans and toss carefully with a wooden spoon. Season with salt and black pepper.

Serve garnished with sage sprigs and bell pepper. (The salad may be refrigerated up to 24 hours. Bring back to room temperature and garnish before serving.)

VARIATION

Substitute 3 (15-ounce) cans cannellini beans, rinsed and drained, for the dried Great Northern white beans. Warm in the microwave on high for 2½ to 3 minutes before adding to the warm vegetables. Omit the bay leaf and 1 cup of chicken broth.

Herb-Roasted Corn on the Cob

A delicious, easy side dish for any party casual enough to allow for eating with your hands. It is important to purchase unshucked corn for this preparation. Leftover roasted kernels, cut from the cob, provide an exceptionally flavorful ingredient for salads, sauces, and salsas.

MAKES 8 SERVINGS

2 tablespoons freshly ground coarse black pepper

5 tablespoons minced fresh basil, cilantro, thyme, tarragon, or chives, or a combination

8 ears yellow or white corn with husks

1 tablespoon extra-virgin olive oil

Preheat the oven to 400F (205C) or a grill to medium-hot.

In a small bowl, combine the pepper and the herbs.

Loosen the husks and pull them down without detaching them from the stem end of the corn. Pull away and discard as much of the silk as possible. Using a pastry brush, lightly coat each cob with the olive oil. (If you have natural olive oil spray, lightly spray each ear.) Liberally sprinkle each ear with the pepper/herb mixture, pressing to the oil. Pull the husks back up to encase the corn and tie securely at the top with kitchen twine.

Use a plant mister, or your hand, to lightly moisten the husks with water.

Put the ears directly on the middle rack of the oven or on the grill. Cook for 15 to 20 minutes, rotating once or twice with tongs. Remove from the heat and serve immediately or let cool for use in other recipes.

Sebastian's Green Corn on the Cob

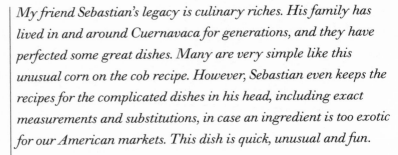

My friend Sebastian's legacy is culinary riches. His family has lived in and around Cuernavaca for generations, and they have perfected some great dishes. Many are very simple like this unusual corn on the cob recipe. However, Sebastian even keeps the recipes for the complicated dishes in his head, including exact measurements and substitutions, in case an ingredient is too exotic for our American markets. This dish is quick, unusual and fun.

MAKES 8 SERVINGS

2 serrano chiles

4 fresh tomatillos

1 cup mashed avocado (1 to 2 avocados)

1 teaspoon fresh lime juice

4 cloves garlic, peeled

½ teaspoon ground coriander

8 ears white corn, husk removed

½ cup freshly grated Parmesan cheese

½ cup chopped pepitas (shelled pumpkin seeds), toasted (page 315)

Roast chiles and peel (see instructions page 315). Remove the papery husks from the tomatillos and roughly chop. Using a fork, mix the avocado with the lime juice.

Put the tomatillos, roasted chiles, garlic, and coriander in the blender and blend until pureed. Pour into a bowl and stir in the avocado.

Boil the corn in lightly salted water until tender, 3 to 4 minutes. Stick corn holders in each ear and use to hold them while you brush the avocado mixture in a thin coating all over each ear.

Sprinkle the Parmesan cheese and pepitas on the corn. Serve immediately.

Pear and Potato Gratin with Horseradish

This is the perfect starch with beef or pork or roast duck. A potato gratin is always a richly satisfying dish; the elegant addition of pears and horseradish makes this one a little different.

MAKES 8 SERVINGS

1 tablespoon chopped fresh thyme

½ teaspoon Kosher salt

½ teaspoon ground white pepper

2 cloves garlic, minced

3 tablespoons grated fresh or prepared horseradish

1 cup half-and-half

2½ pounds Yukon gold or other boiling potato

3 (about 1½ pounds) Bosc or other firm, ripe pear

2½ cups milk

Kosher salt

Freshly ground coarse black pepper

1½ cups (6 ounces) shredded Gruyère cheese

2 tablespoons unsalted butter

⅓ cup freshly grated Parmesan cheese

Add the thyme, salt, white pepper, garlic, and horseradish to the half-and-half; set aside. (If using bottled horseradish, rinse and drain before measuring.)

Peel the potatoes and slice into about ¼-inch-thick slices.

Put the milk into a large saucepan and bring to a rolling boil over medium heat. Add the potatoes. If the milk doesn't cover the potatoes, add additional milk to cover. Simmer 10 to 15 minutes, adjusting the heat if necessary to keep the milk from boiling over. Simmer until the potatoes are easily pierced with a knife tip but still firm. Drain the potato slices in a colander, discarding the milk. Cool slightly.

Preheat the oven to 350F (175C). Peel the pears and remove the cores. Slice the pears into about ¼-inch-thick slices; it is important that the pears and potatoes be the same thickness.

Butter a 13 × 9-inch baking pan. Layer half of the potatoes in the baking pan. Season with salt and pepper. Layer the pears over the potatoes. Sprinkle with half of the Gruyère cheese. Dot with 1 tablespoon of the butter. Pour half of the half-and-half mixture over the pears. Add the remaining potatoes. Season with salt and pepper. Sprinkle with the remaining Gruyère cheese and pour the remaining half-and-half mixture over everything. Press the ingredients into the half-and-half. The top must be below the rim of the pan. Cover well with a lid or foil. (The dish can be covered and refrigerated for up to 24 hours.)

To cook: Bake for 45 minutes or until bubbling. Uncover, sprinkle on the Parmesan cheese, and dot with the remaining 1 tablespoon butter. Bake until browned, about 12 minutes. Let rest 10 minutes before cutting to serve.

Classic Mashed Potatoes

Mashed potatoes are more popular than ever. Some of the country's most exciting chefs serve mashed potatoes as the backdrop for everything from honey-seared duck breast to poached turbot wrapped in leeks, or, in the foreground, glorified with grilled lobster and filet mignon. Mashed potatoes with roast garlic, celery root, or truffle oil have recently added glamour to their already solid place in our hearts. Serve them at the most elegant occasion, and you will both impress and charm your guests.

MAKES 8 SERVINGS

---

4 pounds medium russet potatoes

5 to 8 tablespoons unsalted butter, softened

¾ cup heavy cream or milk

1 teaspoon Kosher salt

¼ teaspoon ground white or black pepper

Scrub the potatoes and stick all over with a knife. Put them in the microwave and cook on high for 10 minutes; turn the potatoes. Cook 5 to 10 minutes more, until the potatoes are tender without being mushy, a sharp knife should slip in easily.

Cool the potatoes enough to handle and peel. Cut the potatoes into a rough dice and put in the bowl of an electric mixer (see Tip on page 257). Beating on low speed, add 5 tablespoons of butter, 1 tablespoon at a time, and beat to incorporate.

Warm the cream in the microwave on high for 20 seconds. Beating on low speed, slowly add the warm cream. Add the remaining 3 tablespoons butter if you prefer a more buttery flavor. Season with salt and pepper.

Serve the mashed potatoes immediately or keep warm in a tightly covered, buttered casserole in a 200F (95C) oven for up to 1 hour.

(To hold until the next day; cool the potatoes slightly, cover tightly with plastic wrap, and refrigerate. To reheat: About an hour before serving, remove potatoes from the refrigerator. Brush the top with melted butter and add 1 tablespoon of cream or milk. Cover with a paper towel and heat in the microwave on high for 45 to 60 seconds. Remove towel and stir to blend. Replace paper towel and heat for 20 to 30 seconds to finish heating through.

TIP

If you prefer very smooth mashed potatoes (no lumps), put them through a ricer, or press through a strainer, before putting into the mixer bowl.

VARIATION

Roasted Garlic Mashed Potatoes with Crispy Shallots

Crispy Shallots (page 281)
24 cloves garlic, unpeeled

1 tablespoon extra-virgin olive oil
Classic Mashed Potatoes

Prepare the Crispy Shallots up to 3 days ahead and store in an airtight container. If made ahead, rewarm in a 300F (150C) oven before using.

Preheat the oven to 325F (165C). Toss the garlic cloves with olive oil to coat. Spread out on a baking sheet and roast for 15 to 20 minutes, until soft and golden. Slip the paper skins off the garlic. Puree the roasted garlic with the cream in a blender or food processor and use it instead of plain cream in the basic potato recipe. Top each serving with Crispy Shallots.

Mashed Mapled Sweet Potatoes with Glazed Nuts

Topped with maple-glazed nuts, this is especially great with game and turkey.

MAKES 8 SERVINGS

2 pounds orange sweet potatoes (sometimes called garnet yams)

2 pounds russet potatoes

5 to 8 tablespoons unsalted butter, softened

¾ cup heavy cream or milk

2 tablespoons pure maple syrup

1 teaspoon minced fresh thyme

1 teaspoon Kosher salt

¼ teaspoon ground white or black pepper

GLAZED NUTS

1 tablespoon butter

½ cup pecan pieces

¼ cup pine nuts

1 tablespoon pure maple syrup

½ teaspoon Kosher salt

Freshly ground coarse black pepper

Scrub the potatoes and stick all over with a knife. Put them in the microwave and cook on high for 10 minutes; turn the potatoes. Cook 5 to 10 minutes more, until the potatoes are tender without being mushy, a sharp knife should slip in easily.

Cool the potatoes enough to handle and peel. Cut the potatoes into a rough dice and put in the bowl of an electric mixer.

Beating on low speed, add the butter, 1 tablespoon at a time, and beat to incorporate.

Warm the cream in the microwave on high for 20 seconds. Beating on low speed, slowly add the warm cream. Add the maple syrup, thyme, salt, and pepper.

Serve the mashed potatoes immediately or keep warm in a tightly covered, buttered casserole in a 200F (95C) oven for up to 1 hour.

(To hold until the next day; cool the potatoes slightly, cover tightly with plastic wrap, and refrigerate. To reheat: About an hour before serving, remove potatoes from the refrigerator. Brush the top with melted butter and add 1 tablespoon of cream or milk. Cover with a paper towel and heat in the microwave on high for about 5 minutes. Remove towel and stir to blend. Replace paper towel and heat for about 2 minutes or until hot.)

Prepare the Glazed Nuts: Melt the butter in sauté pan over medium heat until foaming. Add the nuts, toss to coat, and sauté for 1 to 2 minutes, moving the pan rapidly. Reduce the heat to medium-low, add the maple syrup, salt, and pepper. Cook, stirring, until the nuts are glazed, 1 to 2 minutes. Use immediately or cool on a baking sheet.

Top each serving with the Glazed Nuts.

Deberah's Quick Orange Rice

This is a simple wonderful recipe. It meets all of the entertaining criteria: delicious, pretty, easy, and it can be made ahead. I like it with the mint or green onions sprinkled on top. The addition of carrots or snow peas makes it into more of a complete side dish. I have even added shrimp, chicken, and sliced vegetables to use this as the basis for a great, quick stir-fried entrée.

MAKES 4 TO 6 SERVINGS

1 cup uncooked basmati rice

2 cups fresh orange juice

1 tablespoon grated orange zest

¾ cup blanched julienned carrot or snow peas

Kosher salt

Freshly ground coarse black pepper

2 tablespoons chopped fresh mint or green onion

Cook the rice according to package directions, replacing the water with the orange juice, about 20 minutes. Remove from the heat and stir in the orange zest and carrot, fluff with a fork, and season with salt and pepper. Sprinkle with the mint and serve. (The rice can be prepared a day ahead and refrigerated. Heat, covered, in a low oven for about 20 minutes.)

Caribbean Rice

I have made this dish, with some variation, for over twenty-five years. It is a satisfying vegetarian entrée and a great complement to curries, saté, and grilled fish. For buffets I like to serve it on a platter lined with banana leaves.

MAKES 8 SERVINGS

1½ cups uncooked basmati or jasmine rice

2 tablespoons peanut oil

2 tablespoons unsalted butter

1 teaspoon ground cinnamon

1 teaspoon curry powder

¼ teaspoon saffron threads

¼ teaspoon ground cardamom

2 tablespoons slivered fresh ginger

1½ cups finely sliced red onions

1 teaspoon minced serrano chile (optional)

1½ cups diced firm bananas

Kosher salt

Freshly ground coarse black pepper

½ cup peanuts, toasted (page 315)

3 tablespoons minced fresh cilantro

Cook the rice according to package directions, about 20 minutes. Remove from the heat and let stand, covered, for 5 minutes.

Meanwhile, heat the oil and butter in a large sauté pan over medium heat. Add the cinnamon, curry powder, saffron, cardamom, and ginger and cook for about 2 minutes. Add the onions and sauté until the onions are softened. Add the chile if desired. Add the bananas and sauté just until heated through; do not overcook or the bananas will fall apart. Season with salt and pepper; set aside.

Toss the rice with the banana mixture. Taste for salt and pepper. (The rice dish can be prepared a day ahead and refrigerated. Heat, covered, in a low oven for about 20 minutes.)

To serve: Top with the peanuts and cilantro.

Aromatic Basmati Pilaf

This simple pilaf perfumes the whole house as it cooks. I have served it to oohs and aahs with Tandoori-Flavored Chicken (page 206), and Skewered Lamb Ruffles with Almond Mint Pesto (page 219). It would be equally satisfying with a simple grilled fish.

MAKES 8 SERVINGS

2 tablespoons vegetable oil

1 tablespoon unsalted butter

1 large stick cinnamon

2 whole cloves

¾ cup minced onion

½ teaspoon ground cardamom

2 cups uncooked basmati rice

1 cup water

2 cups chicken broth

¼ cup seedless raisins or chopped dates

½ teaspoon salt

1 tablespoon grated orange zest

¼ cup unsalted pistachios, toasted (page 315)

Heat the oil and butter in a 3-quart Dutch oven over high heat. Add the cinnamon and cloves and cook, stirring, until the cinnamon stick puffs up, 1 to 2 minutes. Reduce the heat and add the onion and cardamom and sauté until the onion is clear, about 3 minutes. Stir in the rice and mix to coat all the grains with the other ingredients. Cook until it begins to be aromatic, 1 to 2 minutes.

Add the water, chicken broth, raisins, salt, and orange zest and bring to a boil. Reduce the heat to low and cover tightly. Simmer until all of the liquid has been absorbed, 13 to 15 minutes. Remove from heat and let stand, covered, for 10 minutes to allow the rice grains to stabilize.

Uncover and fluff with a fork before serving. Remove the cinnamon stick and cloves. (The rice can be held, covered, before serving in a lightly oiled casserole or serving dish in a 200F (95C) low oven for up to 30 minutes. The pilaf can also be reheated in the microwave.)

Garnish with the pistachios before serving.

Grilled Vegetables with Balsamic Vinaigrette

This very popular preparation makes a beautiful do-ahead platter for a buffet, garnished with fresh thyme sprigs and pine nuts. These vegetables are also a wonderful side dish on an entrée plate or as a pizza topping. The recipe may appear complicated, but most of the instructions are teaching the technique. When you have followed the directions once or twice, you will easily proceed with your own variations.

MAKES 8 TO 14 SERVINGS

MARINADE

4 teaspoons chopped fresh thyme

3 cups canola oil

6 cloves garlic, minced

1 teaspoon freshly ground coarse black pepper

2 teaspoons Kosher salt

Balsamic Vinaigrette (page 197)

VEGETABLES

1 ¼ pounds orange sweet potatoes (sometimes called garnet yams)

2 pounds eggplant (globe or Japanese)

1 pound red bell peppers

1 ¼ pounds carrots

1 ¼ pounds zucchini

2 bunches green onions

8 ounces portobello mushrooms

Prepare the marinade: Combine all the ingredients in a small bowl and whisk thoroughly. Set aside. (This can be made up to 48 hours in advance and kept refrigerated. The flavors blend and improve with time.)

Prepare the Balsamic Vinaigrette at least the day before using, cover and refrigerate; it will keep for up to 1 week.

Prepare the vegetables: First scrub the sweet potatoes, then cut into either ¼-inch-thick rounds or long slices.

Slice the eggplant into ¾-inch-thick rounds. Core the bell peppers and cut each lengthwise into 6 wide spears. Scrub the carrots and cut on the diagonal into about ½-inch-thick slices. Wash and slice the zucchini into ¾-inch-thick rounds. Trim the root end off the green onions, then rinse and trim the green tops to a 4- to 5-inch length.

The mushrooms can be wiped clean with a dry towel and left whole, unless they are over 3 inches in diameter; cut large mushrooms in half through the stem.

Put the raw, cut vegetables into a large flat dish with room for the marinade. Cover the vegetables with the marinade and loosely cover the dish with plastic wrap. Marinate for 1 to 3 hours, basting with the marinade occasionally to keep the vegetables moist. The more time the vegetables are in the marinade, the more flavors will come out in the finished dish.

Preheat the oven to 375F (190C). Preheat the grill. (The grill must be very hot and very clean. Scrape with a wire brush, if necessary, and spray the grill with nonstick cooking spray before you begin grilling.) If there are especially wide openings on your grill, place a cake cooling rack on the grill as a screen to keep small pieces from falling through.

To cook the vegetables: About 1 hour before grilling the rest of the vegetables, put the sweet potato slices on the hot grill and cook, turning once, until there are brown grill marks on both sides. They will still be hard in the middle. Lay the sweet potato slices on a greased sheet pan and cover with foil. Bake for about 40 minutes or until soft when pierced with a fork, but not falling apart. Remove from the oven and add to the other grilled vegetables.

When the sweet potatoes have been in the oven about 20 minutes, start to grill the other vegetables. Grill all of each kind of vegetable separately, as they cook at different rates. Make sure that you have tongs or a long-handled spatula ready, because there is a lot of checking and turning required for these fast-cooking pieces.

Begin with the carrots because they take the longest to cook, about 10 minutes, and retain heat well. The eggplant should be done next; it cooks in 5 to 6 minutes. Then add a combination of the zucchini, green onions, and bell pepper. The mushrooms should go on last and will finish in about 2 minutes per side. Grill each vegetable just long enough to color and soften without drying it out. As they are removed from the grill, place the vegetables on a serving platter or baking sheet and tent with foil.

The vegetables can be served immediately, drizzled with the vinaigrette, as individual warm salads, as a side dish to accompany an entrée, or as a very satisfying vegetarian entrée over steamed rice.

To serve as a cold salad, store the grilled, wrapped vegetables in the refrigerator for up to 24 hours. Serve the vegetables on a bed of field greens or torn spinach, with a pitcher of the vinaigrette on the side.

Easy Make-Ahead Steps for the Grilled Vegetables
- **Prepare the marinade and vinaigrette up to several days ahead.**
- **Cut up the vegetables and marinate for 1 to 3 hours.**

- Preheat the oven and grill.

- Quick grill the sweet potatoes and bake for 40 minutes or until done.

- Grill remaining vegetables.

- Serve warm, topped with vinaigrette, or wrap and refrigerate for service the next day.

Garlic Flans

A delicate cloud of garlic-scented custard makes a delicious surprise in my traditional Onion Soup with Garlic Flans (page 175). It's also fun as a side dish with a tempura supper.

MAKES 24 MINI FLANS

2 cups heavy cream

8 large cloves garlic, minced

8 large egg yolks

⅓ cup freshly grated Parmesan cheese

¼ teaspoon Kosher salt

Freshly ground coarse black pepper

Generous pinch freshly ground nutmeg

Preheat the oven to 325F (165C). Spray 24 mini muffin cups (1 or 2 pans) with vegetable spray.

In a small saucepan, bring the cream and garlic to a simmer over low heat. Remove from heat and let stand 5 minutes.

In a bowl, whisk together the egg yolks, Parmesan cheese, salt, pepper, and nutmeg.

Strain the cream into the egg yolk mixture, whisking constantly. Pour into the muffin cups. Place the muffin pan in a flat roasting pan. Add enough water to reach halfway up the muffin pan.

Bake for 25 to 27 minutes, until the flans are golden and set. Remove the muffin pan from the water bath and cool the flans before unmolding.

Grandma Morgan's Thanksgiving Stuffing

This is basically the same turkey dressing that my mother's mother made. I have added the chestnuts and dried cherries because my husband loved them. The crunch of the nuts, the juicy apples, and the earthy herbs conspire to evoke holiday memories for me of the great Thanksgiving dinners that my grandma turned out every year.

MAKES 10 TO 12 SERVINGS

About 15 large chestnuts

4 tablespoons unsalted butter

3 cups chopped yellow onions (about 3 large)

2 cups chopped celery

1 tablespoon minced garlic

6 slices thick-cut bacon

1½ cups chopped green apples

2 cups cubed baked russet potatoes

1 cup hazelnuts, toasted (see 315)

1 cup dried cherries

6 cups cornbread cubes

2 tablespoons dry sage

2 teaspoons minced fresh thyme

1 teaspoon ground white pepper

½ cup Madeira

1 to 1½ cups low-sodium chicken broth

Kosher salt

Preheat the oven to 400F (205C). Cut an X in the flat side of each chestnut, place on a baking sheet, and roast for 25 to 35 minutes, depending on their size, until tender when pierced with the tip of a knife. Cool and peel; set aside.

Melt 2 tablespoons of the butter in a large skillet over medium heat. Add the onions, celery, and garlic and sauté 4 to 5 minutes until the onions are soft. Using a slotted spoon, remove the vegetables to a large bowl.

Roughly chop the bacon and add to the same pan and sauté for 6 to 7 minutes. Add the apples to the pan and sauté until the bacon is fully cooked, 3 to 4 minutes. Remove the bacon and apples with a slotted spoon to the bowl with the vegetables; let stand until cooled.

Add the chestnuts, potatoes, hazelnuts, cherries, cornbread, herbs, and pepper to the vegetables and toss to mix well.

Melt the remaining 2 tablespoons of butter. Drizzle the Madeira, melted butter, and some of the broth over the mixture and toss to combine. The stuffing should be moist but not gooey or mushy. It will pick up a great deal of moisture from the cavity of the turkey during cooking. If it is too wet now, your finished dressing will be sodden. Salt for taste. (The dressing can be covered and refrigerated at this point up to 24 hours before using in the bird.)

Sauces, Relishes, and Condiments

I believe that if ever I had to practice cannibalism, I might manage if there were enough tarragon around.

—Attributed to James Beard as part of his eulogy

These recipes reflect my affinity for intensely flavored condiments and sauces each of which asserts its personality whenever served. Adding one of these homemade sauces or relishes to your menu is an easy way to transform simple grilled meat, pasta, or baked fish into a sophisticated main course. Sauces like these are entertaining basics that can be used to brighten up a variety of different preparations with success. Most of them also meet another entertaining criteria: They not only can be made in advance; they also improve with age.

For example, I use the Rosemary Pesto (page 277) to coat a rack of lamb for roasting, mashed with chevre as a spread for crostini, and melted onto angel hair pasta with mushrooms and sun-dried tomatoes.

As a condiment, my current favorite is Whole Roast Garlic with Herbs. Serve the whole cloves alongside mashed potatoes, a steak, or a pasta dish. For those of us who love garlic—and we are legion—this is the ultimate in creative condimentry. And the golden brown cloves look beautiful on the plate, too.

Fresh Tomato Sauce

This is especially good with the Chevre and Prosciutto Ravioli (page 142), but complements many pasta dishes.

MAKES ABOUT 2 CUPS

3 tablespoons extra-virgin olive oil

1 onion, chopped

3 cloves garlic, minced

2½ cups chopped, seeded fresh tomatoes or 1 (28-ounce) can whole tomatoes, drained and chopped

1 tablespoon tomato paste

¼ cup chopped fresh basil

Salt

Fresh coarsely ground black pepper

Heat the oil in a skillet over medium heat. Add the onion and cook until softened, 2 to 3 minutes. Add the garlic and cook until aromatic, 1 minute. Add the tomatoes and simmer for 4 to 5 minutes. Stir in the tomato paste and basil. Cook 1 to 2 minutes. Taste and season with salt and pepper.

Tapenade

Tapenade is so flavorful that it can be employed to add a Mediterranean flair to everything from roast chicken to broiled tomatoes to a rustic pizza. Many Italian trattorias in California serve tapenade in place of butter with bread at the table. It is better if prepared the day before using.

MAKES ABOUT 1¼ CUPS

1 cup pitted, niçoise olives

2 tablespoons capers, rinsed

2 tablespoons chopped, rinsed anchovy fillet

1 tablespoon minced garlic

1 teaspoon minced lemon peel

½ teaspoon ground white pepper

½ teaspoon dried rosemary

2 teaspoons fresh lemon juice

¼ cup extra-virgin olive oil

1 tablespoon brandy or aquavit (optional)

Combine all the ingredients, except the oil and brandy, in a food processor or blender and process until pureed. With the motor running, slowly add the oil and process until incorporated.

Add the brandy, if desired. Although it is not strictly traditional, I prefer to add it. Cover and refrigerate for up to 1 week.

Peanut Sauce

This is best if made a day or two ahead and stored in the refrigerator. If it is made ahead of time, warm the sauce in the microwave for 40 to 50 seconds before serving. Serve with Beef Saté (page 151). It's also good as a salad dressing on a cold beef, cucumber, red onion, and mint salad.

MAKES ABOUT 2 CUPS

5 to 6 dried Thai chiles

3 shallots, finely chopped

2 teaspoons minced fresh ginger

4 cloves garlic, minced

2–3 tablespoons peanut oil

½ teaspoon ground cinnamon

1 teaspoon ground cumin

2 teaspoons ground coriander

1 cup unsweetened coconut milk

¾ cup chicken broth

2 tablespoons light brown sugar or to taste

2 tablespoons fresh lime juice

1 teaspoon fish sauce (nam pla) or soy sauce or to taste

⅔ cup chunky peanut butter

Remove the stems and seeds from the chiles and discard. Finely grind the chiles in a spice grinder.

Add the shallots, ginger, and garlic to a mortar. Grind with the pestle until smooth. (A mini food processor can be used but be careful not to overprocess or the mixture will become watery.)

Add 2 tablespoons of the peanut oil to a heavy skillet over medium-high heat. Add the shallot mixture and sauté, stirring occasionally, until softened and starting to color, about 5 minutes. Reduce the heat to medium and add the cumin and coriander and ground chile. Sauté until aromatic, 3 to 4 minutes, adding more oil if necessary.

Reduce the heat to low and add the coconut milk, broth, brown sugar, lime juice, and fish sauce. Stir well to mix with seasonings. Stir in the peanut butter. Simmer, stirring occasionally, until thickened, about 10 minutes. Taste and add more sugar or fish sauce if needed. Serve warm.

Mustard-Horseradish Sauce

Serve with Carpaccio (page 149) or any grilled steak or beef roast.

MAKES ABOUT 1 CUP

2 tablespoons Dijon or Pommery mustard

⅓ cup sour cream

2 tablespoons extra-virgin olive oil

2 tablespoons bottled horseradish, drained

Pinch sugar

Freshly ground coarse black pepper

1 tablespoon minced fresh tarragon or rosemary (optional)

Prepare the sauce: Combine all ingredients in a small bowl and whisk to mix. Cover and refrigerate 1 hour or overnight.

Dill-Mustard Sauce

Serve with the Gravlax (page 153). This can be made and refrigerated up to a week in advance.

MAKES 3 CUPS

⅓ cup cider vinegar

7 tablespoons sugar

¼ cup minced fresh dill

1¼ cups Dijon mustard

2 tablespoons ground white pepper

2 tablespoons minced capers

1½ cups extra-virgin olive oil

Whisk together all the ingredients except the oil. When well combined, drizzle in the oil, while whisking. Whisk until slightly thickened.

Green Sauce

This is a beautifully green, creamy rendition of the most traditional of seafood condiments. Brushing it on fish fillets before they go on the grill adds a touch of zest. This will keep well in the refrigerator for 3 to 4 days.

MAKES ABOUT 1½ CUPS

1 cup mayonnaise

¼ cup chopped fresh parsley

¼ cup chopped fresh chives, cilantro, or chervil

2 tablespoons minced shallot

2 tablespoons fresh lemon juice

2 tablespoons capers, drained

Tabasco sauce

¼ teaspoon Kosher salt

¼ teaspoon freshly ground coarse black pepper

Put the mayonnaise, parsley, chives, and shallot into the food processor and pulse to blend. Stir in the remaining ingredients and taste for spiciness, salt, and pepper. Refrigerate until ready to use.

Orange-Ginger Marmalade Dip

Use as a dip or sauce. It is actually improved by aging a couple of days in the refrigerator.

MAKES ABOUT 1½ CUPS

1 cup rough-cut orange marmalade

4 teaspoons minced fresh ginger

1 tablespoon minced garlic

⅓ cup fresh lemon juice or tamarind pulp

2 tablespoons Madeira

¼ teaspoon freshly ground black pepper

½ teaspoon red pepper flakes

In a medium bowl, combine all the ingredients until well mixed. Cover and refrigerate up to 2 days. Bring to room temperature before serving.

Tonnato Sauce

This sauce may be prepared in advance and then refrigerated up to two days.

MAKES 2¼ CUPS

1 (6- to 7-ounce) can tuna packed in olive oil

5 anchovy fillets in olive oil

2 tablespoons minced fresh Italian parsley

2 tablespoons extra-virgin olive oil

1 tablespoon fresh lemon juice

1 cup mayonnaise

2 tablespoons capers, or to taste, drained

¼ teaspoon ground white pepper

About ½ cup whipping cream

Using short pulses, puree the tuna, anchovies, parsley, olive oil, and lemon juice in a blender. Scrape the sides down frequently and stir to ensure even blending. When smooth, add the mayonnaise, capers, and white pepper and blend. Add the cream, a little at a time until you have the desired texture and flavor. Additional white pepper, lemon juice, or anchovies may be added at this point as desired.

Herb Butter

This simple herb butter complements the Frogmore Stew (page 215), grilled fish, and chicken.

MAKES ABOUT 2 CUPS

½ cup chopped fresh parsley

½ cup minced fresh thyme

1 cup (2 sticks) unsalted butter, melted

⅓ cup fresh lemon juice

Combine the parsley and thyme in a small bowl. Pour the butter over the herbs. Stir in the lemon juice.

Harissa

This Tunisian sauce is one of the most flavorful hot sauces in the world. It is a traditional accompaniment to couscous, but I use it for everything from energizing guacamole to drizzling on a simple bowl of bean stew. It is also a great wet rub for barbecued meats. A little goes a long way!

MAKES 1⅓ CUPS

8 to 10 red serrano or Thai chiles

7 cloves garlic, peeled

1 teaspoon ground cumin, toasted (page 315)

1½ teaspoons coriander seeds, toasted (page 315)

½ teaspoon chili powder

1½ teaspoons Kosher salt

2 red bell peppers

3 tablespoons cider vinegar

½ teaspoon freshly ground coarse black pepper

2 tablespoons extra-virgin olive oil

Wearing rubber gloves, remove the ribs, seeds, and stems from the chiles. In a food processor, grind the chiles, garlic, cumin, coriander, chili powder, and salt to a smooth paste.

Preheat the grill or broiler to high.

Place the whole bell peppers to char on the hot grill or under the broiler. Using tongs, turn them from side to side to roast evenly. Grill until charred and blistered, 3 to 5 minutes, remove from the heat, and enclose tightly in a plastic or paper bag to steam until cool.

Remove skins, stems, and seeds from the bell peppers. Add the peeled peppers to the processor along with the vinegar, black pepper, and olive oil. Pulse to a chunky puree. Harissa is best if prepared at least 1 to 2 days before serving. It can be frozen or kept in the refrigerator for up to 10 days.

Healthy Party Food

There are some healthy recipes that also meet all of my party criteria—beautiful to look at, prepared ahead of time, and delicious. Most people are happy to forgo their normal diet at a party, but if you serve something yummy and healthy, it's another feather in your cap. Healthy food is a creative way to show your guests you care for them.

Orange-Dill Sauce

This blushing, rosy cream sauce can be used to enhance either hot or cold seafood preparations. I serve it on cold poached salmon or shrimp and on grilled scallops. It is also an unusual dressing for a Crab Louis–style salad.

MAKES 2¼ CUPS

1½ tablespoons orange juice concentrate

1 cup sour cream

1 (3-ounce) package cream cheese, softened

1 tablespoon minced fresh dill

¼ teaspoon Tabasco sauce

1 tablespoon minced garlic

2 teaspoons tomato paste

¼ cup plus 2 teaspoons water

2 tablespoons fresh lemon juice

¾ teaspoon freshly grated nutmeg

½ teaspoon Kosher salt

¼ teaspoon cayenne pepper

5 tablespoons canola oil

Combine all the ingredients except the oil in the bowl of a food processor. Pulse until well mixed. With the motor running, slowly pour the oil in through the feed tube and process until sauce thickens, about 1 minute. Cover and refrigerate up to 1 week.

Barbecue Sauce

I use this sauce, based on Ted Gray's recipe, for Barbecued Pork Ribs (page 231) and on flank steak and chicken as well. It imparts an Asian flavor, which is unflaggingly popular.

MAKES ABOUT 2¾ CUPS; ENOUGH FOR 6 POUNDS OF MEAT

½ cup hoisin sauce

½ cup applesauce

½ cup Asian garlic chili sauce

½ cup tomato ketchup

2 cloves garlic, minced

1 tablespoon minced ginger

2 green onions, chopped

¼ cup dry sherry

¼ cup rice wine vinegar

¼ cup honey

½ tablespoon sesame oil

2 teaspoons soy sauce

Fresh cracked black pepper

Combine all the ingredients and mix well. The sauce can be prepared, covered, and refrigerated for up to 1 week.

Jejeruk (Fresh Coconut Relish)

I first tasted this sweet, crunchy, zingy coconut relish as one of dozens of condiments served to complete a Balinese rijsttafel dinner. Each of the little dishes, offered from an intricately carved wooden tray, presented a strong, bright taste, but I particularly loved this combination of nutty-sweet coconut and hot chiles. I asked chef/restaurateur Joe Schultz, who was sharing the meal, if he had a recipe to re-create this unusual relish. Being a master of all things exotic, especially Balinese, he had this at his fingertips. Serve this with Pepes (page 208) or as one of numerous condiments with a curry-type meal. This must be made with fresh coconut.

MAKES ABOUT 2 CUPS

1 cup low-sodium chicken broth

½ yellow onion, sliced

2¼ teaspoons minced garlic

1 whole fresh coconut, drained

½ teaspoon minced fresh ginger (see Notes below)

¼ teaspoon white pepper

1 teaspoon fresh lime juice

⅛ to ¼ teaspoon ground dried Japanese or Thai chile (see Notes below)

½ serrano chile, seeded and minced

Pinch sugar

Kosher salt

Simmer the chicken broth, onion, and 2 teaspoons of the garlic over medium heat until reduced by half, about 15 minutes. Remove from heat and set aside to cool.

Remove the coconut meat from the shell and peel off the inner dark skin with a vegetable peeler. Coarsely grate the coconut meat into long strips. (Use the large round holes on a grater/shredder if you don't have an actual coconut grater.)

Mix the coconut, the broth mixture, and remaining ingredients. Cover and refrigerate for 30 minutes. Taste for seasoning; add salt or more chiles as needed. Serve immediately or refrigerate up to 24 hours.

NOTES

Ginger: The more traditional ingredient is **kencur**, sold dried and sometimes frozen in Asian markets—as lesser **galangal** or **sha ginger** in Chinese markets, **rhizome** in Thai markets.

Chiles: Remove the seeds and stems from the dried chiles and grind in a spice grinder.

About Chiles

For most practical purposes there are two chile flavors. Green chiles, hot and slightly to very bitter, are always fresh (well, almost always). The difference in the "fieriness" between the hotter green chiles like jalapeño, serrano, Fresno, and Thai is fairly subtle and they're interchangeable on a volume basis. However, the hotness is surprisingly variable within a single type. Even individual chiles picked from one plant may exhibit entirely differing levels of heat. For this reason, the exact quantity of green chile called for in a recipe can be very misleading.

Red chiles, available both fresh and dried, are sweetly aromatic and hot. Fresh red chiles are more variable in heat between varieties than green; not surprising, as they are more mature, both as to flavor and aroma and sheer firepower. Ultra-hot habaneros are especially treacherous. Their aroma is so wonderful it is easy to get carried away and ruin a dish by adding too much.

If you are preparing a large quantity of fresh chiles remove the seeds then puree in a blender and use the resulting paste. This gives you an "averaged" hotness by mingling a number of individual chiles and is a more stable ingredient. Chile puree can also be stored in the refrigerator or freezer for later use.

There are two methods for utilizing dried (red) chiles. Either remove the seeds and stems and grind the chiles to a powder in a spice or coffee grinder, or soak in hot water until softened, then chop or puree to use.

Another very reliable source of chile heat is a combination of cayenne pepper and chopped red bell peppers in place of the fresh chiles called for in a recipe.

by Joe Schultz

Dry Rub

To add an intense flavor, liberally sprinkle the rub on both sides of pork, beef, or chicken. Rub in and let rest an hour before grilling.

MAKES ABOUT 1¾ CUPS; ENOUGH FOR 6 POUNDS OF MEAT

1 cup sugar

½ cup salt

2 tablespoons ground cayenne

1 tablespoon ground celery seeds

1 tablespoon ground cumin

Combine all the ingredients and mix well. The rub can be prepared, tightly sealed, and stored for up to 1 week.

Artichoke Pesto

This pesto is extraordinarily multipurpose. Brush it on grilled ears of corn when serving. Toss it with a warm, all-green vegetable melange and you have created a spectacular side dish. Artichoke Pesto is an excellent dressing for pasta salad or for warm fettuccine with poached chicken. The pesto can also be mixed into goat cheese to make a dip for crudités. I keep some in my freezer at all times.

MAKES 3 CUPS

2 tablespoons chopped garlic

½ cup minced fresh parsley

½ cup chopped fresh basil

1 (14 ½-ounce) can water-packed artichoke hearts, drained

½ cup pine nuts plus 2 tablespoons, toasted (page 315)

½ cup freshly grated Parmesan cheese

2½ tablespoons fresh lemon juice

⅔ cup extra-virgin olive oil

½ cup whipping cream

¼ teaspoon Kosher salt

½ teaspoon ground white pepper

Place the garlic, parsley, and basil in the bowl of a food processor and puree.

Add the artichoke hearts, pine nuts, and Parmesan cheese and process until pureed. Add the lemon juice and blend.

With the motor running, pour in the olive oil and cream and process until thick and creamy, about 45 seconds. Add the salt and white pepper and season to taste.

Cover and refrigerate for up to 1 week in the refrigerator.

Rosemary Pesto

Rosemary pesto is a natural complement for lamb. I also spread it on grilled ahi sandwiches instead of mayonnaise. It's great on a rustic pizza with smoked mozzarella, mushrooms, eggplant, and olives. I spread it under the skin of chicken before roasting.

MAKES ABOUT 1½ CUPS

⅓ cup chopped fresh rosemary

1½ cups chopped fresh parsley

4 cloves garlic, peeled

½ cup freshly grated Parmesan cheese

½ cup chopped pine nuts or walnuts

½ cup extra-virgin olive oil

½ teaspoon white pepper

Combine all the ingredients, but only half of the olive oil, in a food processor. Process to mix. With motor running, pour in the remaining olive oil and process until smooth with some tiny chunks. Use immediately or cover and refrigerate for up to 1 week. The flavors of this pungent pesto improve over time.

Pistachio Mint Pesto

This pesto can be used as the dressing for a tomato and fresh mozzarella salad, as a last-minute addition to curried lentils, or combined with ground lamb in Lamb and Mint Pesto Borek (page 150)

MAKES 1 CUP

¼ cup unsalted pistachio nuts, toasted (page 315)

¼ cup freshly grated Parmesan cheese

⅓ cup extra-virgin olive oil

¾ cup fresh basil leaves

1¼ cups fresh mint leaves

3 medium cloves garlic

Kosher salt

Freshly ground coarse black pepper (optional)

Put the pistachios, Parmesan cheese, and the olive oil in a food processor and pulse until pureed. Add the basil, mint, and garlic and process to a smooth texture.

Cover and refrigerate for at least 1 hour. Taste for salt and pepper and add if needed. Serve the pesto or refrigerate up to 24 hours.

Roasted Red Pepper Sauce

Wonderful with Barbecued Oysters (page 141), roast chicken, and sautéed halibut it's also spectacular on simple pasta with vegetables. The sauce improves with age and keeps at least three days in the refrigerator.

MAKES ABOUT 2¼ CUPS

1 medium dried pasilla chile

3 medium red bell peppers

6 cloves garlic

3 to 4 tablespoons extra-virgin olive oil

¼ cup minced shallots

½ white onion, minced

2 tablespoons red wine vinegar

1 tablespoon chopped fresh thyme

¼ to ½ teaspoon cayenne pepper

½ teaspoon Kosher salt

Freshly ground coarse black pepper

Cover the pasilla chile with boiling water and set aside to soften.

Roast the bell peppers and unpeeled garlic under the broiler, turning frequently, until the peppers are blistered and charred. Place the peppers and garlic into a plastic or paper bag and seal. Cool 5 to 10 minutes. Peel the garlic and remove the skin, stems, and seeds from the peppers.

Heat 1 tablespoon of the olive oil in a small sauté pan over medium heat. Add the shallots and onion and sauté until soft and barely golden.

Puree the peppers, garlic, and onions in a blender or food processor. With the motor running, slowly add in the remaining olive oil and vinegar, alternately. When the liquids are thoroughly incorporated, add the thyme, cayenne, salt, and pepper and pulse to mix.

Poblano Cream Sauce

In this quick sauce, cream mellows the musky flavor of the poblano chile. I serve this on roast pork loin, swirled in Roasted Eggplant Soup (page 182), or layered with chicken and crepes for an elegant lasagna.

MAKES 1½ CUPS

---

2 tablespoons extra-virgin olive oil

1 poblano chile, minced (about ¾ cup)

¾ cup diced onion

2 tablespoons chopped garlic

¾ cup chopped fresh cilantro

¼ cup whipping cream

½ cup sour cream

Kosher salt

Ground white pepper

GARNISH

¼ cup julienne red bell pepper

¼ cup pepitas (shelled pumpkin seeds), toasted (page 315)

Heat oil in a heavy saucepan over medium heat. Add the chile and onion and sauté about 4 minutes. Add the garlic and sauté for 2 minutes. Add remaining ingredients and simmer for 1 to 2 minutes to blend and thicken. Season with salt and pepper.

Use an immersion blender or pour into a blender to puree.

Serve immediately, garnished with bell pepper and pepitas.

Spicy Vinegar Dipping Sauce

Serve with Chicken Pyramid Dumplings (page 145) or use it to enhance Chinese takeout.

MAKES ABOUT ¾ CUP

½ cup seasoned rice vinegar

¼ cup low-sodium soy sauce

1 tablespoon minced fresh ginger

⅛ teaspoon Chinese chili oil, more if desired

Combine all of the ingredients and taste so that you can adjust the chili oil. This is better if made the day before and stored in the refrigerator.

Vietnamese Chili Sauce

This fresh, tangy sauce is great with the Vietnamese-Inspired Spring Rolls (page 146), Barbecued Oysters (page 141), or any grilled fish.

MAKES ABOUT 1 CUP

---

4 red Thai chiles or 2 jalapeño chiles

2 tablespoons sugar

6 cloves garlic

4 tablespoons fish sauce (*nam pla*)

6 tablespoons fresh lemon or lime juice

Remove the seeds and stems from the chiles. Combine the chiles, sugar, and garlic in a mini food processor and puree. Add the fish sauce and lemon juice. Cover and refrigerate for at least 1 day before using.

Zingy Tartar Sauce

A spicy variation on the typical tartar sauce, it is very good with any kind of fish or shellfish.

MAKES ABOUT 1¼ CUPS

---

2 tablespoons finely chopped capers

¼ cup finely chopped fresh parsley, cilantro, or chervil

2 tablespoons minced shallot

1 tablespoon minced jalapeño chile

1 cup mayonnaise

2 tablespoons fresh lemon juice

Dash Tabasco sauce, or to taste

Kosher salt

Freshly ground coarse black pepper

Combine all the ingredients in a small bowl. Cover and refrigerate for up to 4 days.

Roasted Balsamic and Honey Onions

This sweetly glazed onion relish adds layers of flavor to a hamburger, pizza, or polenta.

MAKES 2 CUPS

5 cups thinly sliced red onions
½ cup balsamic vinegar

6 tablespoons honey

Preheat the oven to 350F (175C). Mix all the ingredients thoroughly in a small roasting pan. Roast for 1 hour, until the vinegar and honey have reduced to a syrup. Serve immediately or refrigerate for up to 4 days.

Crispy Shallots

Sprinkle over the top of the Roasted Garlic Mashed Potatoes with Crispy Shallots (page 257) or Mediterranean Bean Spread (page 163) for a crunchy garnish.

MAKES ABOUT 1¼ CUPS

1 cup vegetable oil

½ cup finely sliced shallots (4 or 5)

Heat the oil over medium-high heat in a small wok or heavy-bottomed saucepan to 360F (180C). Add the shallots and fry, turning frequently, until golden brown, 2 to 3 minutes. Remove from the oil with a strainer or slotted spoon and drain on paper towels. If made ahead, cool and store in an airtight container up to 3 days.

Guacamole

Still wildly popular, guacamole is one of the simplest of dips. There are many variations. This is my favorite recipe, but feel free to experiment; it will always be delicious. Start with perfectly ripe avocados, either Haas or Bacon, and freshly squeezed lime juice, and you can't go wrong. I serve guacamole as a dip with tortilla chips and jicama spears and as a garnish on everything Hispanic from tacos to tamales.

MAKES 2 CUPS

---

2 ripe Haas or Bacon avocados

3 tablespoons fresh lime juice

¼ cup minced red onion

¼ cup minced fresh cilantro

¼ to ⅓ cup chopped tomato

1 serrano chile, minced

Cayenne pepper

Kosher salt

Freshly ground coarse black pepper

Peel and seed the avocados. Combine in a bowl with the lime juice and roughly mash with the back of a fork. Leave it chunky.

Stir in the remaining ingredients and taste for seasoning. Guacamole is best if made shortly before serving. It doesn't hold well in the refrigerator.

Whole Roast Garlic with Herbs

This very simple preparation produces a versatile ingredient that can be used as a spread, garnish, and appetizer.

Select large, firm fresh heads of garlic. If what is available looks shriveled or old, save this preparation for another time.

MAKES 8 SERVINGS

8 heads garlic

3 tablespoons dry sherry

2/3 cup chicken broth

1 tablespoon minced fresh thyme, sage, or rosemary

2 tablespoons extra-virgin olive oil

3 tablespoons unsalted butter, melted

1 teaspoon coarsely ground black pepper

1/2 teaspoon Kosher salt

Preheat the oven to 350F (175C). Remove the loose white, papery outer skins from the garlic and discard. Leave the heads intact.

Set the garlic heads, root end down, in a shallow roasting pan just large enough to hold them. Pour the sherry and chicken broth into the bottom of the pan. The liquid should be about 1/2 inch deep, adjust quantities as necessary.

In a food processor, puree the herbs, olive oil, and butter. Drizzle this mixture over the top of each garlic head. Season with pepper and salt.

Cover the pan with foil. Roast for 1 hour, basting frequently.

Remove the foil, baste the garlic with the pan juices and roast for 15 to 20 minutes more, until the papery skins are golden and the cloves feel very soft.

SERVING SUGGESTIONS

The garlic cloves can now be squeezed (like toothpaste) from the papery skins to be used in a sauce, as a topping for pizza, or simply spread on toast. A whole head of garlic makes a charming appetizer served in a nest of fresh herbs with lemon wedges and toast for spreading.

VARIATION

The garlic can also be prepared in the same way, but cooked on a grill with delicious results. In order to cook it on the grill, omit the pan and just enclose the cloves in heavy-duty foil with the butter drizzle and 1 teaspoon of chicken stock for each head. Place over a hot fire, turning occasionally for about 40 minutes.

Cranberry Kumquat Relish

This beautiful, spicy relish goes together so quickly there is no reason to ever buy cranberry sauce again. The blending of hearty, sweet, and savory flavors makes it perfect with poultry or pork anytime of the year—not just at Thanksgiving. Some traditionalists may object, but my customers love the unusual zing of the kumquats and the ginger.

MAKES 10 SERVINGS

6 cups fresh cranberries

1¼ cups ruby Port wine

¾ cup chopped, seeded kumquats

1¾ cups sugar

¼ teaspoon Kosher salt

¼ teaspoon freshly ground coarse black pepper

2 tablespoons grated orange zest

1 tablespoon plus 1 teaspoon minced fresh ginger

Rinse the cranberries and sort to remove any old or shriveled fruit. Combine the cranberries, wine, kumquats, sugar, salt, and pepper in a large heavy-bottomed saucepan. Bring to a simmer over medium-high heat. Cover and reduce the heat to medium-low. Simmer until most of the cranberries have "popped," 10 to 12 minutes.

Stir in the orange zest and ginger. Simmer, uncovered, until thickened, 5 to 7 minutes. The relish can be refrigerated for up to 1 week.

VARIATION
Substitute orange segments for the chopped kumquats.

Mint-Cilantro Raita

Raita is a refreshing yogurt salad/relish that serves as a soothing accompaniment to spicy curries and other highly flavored dishes. It is best served the same day as it is made; however, the flavor improves if the raita rests in the refrigerator for 1 to 2 hours before serving.

MAKES ABOUT 3 CUPS

---

2 to 3 cups plain yogurt

2 cucumbers

Kosher salt

Freshly ground coarse black pepper

¼ cup chopped fresh mint

½ teaspoon ground cumin

1 small serrano chile, minced

2 tablespoons sliced red onion

2 tablespoons minced garlic

1 tablespoon fresh lemon juice or tamarind pulp

2 tablespoons chopped fresh cilantro

Spoon the yogurt into a strainer lined with a single thickness of cheesecloth. Let drain about 45 minutes to remove excess liquid.

Peel and seed the cucumbers. Slice and toss lightly with salt. Place in a colander and let drain for about 30 minutes.

Combine the cucumbers, yogurt, and the remaining ingredients. Cover and refrigerate for at least 1 hour before using.

Yemenite Zhoug Relish

I first tasted this bright green, Yemenite "relish" in Jerusalem. Surprisingly, even with all of the hot chiles used, it is only pleasantly spicy, with great fresh herb flavors. Zhoug is an excellent marinade for lamb or chicken. It improves with age and will keep for up to 2 weeks in the refrigerator.

MAKES 1 ½ CUPS

1 cup diced seeded fresh jalapeño or de Agua chiles

½ cup chopped fresh parsley

½ cup chopped fresh cilantro

2 tablespoons minced garlic

1 teaspoon salt

1 teaspoon freshly ground coarse black pepper

½ cup chopped fresh mint

½ tablespoon extra-virgin olive oil

1 tablespoon fresh lemon juice

1 teaspoon grated lemon zest

Pinch ground cardamom

Put the chiles in a food processor or a blender and pulse to a puree. Add the remaining ingredients and pulse to a rough puree.

Taste for salt, using a chunk of bread or plain cracker. Cover and refrigerate at least 1 day before using.

SERVING SUGGESTIONS

At casual parties I offer the zhoug and a bowl of Harissa (page 272) as a choice of dipping sauces for grilled lamb, chicken, and shrimp skewers. The meats are simply brushed with a little olive oil, salt, and pepper and a squeeze of lemon before grilling.

TIP

When chopping fresh chiles, wear rubber gloves. Remove the seeds and ribs from the chiles for a milder taste.

Citrus Salsa

The fruit and chiles add a spicy tanginess that is a perfect accompaniment to Fish Tacos (page 220).

MAKES ABOUT 2 CUPS

1 segmented, peeled navel orange

2 segmented, peeled lemons

2 teaspoons minced, seeded serrano chiles

¾ cup diced canned tomatillos, drained

1 medium red onion, diced

3 tablespoons chopped fresh cilantro

1 teaspoon Kosher salt

1 teaspoon minced fresh oregano

½ teaspoon freshly ground coarse black pepper

Roughly chop the orange and lemon segments. Retain all of the juice that accumulates when you are peeling and chopping the citrus. Combine all the ingredients, including the citrus juices, in a medium bowl and toss. Taste for salt and pepper. (The salsa can be prepared up to 2 days in advance.)

Caribbean Salsa

The unusual combination of grapefruit, banana, and chiles takes salsa to a new level with sweet perfectly balanced with tart and hot.

MAKES ABOUT 2 CUPS

1 cup chopped fresh cilantro

½ cup pink grapefruit segments

2 jalapeño chiles, minced

¼ cup fresh lime juice

1 cup minced green onions

Kosher salt

Freshly ground coarse black pepper

1 large ripe banana

Combine the cilantro, grapefruit segments, chiles, lime juice, and green onions in a bowl. Season with salt and pepper to taste. Dice the banana and add just before serving.

Cinnamon Toast Spread

This simple spread exactly re-creates the memory I have of my mother's cinnamon toast. It is lovely served on a brunch buffet with croissants and muffins. I also use it as a filling for a warm dessert crepe topped with shaved chocolate and whipped cream.

MAKES ABOUT 1 CUP

¾ **teaspoon pure vanilla extract**

¾ **teaspoon ground cinnamon**

1 **tablespoon whipping cream**

2 **tablespoons chopped, seedless raisins**

2 **tablespoons light brown sugar**

1 **(8-ounce) package cream cheese, softened**

Mix the vanilla extract and cinnamon; set aside.

Heat the cream in the microwave for 20 to 30 seconds, until bubbling. Stir in the vanilla-cinnamon mixture. Blend well; the result is a very thick paste.

Pulse the raisins with the brown sugar in a food processor until finely chopped. Add the cinnamon mixture and cream cheese and pulse to mix thoroughly.

Refrigerate at least 3 hours or up to 1 week before serving.

Whiskey Caramel Sauce

This luscious caramel recipe is finished quickly and keeps for weeks. Use it to enhance dishes like peach crepes, bread pudding, and ice cream.

MAKES ABOUT 1 CUP

¾ **cup sugar**

¼ **cup water**

⅓ **cup whipping cream, warmed**

2 **tablespoons unsalted butter, at room temperature**

2 **tablespoons Jack Daniels or other good whiskey or dark rum**

Combine the sugar and water in a heavy saucepan and stir to blend. Cook over low heat, using the handle of the pan to swirl the liquid, until the sugar is completely dissolved and the mixture is absolutely clear, about 4 minutes.

Increase the heat to medium-high, bring to a boil, and cook, swirling the pan occasionally, until the caramel turns a dark amber color, like maple syrup, 10 to 12 minutes. Remove the pan from the heat.

Slowly pour the warm cream into the caramel; the caramel will froth and steam.

Return the pan to low heat. Cook, stirring gently with a wooden spoon to dissolve any solid bits of caramel, until the sauce is smooth, about 1 minute. Remove from the heat and stir in the butter and whiskey.

Serve warm. (The sauce can be tightly covered and refrigerated for up to 2 weeks. Warm before serving.)

I doubt whether the world holds for anyone a more soul-stirring surprise than the first adventure with ice-cream.

—Heywood Broun

My client asked me to transform a one-thousand-square-foot tent into an Arabian fantasy on a small budget. With a groan, my designer said, "Well, there's only one way to go. We'll construct a big splashy buffet in the middle and dim the lighting around the perimeter of the tent. The whole budget gets spent on the one big table and we put a spotlight on it."

Over time I integrated his concept of focus-for-effect into my menu planning. I came to realize that if there is only time or money for one elaborate course, make it dessert. The big splash should be the finish. Everyone loves an elegant decadent sweet, and everyone remembers what came last!

Fortunately, the traditional elements of desserts lend themselves to drama. The universal favorite chocolate, white or dark, can be shaved, melted or curled. It is even rolled paper-thin to be used like wrapping paper to enclose a special cake. Fruit is to dessert what flowers are to the forest, the riot of color that makes the muted surroundings seem warm and appealing. Ice cream and cake can be molded, stacked, layered, together or separately, and shaped like everything from a rocket ship to an Easter egg.

In short, a cook's artistry and whimsy find their most fertile opportunities when creating desserts—the queen of the dining room.

Serafina's Tiramisu

My friend Susan Kaufman's Seattle restaurant, Serafina, is famous for its romantic ambience, great food, and this delectable tiramisu. It is well worth the time required, especially since it improves when made a day or two in advance.

MAKES 8 TO 10 SERVINGS

¾ teaspoon pure vanilla extract

3 tablespoons amaretto

8 egg yolks

½ cup plus 2 tablespoons sugar

¾ cup Champagne

8 ounces (1 cup) mascarpone

¼ cup brandy

2 tablespoons coffee liqueur

¾ cup triple-strength coffee or espresso

20 to 24 ladyfingers

1¼ cups whipping cream

½ teaspoon ground cinnamon

¼ cup grated semisweet chocolate

Chocolate curls (optional)

Combine the vanilla and 2½ tablespoons of the amaretto in a small bowl.

In the bowl of an electric mixer, combine the egg yolks and ½ cup sugar. Beat until thick and pale, 3 to 4 minutes. Reduce mixer speed and add in the amaretto mixture. Beat 3 to 5 minutes.

Pour the egg mixture into the top half of a double boiler or a metal mixing bowl and whisk in the Champagne. Place pan over boiling water and cook, whisking constantly, until mixture thickens enough to create ribbons when the whisk is lifted (the ribbons will dissolve quickly), 6 to 7 minutes.

Remove the pan from the heat and place in a bowl of ice and continue to whisk until the custard has cooled slightly, 3 to 4 minutes. Whisk in the mascarpone, mix thoroughly, and allow to cool completely on the ice, whisking occasionally.

Combine the remaining 2 tablespoons sugar, brandy, remaining amaretto, coffee liqueur, and coffee in a bowl. Spread the ladyfingers out on a baking sheet and drizzle thoroughly (to soak) with the coffee mixture.

In the bowl of your electric mixer, whip the cream and cinnamon until stiff peaks form. Using a spatula, fold the cooled custard into the whipped cream.

In a 3-quart trifle bowl, arrange a layer of the soaked ladyfingers, cover with half of the custard, sprinkle with half of the grated chocolate. Repeat the layers. Decorate the top with chocolate curls, if desired. Cover tightly and refrigerate at least 4 hours, and up to 2 days, before serving.

White Chocolate Cheesecake en Croûte

The addition of a ruffled pastry casing adds an element of glamour and drama to an already delicious dessert. Good theater is good entertaining.

This is time consuming, but once you have mastered the phyllo assembly, it's really fun and easy. This cake stores well in the refrigerator, and it may be frozen before cooking.

MAKES 8 SERVINGS

About 8 sheets phyllo dough

FILLING

1 ½ pounds [3 (8-ounce) packages] cream cheese, softened

8 ounces mild fresh chevre, softened

¾ cup unsalted butter, softened

4 eggs

1 pound white chocolate

3 tablespoons Frangelico

2 teaspoons pure vanilla extract

Freshly grated nutmeg

2 tablespoons sugar

RASPBERRY SAUCE

2 cups fresh or frozen, thawed raspberries

¼ cup Framboise or Grand Marnier

Powdered sugar to taste

Thaw the phyllo, if frozen, overnight in the refrigerator. This is very important. If thawed more quickly, at room temperature, the leaves tend to stick together and tear.

Preheat the oven to 325F (165C). In a medium bowl, combine the cream cheese, chevre, and ¼ cup of the butter. Using an electric mixer, gently whip until well mixed and fluffy. Add the eggs, one at a time, and beat until combined. Set aside.

Chop the white chocolate into rough chunks and heat in the microwave on high for 30 seconds at a time. Stir between heatings, until melted, for a total of about 2 minutes.

Stir the Frangelico and the vanilla into the melted chocolate until well combined. Set aside to cool. Once the Frangelico mixture has cooled, stir into the cheese mixture.

Melt the remaining butter. Butter a 6- to 8-inch springform pan. Smooth 1 sheet of phyllo across the bottom of the pan and up the sides. Brush with melted butter and sprinkle with nutmeg. Repeat with 2 more sheets of phyllo.

Place the corner of 1 sheet of phyllo in the center of the pan and smooth into the corners and up the side. There will be a 4- to 5-inch tail hanging over the edge of the pan. Brush all over with melted butter, including the overhang. Repeat with 3 more sheets, overlapping them as you work around the pan.

When the pan is completely lined, with about 4 inches hanging over all around, pour in the filling to 2 inches below the rim.

Gently fold over the phyllo ends so that they meet in the center of the pan over the cheese filling. Gently twist the ends together to form a knotted "rosette." An extra strip of phyllo can be buttered and wound into this design. Brush the whole top with melted butter and dust with the sugar.

Put the cheesecake on a sheet pan. Bake for about 1½ hours, until firm and puffed. If the rosette starts to brown before the cake is set, cover loosely with foil. To test for doneness, gently shake the sheet pan. If the cake still jiggles, it's not done. Remove and let cool on a rack for 1 hour before slicing. (The cheesecake can be made the day before and refrigerated.)

To prepare the sauce: Combine the raspberries and liqueur in a blender and puree. Taste for sweetness and add sugar to taste. Mix to combine and strain the sauce to remove the seeds. (This can be made up to 2 days in advance and refrigerated.)

To serve: Loosen the sides of the springform pan and remove. Use a serrated knife to slice through the pastry and cheesecake. Lay each piece on its side and drizzle with the sauce.

Individual Citrus Shells

Hollowed out citrus fruit filled with a sorbet or gelato make a beautiful presentation and can be prepared up to 2 weeks in advance. Cut the tops off whole limes, lemons, and oranges and scoop out the pulp with a grapefruit spoon. If necessary, take thin slices off the bottoms so the fruits will set flat. Then pack the shell with the frozen dessert. Cover well and freeze. It works equally well if the shell and the filling are the same flavor or complementary flavors, like limes filled with mango. A blood orange filled with a dark chocolate gelato is a favorite. To serve, I scatter raspberries and white chocolate curls on the plate.

Meringue Boxes Filled with Lime Curd

This beautiful, fanciful dessert can be finished the day before your party. At the last minute, assemble to serve. The meringues can be made in any shape you fancy. I like the idea of a box with a "lid," but meringue will assume the shape of a haystack or a heart just as easily. The Whiskey Caramel Sauce (page 288) can be made up to 2 weeks ahead. It is drizzled across the boxes in a delicate spider web and blackberries or raspberries decorate the corners.

If the weather is humid, meringues are not a good idea since they become sticky.

MAKES 8 TO 10 SERVINGS

MERINGUE

8 egg whites

Pinch salt

1½ cups superfine sugar

LIME CURD

¾ cup superfine sugar

3 eggs

3 egg yolks

1 cup fresh lime juice (about 7 limes)

¼ cup grated lime zest

½ cup unsalted butter

Whiskey Caramel Sauce (page 288)

Fresh blackberries or raspberries

Prepare the Meringue: Preheat the oven to 250F (120C). Line 2 baking sheets with parchment paper. On 1 sheet, trace around a small square or other form to create 8 shapes for meringues.

The egg whites will whip more easily if they are room temperature before you begin. With an electric mixer on high speed, whip the egg whites and salt until they begin to foam. Slowly add in the sugar, 1 tablespoon at a time, until it's all incorporated. Beat the egg whites until stiff and glossy, about 6 minutes total.

Transfer the meringue to a pastry bag with a large tip. Following your outlines, fill in the squares at an even thickness. When you have 8 squares, go back and pipe the 4 sides of each "box." On the second sheet pan, create 8 free-form lids in any shape that amuses you: a swirl, a triangle, a figure eight, or a circle.

Bake for 1½ to 2 hours. Turn off the oven and leave the meringues in the warm oven to continue drying for several hours or overnight, until crisp.

Prepare the Lime Curd: In a bowl, lightly whisk the sugar, eggs, and egg yolks. Combine the lime juice, lime zest, and butter in a heavy-bottomed saucepan. Bring the liquid to a rapid simmer over high heat. Remove from the heat. Whisk half of the lime butter into the egg mixture. Then whisk this back into the remaining lime butter in the saucepan.

Cook over medium-high heat, whisking vigorously, until thick and creamy.

Strain the curd into a nonreactive bowl, press plastic wrap onto the top to avoid forming a skin, and let cool. Wrap well and refrigerate for up to 3 days.

Prepare the Whiskey Caramel Sauce.

To serve: Place a meringue box on each plate, fill with cold lime curd, and place the lid at a rakish angle. Use a fork to drizzle the sauce from side to side across the plate to form a lacy web over the box. Garnish with the berries.

TIP
If you can't find superfine sugar in the market, grind regular sugar in your spice mill or coffee grinder.

Date and Orange Wontons

Crisp and sugary on the outside and creamy in the middle, these are great with green tea ice cream as a creative conclusion to a Chinese meal.

MAKES 50 TO 60 WONTONS

1 cup chopped walnuts

1 cup pitted dates

2 tablespoons fresh orange juice

1 tablespoon grated orange zest

½ teaspoon ground cardamom

2 tablespoons cream cheese, softened

½ cup powdered sugar

¼ teaspoon ground ginger

60 (3 ½-inch) wonton wrappers

1½ to 2 cups vegetable oil

In a food processor, grind the walnuts, dates, orange juice, orange zest, and cardamom to a creamy paste. Add the cream cheese and pulse to combine.

Combine powdered sugar and ginger in a small bowl and stir to mix.

Place a wonton wrapper on your work surface and put 1 teaspoon of the date filling in the middle. Brush the edge of the wonton with water. Fold over to form a triangle and press the edges to seal. Bring the 2 long points together, brush with water, and press together. Fold over the remaining point. (This fold is usually illustrated nicely on the back of wonton packages).

Heat the oil to 350F (175C) in a wok or electric frying pan. Cook the wontons, a few at a time, until golden, 2 to 3 minutes. Transfer to paper towels to drain and sprinkle generously with the gingered powdered sugar. Serve immediately.

Susan's Apple Bread and Butter Pudding

Good bread pudding is just so rainy-day yummy and gratifying. It's comfort food defined. It is also simple to prepare and economical since it is based on stale bread. I often serve this as the conclusion to a simple, grilled supper. This should be served warm topped with rum raisin ice cream, whipped cream, or the Whiskey Caramel Sauce (page 288).

MAKES 8 TO 10 SERVINGS

1 (14-ounce) loaf challah or a mild white bread

¾ cup unsalted butter, melted

4 egg yolks

1 egg

½ pound sugar

2½ cups whole milk

1 (12-ounce) can evaporated milk

½ teaspoon pure vanilla extract

1½ cups chopped peeled pippin apples (about 2 apples)

½ cup raisins

½ cup light rum

Ground cinnamon

Cut bread into 1-inch chunks and let sit out overnight to dry or toast in a 300F (150C) oven until dry.

Beat half of the butter, the egg yolks, egg, and sugar in a mixing bowl until creamy. Add the whole and evaporated milks and vanilla and beat to mix well.

Combine the apples, raisins, and dry bread in a large bowl. Drizzle the rum and remaining butter over the bread mixture. Toss to mix. Add the egg mixture and toss to coat. Let rest 30 minutes or until the bread is soft and spongy.

Preheat the oven to 350F (175C). Butter a 3-quart casserole. Pour in the bread mixture and sprinkle the top liberally with cinnamon. Set the casserole in a larger pan. Add enough hot water to come halfway up casserole sides. Bake for about 1 hour, until a knife inserted in the middle comes out clean.

Let rest about 10 minutes before serving. Serve warm. Any leftovers should be refrigerated and can be reheated in the microwave.

Will's Hot Banana Split

A great topping for ice cream because it's quick, easy, and delicious. It's a great opportunity for a flaming dessert (see the Variation below). This dessert is the exception to my rule about not serving flaming food.

MAKES 4 SERVINGS

4 medium ripe bananas

¼ cup unsalted butter

¾ cup packed light brown sugar

Juice of 1 orange

Juice of ½ lemon

¼ cup banana liqueur

Ground cinnamon

1 quart coconut or French vanilla ice cream

Split the bananas lengthwise into 2 pieces and cut each piece in half.

In a sauté pan over medium heat, combine all the ingredients except the bananas, cinnamon, and ice cream. Stir to mix and cook over low heat until combined and bubbly, 1 to 2 minutes.

Slip the bananas into the pan and sauté, turning once, until golden, 2 to 3 minutes. Dust with cinnamon. Serve over ice cream.

VARIATION

To flambé: Remove the pan from the heat, add an additional ¼ cup rum or banana liqueur, and use a long match to ignite the liquid in the pan. It will flame up for a few seconds, during which time you spoon it over the ice cream to guests' oohs and aahs.

Almond Orange Tea Cake

My friend Anne is one of the few caterers I know who makes virtually every bite of food she serves her clients. This light, orange-scented teacake is the kind of dessert that both Anne and I enjoy, not too sweet and not too difficult to prepare. It's lovely for a brunch or tea party.

MAKES 2 (8-INCH) CAKES

CAKE
2 large navel oranges
1 cup sugar
6 eggs
1½ cups ground almonds (about 6 ounces)
Pinch salt
1 teaspoon baking powder

3 tablespoons orange juice concentrate
2 tablespoons Triple Sec

TOPPING
⅓ cup whipping cream
¼ cup purchased orange curd
½ cup cream cheese, softened

Prepare the cake: Place the whole oranges in a saucepan and cover with water. Bring to a slow boil and cook until they are very soft, about 60 minutes.

Drain the oranges and cool. Cut the oranges into quarters and remove any seeds.

Put the oranges and sugar into the bowl of the food processor and process into a puree; some little pieces are okay. They add a pleasant flavor, because all of the bitterness has boiled out.

Preheat the oven to 400F (205C). Butter and flour 2 (8-inch-round) cake pans.

In a large bowl, beat the eggs until thickened. Add the almonds, salt, baking powder, and the orange puree. Mix well and pour into the prepared cake pans.

Bake for 1 hour, until firm when pressed and a wooden pick or cake tester comes out clean. (The top will get quite dark brown, which is okay, but if you are concerned that it is getting too dark, cover the top lightly with foil.)

Cool the cakes in the pans on a wire rack for 10 minutes, then turn out onto the rack to finish cooling.

Combine the orange juice concentrate and the Triple Sec. When completely cooled, turn the cakes right side up and brush the tops lightly with the orange juice mixture. Wrap in plastic wrap and refrigerate at least 2 hours or overnight before serving.

Prepare the Topping: Whip the cream until soft peaks form. Fold in the orange curd and cream cheese.

To serve: Cut the cake into small slices; serve with a dollop of the topping on the side.

Peach-Caramel Crepes

Peach with ginger and caramel is an enticing combination. The crepes and caramel sauce are basic recipes that can be prepared up to 2 weeks before using in this recipe.

MAKES 8 SERVINGS

Dessert Crepes (page 312)
Whiskey Caramel Sauce (page 288)
¼ cup unsalted butter
2 cups chopped fresh or thawed frozen peaches

¼ cup sugar
1 teaspoon minced fresh ginger
1 quart French vanilla ice cream

The Dessert Crepes and Whiskey Caramel Sauce can both be prepared in advance.

Preheat the oven to 375F (190C). In a large sauté pan, bring the butter to a simmer over low heat. Add the peaches, sugar, and ginger and sauté 3 to 4 minutes until the peaches have softened slightly.

Put 1 tablespoon of the peach mixture in a crepe and fold in half. Fold in half again and put in a jelly-roll pan. Arrange the folded crepes slightly overlapping in the pan.

Drizzle the caramel sauce over the crepes and bake for 5 to 6 minutes, until sizzling.

Serve 2 crepes per person topped with a scoop of French vanilla ice cream.

Ankica (Anne Dreyer) has refined this simple yet sumptuous dessert. The recipe creates a homey, comforting fruit crisp in practically no time. If you are really in a hurry, you can pull a package of berries out of the freezer, drain for about 10 minutes, add sugar and spice, cover with the topping from your freezer, and put the dish directly in a preheated oven. This is great on a dessert buffet following a casual meal.

MAKES 6 TO 8 SERVINGS

TOPPING

¼ cup all-purpose flour

¼ cup unsalted butter

¼ cup rolled oats

¾ cup packed light brown sugar

½ cup chopped pecans or walnuts

¾ teaspoon ground cinnamon

½ teaspoon freshly grated nutmeg

Filling of choice (see below)

Ice cream or whipped cream (optional)

Prepare the topping: In a food processor, pulse the flour and butter until the texture of coarse cornmeal. Remove to a bowl and toss with remaining ingredients until mixed. (This can be refrigerated for 1 week or frozen for 6 months.)

Preheat the oven to 350F (175C). Butter a 10 × 8-inch casserole.

Prepare a fruit filling: Combine all the filling ingredients in a bowl and mix well.

To assemble: Place the fruit filling in the buttered dish. Cover the filling with a ¾-inch layer (or more) of the topping.

Bake until bubbling and the fruit in the middle is tender, 40 to 45 minutes. (The Mixed Berry Crisp will take only about 25 minutes.)

To Serve: Serve warm for the best flavor. Serve with ice cream, if desired.

FILLINGS

PEACH FILLING

2 pounds peaches, peeled and thinly sliced

1 tablespoon fresh lemon juice

3 to 4 tablespoons sugar

3 tablespoons cornstarch

½ teaspoon ground ginger

GREEN APPLE FILLING

2 pounds green apples, peeled and thinly sliced

1 tablespoon fresh lemon juice

½ cup sugar or to taste

1 teaspoon ground cinnamon

1 tablespoon grated lemon zest

MIXED BERRY FILLING

2 pounds fresh or frozen blackberries, boysenberries, raspberries, or a combination

½ cup sugar or to taste

¼ teaspoon ground ginger or to taste

PEAR-CRANBERRY FILLING

1½ pounds pears, peeled and thinly sliced

1 cup cranberries

1 tablespoon fresh lemon juice

¼ cup sugar or to taste

3 tablespoons cornstarch

1 teaspoon ground ginger

½ teaspoon ground cardamon

Pignola Lemon Tarte

This is an ultra-lemon tart with the sophisticated addition of a pine nut crust, Frangelico, and candied pine nuts on top. It is beautiful all on its own or garnished with fresh blackberries or boysenberries. This crust is quick and easy and works beautifully for cheesecake as well.

MAKES 8 TO 10 SERVINGS

CRUST

1 cup all-purpose flour

½ cup powdered sugar

¼ teaspoon salt

½ cup plus 2 tablespoons finely ground pine nuts

6 tablespoons unsalted butter, chilled and cut into pieces

2 egg yolks, slightly beaten

Ice water, if needed

FILLING

⅔ cup sugar

1 egg plus 4 yolks, slightly beaten

⅔ cup fresh lemon juice

3 tablespoons grated lemon zest

6 tablespoons butter, melted

1 tablespoon Frangelico

GLAZED PINE NUTS

1 teaspoon unsalted butter

¼ cup pine nuts

1 teaspoon sugar

Whipped cream or fresh berries (optional)

Prepare the crust: Preheat the oven to 400F (205C).

Sift the flour, sugar, and salt into the bowl of a food processor. Add the pine nuts and butter and pulse until the texture resembles coarse cornmeal, 10 to 15 seconds. With the motor running, add the egg yolks. If the dough is too dry to form a soft ball when pressed, add ice water

1 tablespoon at a time and pulse to mix. Do not overprocess; the dough should not be processed for more than 30 to 40 seconds after adding the liquids.

Transfer the dough to a sheet of waxed paper or plastic wrap. Form the dough into a flat circle. Enclose tightly and refrigerate at least 1 hour or up to 1 day.

Place the chilled dough in a 10- to 11-inch tart pan and use your fingers to press it over the bottom and up the side of the pan. Roll over the edges and crimp with your fingers to form a pretty ruffled edge. Use a fork to prick the shell all over. Cover and chill for 1 hour.

Line the chilled dough with foil or parchment paper smoothed carefully into all of the corners. Line with dry beans, rice, or pie weights. Bake for 10 to 12 minutes, just to set the crust. Remove from the oven and carefully lift out foil and weights. Return to the oven 8 to 10 minutes, until the edges barely begin to color. Set aside to cool.

Prepare the filling: Add the sugar to a large bowl. Whisk in the eggs, 1 at a time. Whisk until the mixture is pale gold, thick, and creamy. Add the lemon juice, lemon zest, and butter. Whisk to blend.

Transfer the mixture to a nonreactive saucepan over medium-low heat. Cook the filling, stirring constantly with a wooden spoon until it begins to thicken, 4 to 5 minutes. Do not let the filling boil. Remove from the heat, stir in the Frangelico and let cool.

Prepare the pine nuts: Heat the butter in a large sauté pan over medium heat. Add the pine nuts and toss to coat. Sprinkle with the sugar and sauté until nuts are a golden tan and aromatic. Remove to a sheet pan to cool.

Preheat the oven to 350F (175C). Pour the filling into the prebaked crust. Bake for 25 minutes, until just starting to set. Remove the tart from the oven and sprinkle with the glazed pine nuts. Return to the oven. Bake for an additional 15 to 20 minutes, until firm.

Let cool, then wrap and refrigerate for at least 2 hours before serving or up to 2 days. Serve with whipped cream or fresh berries, if desired.

Cappuccino Tart

The chocolate, coffee, and cream combined in this dessert will satisfy chocaholics and coffee fans alike.

MAKES 8 TO 10 SERVINGS

Crust from Pignola Lemon Tarte (page 301)

FILLING

1 egg

1 egg yolk

¼ cup plus 1 tablespoon sugar

8 ounces semisweet chocolate, coarsely chopped

¼ cup unsalted butter

2 tablespoons Kahlúa

½ teaspoon pure vanilla extract

⅓ cup whipping cream

2 tablespoons triple-strength coffee

TOPPING

½ cup whipping cream

1½ tablespoons sugar

3 tablespoons triple-strength coffee

Chocolate-covered coffee beans (optional)

Prepare and bake crust in a tart pan as directed; set aside.

Prepare the filling: In a mixing bowl, beat the egg, egg yolk, and the ¼ cup sugar until they double in volume and become pale in color.

In a double boiler over medium heat, melt the chocolate and butter. Slowly whisk in the Kahlúa and vanilla until completely blended. Slowly whisk the egg mixture into the double boiler and cook, whisking constantly, 3 to 4 minutes. Remove the top pan from the heat and set aside to cool.

Whip the cream with the 1 tablespoon sugar until soft peaks form. Slowly drizzle in the coffee and beat until stiff peaks form.

Fold the whipped cream into the cooled chocolate mixture. Pour the filling into the tart shell, cover, and refrigerate for at least 3 hours before serving, or up to 3 days.

Prepare the topping: Whip the cream with the sugar until soft peaks form. Slowly drizzle in the coffee and beat until stiff peaks form.

To serve: Cut the tart into wedges. Spoon a generous dollop of the whipped cream on each slice and decorate with a chocolate-covered coffee bean, if desired.

Cocoa Roca Cloud Cake

This is a family recipe from my friend and recipe tester Evan. It goes together in less than 10 minutes (not counting freezing time) and can be held in the freezer for up to a week before serving.

MAKES 8 TO 10 SERVINGS

---

2 cups whipping cream
½ cup sweetened cocoa mix

1 (7-ounce) can Almond Roca candy
1 (10-inch) angel food cake

Place the whipping cream in bowl of an electric mixer and whip on low speed. Slowly sprinkle in the cocoa mix and whip until stiff peaks form.

Unwrap the candy and place it in a heavy plastic or paper bag. Put the candy in the freezer for 15 minutes. Roughly crush the candy with a hammer or mallet.

Slice the cake in half to make 2 layers. Put about ¾ inch of the cocoa cream on the cut layer, and sprinkle generously with the crushed candy. Replace the top half and frost the cake with at least a ½-inch-thick coating of the cocoa cream. Press the remaining candy over the top and sides.

Wrap lightly with plastic wrap and refrigerate for at least 4 hours before serving. For easier slicing, after this initial chilling, freeze the cake for at least 1 day. It will then slice like an ice cream cake.

Chocolate Decorations and Garnishes

To create a charming decoration for a cheesecake, fruit tart, or birthday cake, brush an even coat of melted white or dark chocolate on clean lemon leaves, geranium leaves, or rose leaves. When the chocolate is set, about 5 minutes, carefully peel off the leaf and you have a sturdy, chocolate reproduction of the fresh leaf. Place the finished leaves on a tray lined with waxed paper. Don't use your fingers to move the finished leaves. A small spatula or knife will be much gentler and less likely to melt the delicate chocolate. The leaves can be kept covered in a cool, dark place for 2 to 3 days. Do not refrigerate unless you absolutely must. Arrange the chocolate leaves in clusters or create a border around the edge of a cake.

Chocolate Pâte with Fresh Plum Sauce

This extremely simple, extremely rich dessert is excellent for a novice cook. It can also be used as the basis for numerous extravagant variations. If you have a little time and ambition, fold in some diced candied ginger, dried cherries, or orange peel.

MAKES 10 TO 12 SERVINGS

PÂTE

1 pound best-quality bittersweet chocolate or 12 ounces semisweet plus 4 ounces unsweetened chocolate, coarsely chopped

¾ cup ruby Port wine

¾ cup chopped unsalted macadamia nuts or almonds

½ cup whipping cream

SAUCE

2 tablespoons unsalted butter

1½ cups chopped plums (about 1 pound) or pitted cherries

⅓ cup sugar

½ cup ruby Port wine

Pinch freshly grated nutmeg

TOPPING

1 cup whipping cream

2 tablespoons sifted powdered sugar

1 teaspoon pure vanilla extract

Prepare the pâte: Line a 9 × 5-inch loaf pan with parchment paper or foil; set aside. Melt the chocolate in a double boiler over low heat. Add the wine and whisk to blend. Remove from the heat and stir in the nuts. Cool to room temperature.

Whip the cream until soft peaks form. Gently fold the chocolate mixture into the whipped cream.

Pour into lined loaf pan, cover, and refrigerate overnight or at least 3 hours. (The pâte can be made up to 5 days in advance.)

Prepare the sauce: Melt the butter in a sauté pan over medium heat. Add the plums and sauté until the plums begin to soften, 2 to 3 minutes. Add the sugar and cook until the sugar begins to caramelize, 4 to 5 minutes. Add the wine and simmer over low heat until slightly thickened, 3 to 5 minutes. Remove from the heat and stir in the nutmeg. (The sauce can be prepared and refrigerated up to 24 hours in advance. Serve at room temperature.)

Prepare the topping: Whip the cream until soft peaks form. Sprinkle in the sugar and vanilla and whip just to blend.

To serve: Use a warm knife to slice the pâté into ½-inch slices. Top each serving with plum sauce and whipped cream.

Pumpkin Chiffon Pie

My mother served this pie at every Thanksgiving. She never had a recipe, so I had to re-create my childhood favorite. To my delight my family loves it. It is extremely simple, and remains my favorite pumpkin pie.

MAKES 8 SERVINGS

1 (1-pound) box gingersnap cookies

3 tablespoons apple juice

2 tablespoons bourbon or dark rum

1 envelope unflavored gelatin

2 cups canned or cooked pumpkin

1 teaspoon pure vanilla extract

¼ cup granulated sugar

½ cup packed light brown sugar

1 teaspoon ground cinnamon

1 teaspoon ground ginger

¼ teaspoon salt

Pinch freshly grated nutmeg

¾ cup whipping cream

Whipped cream, to decorate

Butter a 9- to 10-inch pie pan. Cover the bottom and sides of the pan with gingersnaps. Break small pieces to wedge into the spaces left between the circles.

Combine the apple juice and rum in a microwave-safe container. Heat in the microwave on high for 1 minute. Sprinkle the gelatin over the hot liquid and stir until dissolved. The consistency will be about as thick as an egg white.

In a large bowl, whisk together the gelatin mixture and all of the remaining ingredients, except the whipping cream, until completely blended.

Whip the cream until stiff peaks form. Stir 2 tablespoons of the whipped cream into the pumpkin mixture to lighten it. Then gently fold the remaining whipped cream into the pumpkin mixture. Pour the pumpkin mixture into the gingersnap pie shell. Cover and refrigerate at least 4 hours, preferably overnight.

To serve: Decorate the top with whipped cream.

Coconut Mango Crème Brûlée

There are many variations on this classically popular dessert. Seasonal fruits combined with your favorite liqueur, espresso, chocolate, or even mint make great choices.

MAKES 8 SERVINGS

1 teaspoon unsalted butter

1 cup ripe mango or peach slivers

1 cup coconut milk

5 eggs

3 egg yolks

1 cup whipping cream

2 tablespoons amaretto

⅓ cup granulated sugar

½ teaspoon pure vanilla extract

Pinch salt

½ cup packed light brown sugar

Tiny orchids or nasturtiums, for decoration (optional)

Preheat the oven to 300F (150C). Lightly brush 8 (3-inch) ramekins with melted butter and place in a large roasting pan. Divide the fruit evenly among the ramekins.

Stir the coconut milk to blend in the solids before measuring. Whisk the eggs and yolks until slightly thickened. Stir in the cream, coconut milk, amaretto, sugar, vanilla, and salt. Pour the egg mixture over the fruit in the ramekins.

Carefully pour enough water into the baking pan to reach halfway up the sides of the ramekins. Bake about 55 minutes, until barely set when you gently jiggle them.

Remove from the oven and remove the ramekins from the hot water. Cool the custards. Cover with plastic wrap and refrigerate at least 2 hours or up to 2 days. The custard will remain slightly soft in the center, even when cool.

To serve: Preheat the broiler (see Tip below). Sieve an even ¼-inch-thick layer of the brown sugar over the custard to completely cover. Place the sugared custards on a baking sheet and broil until the sugar caramelizes, 3 to 5 minutes. Depending on your broiler you may need to rotate them to color evenly. Remove and let cool. The sugar top will harden.

Served immediately or, for the best flavor, chill loosely covered for up to 1 hour, but no more or the caramel will begin to soften. Decorate with orchids, if desired.

TIP

If you have a small blowtorch, the type now sold in gourmet stores, it produces a nice crisp caramel crust with much less fuss than the broiler. Plus, they are fun to use.

Mary Medved's Nut Roulade

My friend Anne Dreyer is a very accomplished cook and caterer. Her family emigrated here from Yugoslavia. She is very proud of this heritage and of the recipes her mother, Mary, brought with her. This nut roulade could be filled with a variety of flavors and work well, but the cake itself is a soufflé-like jewel, unlike any I've ever tasted.

MAKES 8 TO 12 SERVINGS

FILLING

¼ cup sugar

2 tablespoons almond or chestnut paste

1 teaspoon pure vanilla extract

⅛ teaspoon rum extract

½ cup unsalted butter, softened

2½ tablespoons all-purpose flour

½ cup whole milk

CAKE

6 eggs, separated

6 tablespoons sugar

1 teaspoon pure vanilla extract

1 tablespoon honey

Pinch cream of tartar

6 tablespoons ground walnuts

4 tablespoons fresh bread crumbs

2 tablespoons all-purpose flour

2 teaspoons baking powder

Pinch salt

Unsweetened cocoa powder

Sliced almonds, toasted (page 315)

Prepare the filling: In a food processor, pulse the ¼ cup sugar, the almond paste, vanilla, rum extract, and butter until combined.

Whisk the flour and milk in a small saucepan over low heat until it forms a smooth paste, 1 to 2 minutes. Remove from the heat and add to the butter mixture in the processor. Process until the filling is fluffy and all of the sugar crystals are dissolved, 2 to 3 minutes. Refrigerate the filling until it has a thick, spreadable consistency, about 45 minutes.

Prepare the cake: Preheat the oven to 350F (175C). Line a 13 × 9-inch baking pan with parchment paper and grease heavily with butter.

In a large bowl, whisk together the egg yolks, sugar, vanilla, honey, and cream of tartar until smooth and golden. Add the ground walnuts and bread crumbs and mix to combine.

Sift together the flour, salt, and baking powder and stir into the nut mixture.

Beat the egg whites until soft peaks form. Gently stir ¼ cup of the egg whites into the nut mixture to lighten, then fold in the remaining egg whites.

Evenly spread the mixture in the prepared pan. Bake for 10 to 15 minutes or until light golden brown and springy to the touch. Turn out on a wire rack and cool completely.

To assemble: Turn cake, top side up, but do not remove the parchment paper. Spread the chilled filling evenly to the ends of the cooled cake. Use the parchment paper to help you lift the end of the cake to start the roll, jelly roll fashion. Roll the cake as tightly as possible, removing the parchment paper as you roll. Wrap the finished roulade in plastic wrap, then foil, and freeze until firm or up to 1 month.

To serve: Unwrap and let partially thaw for about 15 minutes. Dust the top heavily with cocoa powder and sprinkle with almonds. Cut into slices and serve; it's best very cold.

Evan's Summer Cooler

This simple dessert is a refreshing tribute to Provence. It is wonderful accompanied by almond biscotti.

MAKES 8 SERVINGS

2 tablespoons finely ground fresh rosemary

2 quarts lemon sorbet or gelato

½ cup amaretto

2 cups fresh raspberries

Using a spice or coffee grinder, grind the fresh rosemary into "dust." It is important that it is ground very fine.

Scoop the sorbet into 8 chilled bola grande or tulip glasses. Drizzle with the amaretto. Sprinkle with the rosemary. Top with the berries.

VARIATION

If you want to make a dramatic presentation, cut the top quarter off of 8 beautiful lemons. Scoop out the flesh. Slice off the pointed bottoms so that the lemon shells sit flat. Pack softened sorbet into each shell and mound it up. Cover in plastic wrap and freeze until solid. Add the amaretto and rosemary before serving.

Rum Raisin Cheesecake

The crust is crunchy and nutty and the filling just the best of the creamy (not New York) style cheesecakes.

MAKES 8 TO 10 SERVINGS

CRUST

1 cup graham cracker crumbs

¾ cup ground almonds

5 tablespoons sugar

½ cup unsalted butter melted

SOUR CREAM LAYER

2 tablespoons dark rum

⅓ cup sultana raisins or dried cherries

1 teaspoon grated lemon zest

2 cups sour cream

¼ cup sugar

1 teaspoon pure vanilla extract

CREAM CHEESE LAYER

2 eggs

1 teaspoon pure vanilla extract

⅓ cup mild honey

2 (8-ounce) packages (2 cups) cream cheese, softened

Prepare the crust: Preheat the oven to 350F (175C). Combine all the ingredients in a bowl and mix well. Press the crumb mixture into a 10-inch pie plate, going all the way up the sides. Bake 8 to 10 minutes. Let cool.

Prepare the sour cream layer: Combine the rum, raisins, and lemon zest in a microwave-safe bowl. Cover loosely and heat on high for 1 minute. Let cool.

Add the sour cream, sugar, and vanilla to a blender and blend until combined. Transfer to a bowl and stir in the raisin mixture. Set aside.

Preheat the oven to 325F (165C).

Prepare the cream cheese layer: Add all the ingredients to the blender and blend until combined. Pour the cream cheese layer into the crust and bake for 25 minutes, until set in the middle. Remove from oven and let cool.

Increase the oven temperature to 425F (220C). Stir the sour cream mixture and pour over cooled cream cheese layer to cover. Bake for 5 minutes. Cool on a wire rack. Cover with plastic wrap and refrigerate for at least 2 hours before serving or up to 4 days.

VARIATIONS

I like this rum raisin flavor, but you can personalize a cheesecake with ripe bananas, dates, lime juice and zest, or amaretto and figs, just to name a few of the possibilities. The recipe is so stable and forgiving, you can add ⅓ to ½ cup of these ingredients to the sour cream layer with impunity.

Ice in Heaven

Sometimes called Persian pudding, this is the perfect conclusion to a rich meal, and another luscious recipe from my friend Jozseph Schultz, chef and culinary scholar. To quote Joe, "This unlikely sounding dessert is ridiculously easy to prepare and always popular."

It makes a refreshing foil to richer desserts on a buffet, with the pomegranate garnish adding bright color and texture to the soothing pudding. Whipped cream on the side is excellent.

MAKES 8 SERVINGS

3 cups whole milk

2 cups water

½ cup cornstarch

½ cup rice flour

1 cup sugar

½ cup ground almonds, lightly toasted (page 315)

2 tablespoons rose water (see Note below)

½ teaspoon ground cardamom

Pinch salt

¼ cup slivered almonds

Seeds from 1 pomegranate or pomegranate molasses (see Note below)

Lightly butter 8 small ramekins or crème brûlée molds; set aside.

In a large saucepan, whisk together the milk, water, cornstarch, rice flour, and sugar. Bring to a simmer, stirring constantly over medium-high heat. Reduce the heat and simmer until as thick as a medium white sauce, 4 to 5 minutes. You need to watch this closely, because it goes almost immediately from runny to stiff.

Remove the pan from the heat and stir in the ground almonds, rose water, cardamom, and salt.

Pour the pudding into the prepared molds and refrigerate. When completely cooled, cover loosely with plastic wrap. (The pudding can be made up to 2 days before serving.)

To serve, top each pudding with a sprinkle of the slivered almonds and pomegranate seeds or a drizzle of pomegranate molasses.

NOTE

Rose water and pomegranate molasses are available at Middle Eastern stores.

Basic Crepe Batter

This delicate, yet sturdy crepe forms the basis for a lifetime of recipes. The crepes can be made up to a month in advance, wrapped airtight, and frozen.

MAKES 16 TO 20 (6-INCH) CREPES

1 cup all-purpose flour

1 teaspoon Kosher salt

½ cup water

½ cup plus 1 tablespoon milk

3 eggs

3 tablespoons butter, melted

Vegetable oil, for cooking

Combine the flour and salt in a bowl. Place all the remaining ingredients, except the oil, in a blender and pulse to mix. With the motor running, pour in the flour mixture. Scrape down the sides and blend again to thoroughly mix, about 20 seconds. The batter should be about the consistency of heavy cream. Cover and chill for at least 1 hour before using. (The batter can be made up to 24 hours before cooking.)

If you don't have a special crepe pan, a good nonstick omelet pan will do. The pan should be 5 to 6 inches wide on the bottom with sloping sides. Pour a small amount of vegetable oil in the pan and wipe out with a paper towel. You should not have to grease the pan again.

Place the pan over medium-high heat. When the pan is almost smoking hot, add 2 to 3 tablespoons of the batter. Lifting the pan off the heat, swirl the batter around the pan to form an even, very thin coating. The first side will be golden in about 1½ minutes. Loosen lightly with the edge of a spatula and flip to cook the second side for about 1 minute. Don't worry if the first 1 or 2 crepes don't turn out. That seems to happen to everyone. I usually count on throwing out the first few.

Transfer each completed crepe to a rack to cool and continue cooking the remaining batter, adding oil only if the crepes start to stick. If you are making the crepes for future use, layer them, when cool, with waxed paper and freeze or refrigerate.

DESSERT CREPES

For dessert crepes, add 2 teaspoons sugar and 1½ teaspoons vanilla to the basic recipe and decrease the salt to ½ teaspoon. Sweet crepes should be cooked over medium heat because the sugar causes them to burn more easily.

Basic Pasta Dough

This simple dough produces a tender, silky pasta suitable for a wide noodle like pappardelle or filled pastas like ravioli and tortellini. I recommend the addition of a finely chopped fresh herb like thyme, basil, or oregano. You can also be creative by adding vegetable purees such as spinach, carrot, or red bell pepper to color and flavor the pasta. To prepare this recipe you must have a hand-cranked or electric pasta-rolling machine.

MAKES ABOUT 24 OUNCES DOUGH; ENOUGH PASTA FOR 16 TO 20 LARGE RAVIOLI OR ENOUGH PAPPARDELLE FOR 8 SERVINGS

3 cups all-purpose flour

4 eggs and 2 egg yolks, slightly beaten

2 tablespoons milk

½ teaspoon Kosher salt

1 to 2 teaspoons of cold water

About 4 teaspoons minced fresh herbs (optional)

Combine all the ingredients in the bowl of your food processor. Process until the ingredients are well blended and the dough forms a moist, crumbly texture that can be pressed into a ball, about 10 seconds. If the dough seems dry, add water—1 teaspoon at a time—process quickly and retest.

Transfer the dough to a work surface and knead for 10 to 15 seconds to form a smooth ball, flouring if necessary to keep it from sticking.

Wrap the dough in plastic wrap and let rest 30 minutes before rolling. It can be held in the refrigerator for up to 6 hours, but it must be brought back to room temperature before rolling.

To roll out pasta sheets: Turn the smooth rollers of the pasta machine to the widest setting. Cut the dough into 8 pieces; cover with a damp towel. Working with 1 piece at a time, flatten the dough into a rough square the size of the roller opening and lightly dust with flour.

Run the dough through the pasta rollers. Fold over the ends of the resulting rectangle to form a square again, press down the ends to seal, and run through again at the same setting. Repeat this rolling and folding process, dusting with flour when necessary, 6 or 7 more times.

This repeated rolling on the widest setting conditions the dough. It's now ready to quickly run through the more narrow settings. Adjust the roller to the next setting and run the pasta through as one long sheet. Dust with flour as necessary. Continue to roll this long, narrow ribbon of dough through, flipping the dough over so that you reverse front end and back end of the strip each time. Lowering the setting each time, continue until the pasta is about $\frac{1}{16}$-inch thick and about 18 inches long. (The setting will be number 6 or 7.)

TIPS

As the pasta gets longer and thinner while you roll, it is important to "receive" it with one hand as it emerges from the rollers so it doesn't fold up and stick to itself. I usually put a floured sheet pan under the deposit end of my roller so I can gently ease the sheet out along the pan. As each sheet is finished, I cut it in half for easier handling. I lay the finished pasta on a second baking sheet and cover with a clean towel while I roll the rest.

When fresh herbs have been added to the dough, only roll the dough as far as setting number 6. If the dough gets too thin it will tear around the herb pieces.

Clarified Butter

Clarified butter is unsalted butter, which has been gently heated to separate out the milk solids. Because the milk solids have been removed, clarified butter can be heated to a much higher temperature than regular butter without burning.

To clarify butter, heat it in a heavy-bottomed saucepan over medium-low heat. As it heats, some of the water will evaporate and the milk solids will sink to the bottom of the pan. When the liquid is a clear yellow, remove the pan from the heat. Let it rest for 5 minutes, then skim the foam off the top and carefully pour the clear liquid out of the pan, discarding the milk solids left behind. Clarified butter can be stored, in the refrigerator, for several weeks without becoming rancid.

Lemon Peel Twists

Using a vegetable peeler, remove long narrow strips of peel from a lemon with an unblemished skin. Tie the strips in a simple knot and use to garnish seafood, piccata dishes, or desserts.

Roasted Chiles and Bell Peppers

Place the whole chiles or bell peppers on a hot grill or under the broiler. Using tongs, turn them from side to side to roast evenly, until charred and blistered, 3 to 5 minutes. Remove from the heat and enclose tightly in a plastic or paper bag to steam until cool.

When cool, the blackened skin will easily slip off. Remove the stems and seeds. You now have smoky-flavored peppers ready to be used in sauces, salads, pizza, sandwiches, and more. If you do a large quantity at once, any leftovers can be successfully frozen for later use.

Toasted Nuts

Any nut can be toasted with delicious results. The toasted flavor is most noticeable in desserts or when the nuts are eaten alone.

The procedure is the same as for toasting spices (see below). However, it will take from 3 to 5 minutes to achieve a nice pale golden color (except for pistachios). They will also quickly go from perfect to scorched in less than 1 minute. So, they must be watched until done.

Toasted Spices

Spices, like nuts, can be toasted in the oven or over a burner. The flavor intensity developed by toasting spices is well worth the little time involved. However, strict attention must be given to this process for the 1 to 2 minutes it takes. If overheated, the spices will quickly scorch and have to be thrown out. Spices that benefit from toasting include: coriander, cumin, turmeric, cayenne, curry, cardamom, fennel, caraway seed, chili powder, and paprika.

To toast, place the spices in a dry sauté pan over medium heat. Toast, while shaking the pan to avoid overheating in one spot. Remove from the heat when the spices have become aromatic, 1 to 2 minutes. If the spices start to smoke, immediately dump them out of the pan onto a cool surface to halt the cooking. If there is any burned smell, you should discard them and start over.

Spices can also be toasted in a pie pan or on a baking sheet in a 350F (175C) oven. Oven toasting requires the same watchful eye.

THE COMPANIES AND products listed below can form the backbone of your menu support group. While especially comforting for the novice, the finished dishes or ingredients included here will help any "party planner" round out a menu. Not only are these products delicious, they are from "somewhere else," and by definition exotic and interesting.

This is just another aspect of our new global shopping access. You can browse bookstores on your computer and order the books delivered to your home. How much more exciting to get next-day delivery on Maine lobsters, a Cinderella's slipper made of white chocolate, or Bing cherries that crunch like a Pippin apple, from Olson's farms in California!

These reputable companies generally operate on a "satisfaction guaranteed" basis. So, call all of them that interest you and request information or samples so that you are ready to order when the need arises. All of these businesses will ship to individuals.

As someone who has made and shipped tens of thousands of refrigerated products, I can assure you that the satisfaction level on quality food shipping is extremely high. My company averaged less than one question in one thousand orders placed.

Ingredients, Prepared Foods, and Equipment

Abe's Cajun Market

337-477-5499

337-474-3810 (fax)

Lake Charles, LA

Will fax or mail you a catalog. Tasso (Cajun-cured smoked pork) mild and hot boudin sausage

Adriana's Bazaar

800-316-0820

New York

International gourmet products, exotic spices and condiments

Aidells Sausage Company

www.aidells.com

800-546-5795

Kensington, CA

Stunning array of flavors and spices in the guise of sausages: andouille, chicken, duck and other gourmet flavor combinations

Alaska Sausage & Seafood Co.

www.alaskanet.com

800-798-3636

Meat and fish products that are native to Alaska. Exotic sausages and salami featuring reindeer meat, kippered salmon and halibut, smoked and cured salmon

American Mussel Harvesters

401-789-1678

Narragansett, RI

Cold-water shellfish (oysters, clams, mussels) harvested to order and shipped in ice packs

American Spoon Foods

www.spoon.com

888-735-6700

Petoskey, MI

Spoon fruits, sour cherry jam, cherry-peach salsa, Larry Forgione's products: Smoky Catsup, Mango Grill Sauce, Corn Salsa

Annapolis Seafood Market

www.annapolisseafoodmarket.com

410-269-5380

Annapolis, MD

Maryland blue crab, whole and cleaned meat, oysters, soft-shell crabs, lobster. Overnight shipping.

Balduccis

www.balducci.com

800-balducci

212-673-2600

New York

Prepared entrées and appetizers: frittata, oysters Rockefeller, pâtés, terrines; large dessert selection; New York–style steaks; caviars; fresh sauces; Bella de Cerignola olives, and more

Boudin Bakery

www.boudinbakery.com

800-992-1849

San Francisco, CA

Tangy, crispy-crusted sourdough bread from the famous bakery near Fisherman's Wharf in San Francisco

Chefstore

www.chefstore.com

888-334-chef

Culinary outfitters online

Professional quality equipment: All-Clad, KitchenAid, Restaurant Lulu, Le Creuset, Dextelle, De Buyer. Pans, knives, food covers, French silicone elastomolds, serving platters, table decor, martini kits.

Chefwear

800-568-2433

www.chefwearusa.com

Not edible, but the most wonderful, high quality, stylish professional chef's garb. Includes children's sizes and styles. They will custom-make for special orders.

A Cook's Wares

www.cookswares.com

800-915-9788

412-846-9490

Beaver Falls, PA

Their pledge: "Serving the serious cooks of America since 1981."

Superior gourmet gifts and supplies; good chocolate; spices; chiles; great knives, good selection of All-clad, Sitram professional, Cuisinart cookware; Isabelle Marique blue steel bakeware for crispy crusts and more

Culinary Parts Unlimited

www.culinaryparts.com

800-543-7549

Open twenty-four hours a day, seven days a week. Replacement parts for all major brands of kitchen appliances

D'Artagnan

www.dartagnan.com

800-327-8246

Newark, NJ

Provides foie gras and specialty meats to top chefs around the country; fresh duck, pheasant, quail, partridge, and squab; farm raised game: venison, rabbit, buffalo, and boar.

Dean and DeLuca

www.deandeluca.com

800-221-7714

212-431-1691

New York

Petit fours, miniature chocolates, mandarin chocolate cake. Maple honey glazed ham, Jambon Cru du Beaujolais. Wine. Kitchenware from graters and grinders to hand-embroidered tablecloths.

Demi-Glace Gold

www.morethangourmet.com

800-860-9385 (consumer hotline)

330-761-5939 (Tom-sales)

Akron, OH

Classic French sauce basics: beef, veal, duck, and chicken

Ethnic Grocer (partnered with the James Beard Foundation)
www.ethnicgrocer.com
More than 20,000 ethnic food products: ingredients for Asian, Mediterranean, Latin American, and Middle Eastern cooking; edible wrappings, quail eggs, husks and masa for tamales, Szechuan hot bean sauce, pomegranate molasses

El Cholo Spanish Cafe
888-982-6253
Los Angeles, CA
Fresh tamales, including green corn, duck with guajillo chile, beef or pork; sauces; margarita mix

Fancy Foods Gourmet Club
www.ffgc.com
800-576-3548
Buda, TX
Specialty desserts, crab cakes, smoked salmon and trout, Laderlach truffles, beautiful gift baskets

The Fillo Factory
www.fillofactory.com
800-653-4556
Bergen, NJ
Fresh, no-tear fillo dough shipped fresh frozen, regular or whole wheat; also carry a line of frozen fillo hors d'oeuvres

Formaggio Kitchen
888-212-3224
Cambridge, MA
Specialty food store with an on-site cheese cave; very fresh Parmiggiano-Reggiano and more

Kitchen/Market
E-mail: mail@kitchenmarket.com
888-468-4433
New York
Latin American ingredients: ninety types of chile pepper products, twenty cornmeal products, nine types of tortillas; Caribbean ingredients

King Arthur Flour Baker's Store

www.kingarthurflour.com

800-827-6836

Norwich, VT

Playground for home baking enthusiasts: Real maple syrup, vast array of baking and cooking supplies; recipes; fine tools: pastry blending fork, flour wand, English muffin rings, stainless steel rolling pin, doughnut cutter, alphabet and number cutters; ingredients; equipment; and books for the home baker

Legal Sea Foods

www.legalseafoods.com

800-343-5804

Allston, MA

High-quality fresh seafood: live lobster and excellent New England clam chowder. The Lobster Clambake supreme includes lobster, clams, linguica sausage, clam chowder, and corn on the cob. Simple cooking instructions included in every shipment.

Lee Gelfond Chocolates

310-854-3524

Beverly Hills, CA

Candy as art: Specialty molded chocolates, custom "anything" in chocolate

Los Chileros De Nuevo Mexico

E-mail: info@hotchilepepper.com

505-471-6967

Santa Fe, NM

New Mexico food products and wide variety of dried chiles

Maine Lobster Direct

www.mainelobsterdirect.com

800-556-2783

This is *the* site for lobster lovers. Live lobsters and lobster dinners

Mozzarella Co.

www.mozzco.com

800-798-2954

Dallas, TX

Gourmet cheese producer: cow's and goat's milk mozzarella, smoked scamorza, queso oaxaca, mascarpone; range of fresh goat's milk cheeses including ricotta, feta, and fromage blanc

Olson's

www.cjolsoncherries.com

800-738-BING (2464); ask for Deborah

Sunnyvale, CA

Cherries, cherries, cherries, and other fruit. Famous for the world's most wonderful cherries and jewel-packed boxes of cherries; fresh and dried gift packs; chocolate-dipped fruits, homemade jams; jumbo pistachios, almonds, and walnuts.

The Oriental Pantry

www.orientalpantry.com

800-828-0368

Acton, MA

All of the hard-to-find ingredients for authentic Oriental cooking: thirteen kinds of seaweed; lemongrass; fresh spices; equipment: steamers, woks, Chinese knives, and utensils

Penzey's Spices

www.penzeys.com

Catalog available

800-741-7787

Incredible, vast array of exotic spices and herbs. Every chile, every way. Custom spice mixes.

The Perfect Puree

www.perfectpuree.com

800-556-3707

St. Helena, CA

High-quality cooking bases from field-ripened berries, fruits, and vegetables that are pureed then frozen. Widest selection I've found of all natural essences—from pomegranate to persimmon.

Petrossian Paris

www.petrossianparis.com

800-828-9241

212-337-0007 (fax)

New York

Russian caviar, smoked salmon, truffles, foie gras, luscious handmade French chocolates and the elegant appointments to serve these rare delicacies with elan.

The Republic of Tea

www.republicoftea.com

800-354-5530

Mill Valley, CA

Extravagant and enticing variety of special teas from around the world: organic, herbal, chai

Simply Seafood

www.simplyseafood.com

877-706-4022

Seattle, WA

Ships fresh seafood overnight: soft-shell crab, crawfish, sea bass, lobster, lingcod, ono—depending on supply. Smoked fish, recipes and seafood magazine

The Spice Hunter

www.spicehunter.com

800-444-3061

San Luis Obispo, CA

Broad selection of unusual, all natural, salt free blends and spices. Selected products are carried at national grocers; also available online or call for catalog.

Sur la Table

www.surlatable.com

800-243-0852

Catalog Division

Seattle, WA

Pans, appliances, linens, baking supplies, tools to the max. A very complete and sophisticated selection.

Tavolo

www.Tavolo.com

800-700-7336

Affiliated with the Culinary Institute of America. This site offers gourmet and hard-to-find ingredients plus equipment, recipes, nutritional information, and advice. Very large selection of quality, well researched items.

Uwajimaya

www.uwajimaya.com

800-889-1928

Seattle, WA

Asian ingredients: twenty varieties of miso, bean pastes, noodles, Japanese bread crumbs, fermented black beans, and Asian specialty produce: fresh lemongrass, Thai eggplant, red basil, frozen fresh banana leaves, galangal. Mail order catalog available.

Williams-Sonoma

www.williams-sonoma.com

800-840-2591 (request catalog or store info)

Fine quality cooking and serving equipment, selected sauces, condiments, dry mixes, and more. Wedding registry and shopping online.

Recipe, Restaurant, and Resource Web Sites

www.allaboutbeer.com

All About Beer: An encyclopedic beer info source.

www.cuisinenet.com

Over one hundred best hospitality sites to search for restaurant reviews, and gourmet products, from the Great Eastern Mussel Farm to Chicago's MetroMix to All About Beer

www.culinary.com

The Culinary Connection: Recipes and links to other great food sites.

www.fabulousfood.com

Cooking instruction and problem solving. Great if you're stuck and don't want to search through numerous books to find out how to fix a broken hollendaise sauce or how to carve a turkey.

www.foodweb.com

Links to many, many other great sites

www.restaurantreport.com

If all else fails, go to the Best of the Best report at this site. Ratings from all major reviewers are compiled to come up with a majority vote on the best restaurants in the country.

www.ucook.com

This site searches for recipes through a vast "library" of cookbooks. All recipes are cross-referenced by ingredient, ethnic origin and other variables. (The first 10 recipes are free.)

www.soar.berkeley.edu/recipes

At last count, over 68,000 recipes available on-line. Sorted by nationality, recipe name, ingredients, etc. An incredible source of ethnic and hard-to-find recipes as well as myriad variations on the standards.

www.secretrecipe.com

This site specializes in reproducing famous and secret recipes from major manufacturers.

www.zagat.com

Zagat has come out with Marketplace Survey guides for Los Angeles and New York, with more to come. Rated listings of gourmet stores, caterers, specialty products, and markets. Most of the sources listed will mail order.

Wine.com

www.wine.com

888-946-3789

650-938-9463

Palo Alto, CA

Premier on-line source for wine and wine-related gifts

The World of Cheese

www.worldofcheese.com

800-980-9603

Quality selection of specialty and farmstead cheeses from the United States, Canada, England, Spain, Greece, Norway, Ireland and Italy: Blythdale blue, Morbier, Raclette, Picon, Trentino, Grana, Talegggio

Metric Conversion Charts

COMPARISON TO METRIC MEASURE

When You Know	Symbol	Multiply By	To Find	Symbol
teaspoons	tsp.	5.0	milliliters	ml
tablespoons	tbsp.	15.0	milliliters	ml
fluid ounces	fl. oz	30.0	milliliters	ml
cups	c	0.24	liters	l
pints	pt	0.47	liters	l
quarts	qt.	0.95	liters	l
ounces	oz.	28.0	grams	g
pounds	lb.	0.45	kilograms	kg
Fahrenheit	F	5/9 (after subtracting 32)	Celsius	C

FAHRENHEIT TO CELCIUS

F	C
200-205	95
220-225	105
245-250	120
275	135
300-305	150
325-330	165
345-350	175
370-375	190
400-405	205
425-430	220
445-450	230
470-475	245
500	260

LIQUID MEASURE TO MILLIMETERS

$\frac{1}{4}$	teaspoon	=	1.25	milliliters
$\frac{1}{2}$	teaspoon	=	2.5	milliliters
$\frac{3}{4}$	teaspoon	=	3.75	milliliters
1	teaspoon	=	5.0	milliliters
1-$\frac{1}{4}$	teaspoons	=	6.25	milliliters
1-$\frac{1}{2}$	teaspoons	=	7.5	milliliters
1-$\frac{3}{4}$	teaspoons	=	8.75	milliliters
2	teaspoons	=	10.0	milliliters
1	tablespoon	=	15.0	milliliters
2	tablespoons	=	30.0	milliliters

LIQUID MEASURE TO LITERS

$\frac{1}{4}$	cup	=	0.06	liters
$\frac{1}{2}$	cup	=	0.12	liters
$\frac{3}{4}$	cup	=	0.18	liters
1	cup	=	0.24	liters
1-$\frac{1}{4}$	cups	=	0.3	liters
1-$\frac{1}{2}$	cups	=	0.36	liters
2	cups	=	0.48	liters
2-$\frac{1}{2}$	cups	=	0.6	liters
3	cups	=	0.72	liters
3-$\frac{1}{2}$	cups	=	0.84	liters
4	cups	=	0.96	liters
4-$\frac{1}{2}$	cups	=	1.08	liters
5	cups	=	1.2	liters
5-$\frac{1}{2}$	cups	=	1.32	liters

Index

photo by Sunny Bak

ABOUT THE AUTHOR

NICOLE ALONI has enjoyed an exciting and diverse career in the culinary arts and as a stage actress. She completed the diploma course at La Varenne, École de Cuisine in Paris and stayed on to work as a chef at châteaus in Burgundy. In California, she has owned her own restaurant, directed one of the country's largest catering operations, and produced a line of gourmet food products.

For twelve years, Nicole was owner and director of operations for gourmet catering company, Nicole Cottrell Productions, Inc. Her company catered elegant events for clients such as the Kirov Ballet and the Tournament of Roses. She also created an extensive line of gourmet products for the retail marketplace. These products were featured at fine grocery stores and were one of the most popular and successful items in the Neiman-Marcus catalogues.

Prior to opening her own business, Nicole was the director of catering at the Los Angeles Music Center for five years, where she catered the Academy Awards four times, prepared a state luncheon for Queen Elizabeth II, and produced galas for President Reagan.

Nicole has written articles on entertaining for food magazines, including *Bon Appétit*. She is an active member of the International Association of Culinary Professionals and the Actor's Equity Association.